FROM THE RESERVATION TO WASHINGTON

The Rise of Charles Curtis

DEBRA GOODRICH

TWODOT®

ESSEX, CONNECTICUT
HELENA, MONTANA

A · TWODOT® · BOOK
An imprint of The Globe Pequot Publishing Group, Inc.
64 South Main Street
Essex, CT 06426
www.globepequot.com

Distributed by NATIONAL BOOK NETWORK

British Library Cataloguing in Publication Information available

Library of Congress Cataloging-in-Publication Data

Names: Goodrich, Debra, author.
Title: From the reservation to Washington : the rise of Charles Curtis / Debra Goodrich.
Other titles: Rise of Charles Curtis
Description: Essex, Connecticut : TwoDot, [2024] | Includes bibliographical references and index.
Identifiers: LCCN 2024019719 (print) | LCCN 2024019720 (ebook) | ISBN 9781493075355 (cloth) | ISBN 9781493075362 (epub)
Subjects: LCSH: Curtis, Charles, 1860-1936. | Curtis, Charles, 1860-1936—Family. | United States. Congress. Senate—Biography. | United States. Congress. House—Biography. | Vice-presidents—United States—Biography. | United States—Politics and government—1929-1933. | United States—Politics and government—1919-1933. | Kansas Indians—Biography. | Washington, D.C.—Biography. | Topeka (Kan.)—Biography.
Classification: LCC E748.C982 G66 2024 (print) | LCC E748.C982 (ebook) | DDC 973.91/5092—dc23/eng/20240509
LC record available at https://lccn.loc.gov/2024019719
LC ebook record available at https://lccn.loc.gov/2024019720

For my grandchildren—Laurel, Devyn, Rylan, Eternity, and Ma'Kiah— who are "exceptionally attractive and brilliant," possessed of huge hearts, and each of whom makes the world a more interesting and wonderful place.

For the grandmothers who love their grandchildren above everything.

For the People of the South Wind.

CONTENTS

Contents

ACKNOWLEDGMENTS

This is the most difficult part of this book to write—not because there is so little to acknowledge, but because there is so much. There are people who say nice things and encourage you, and then there are people who put themselves on the line to make your work a reality. I am blessed with those people.

First, I would like to say that I believe the most important quality a biographer or historian can have is humility. My former professor Dr. Glenda Riley said, "We can never know the actual past, we can only know the virtual past." At dinner one evening I told her this was such a profound insight and a wonderful reminder lest we think we know everything. She responded, "We don't even know the actual present! How can we know the actual past?"

That is so true. As thorough as we are, there will always be missing pieces. It is my hope with this book to introduce you to Charles Curtis and inspire others to continue researching his life and legacy. My friend Chris Pascale is writing a biography that I eagerly anticipate. I look forward to the historians and scholars who will continue to build the body of knowledge and understanding of Charles Curtis's role in American history.

When I moved to Topeka, Sarah McNeive was my first connection to the history of Kansas and the Historic Topeka Cemetery. Through that association came so many relationships and opportunities, and eventually to my serving as the president of the Shawnee County Historical Society. I was so privileged to work alongside devoted historians such as Douglass Wallace, Bill Wagnon, Ralph Skoog, June Windscheffel, Chris Meinhardt, Doug Wright, Christine Steinkuhler, Jeanne Mithen, and so many others in the Shawnee County Historical Society. Frank and Sabra Shirrell have done so much to preserve the Territorial history of Kansas and have been so generous to me.

The Civil War Roundtable of Eastern Kansas and the Kansas City Civil War Roundtable likewise provided such wonderful experiences and resources, and I am so grateful to everyone involved with those groups, especially Dan Smith, Deb Buckner, Bob Aufdemberge, Jeff Dunaway, and Randy Thies.

I have so many dear friends with whom I worked or volunteered at Fort Leavenworth, but a handful are still a huge part of my life not only as friends but as valuable resources: Steve and Marianne Tennant, Dave and Teresa Chuber, Ed Kennedy, and Chris Gabel.

I am honored to serve as the publicity chair and chair of the 200th Anniversary for the Santa Fe Trail Association. This group has been such a tremendous resource that I cannot begin to thank them enough, but Joanne VanCoevern and her husband, Greg, deserve special recognition. The Santa Fe Trail figured prominently in Curtis's life and the era in which he was born.

Among the people that I constantly turn to for information is Mark Brooks, the site administrator at the Kaw Mission State Historic Site and Last Chance Store, Museums on the Santa Fe Trail, Council Grove, Kansas. He is a treasure, as are Ken and Shirley McClintock, who are so generous with their knowledge and time.

My colleagues in the Order of the Indian Wars have been valuable resources and friends, especially Mike Koury, Jerry Greene, John Monnett, Danny Martinez, and Tod and Bernadette Noble.

Ken Bellmard has shared personal stories and insights into his Kaw ancestry, current issues, and vision for the future. I am most grateful for his friendship.

James Pepper Henry, as vice chair of the Kaw Nation and executive director of the First Americans Museum in Oklahoma City, is an incredible resource. His insight and perspective are invaluable, and his friendship is priceless.

A special thank-you to Lisa Keyes at the Kansas State Historical Society and Kathy Lafferty with the Kenneth Spencer Research Library at the University of Kansas, outstanding public servants!

Crystal Douglas, formerly the museum director at the Kanza Museum, Kaw City, Oklahoma, was a tremendous resource and friend. Her passing left a void that is impossible to fill.

There are a handful of friends that are "on call" for quick answers and expertise: Tim Rues, Bryce Benedict, Mike Baughn, Michael Grauer, Holly Zane, Ramon Powers, Mike Sheriff, Dave Bennett, Matt Matthews, Greg Higginbotham, Terry Beck, Dee Cordry, and Andy Obermueller. Likewise, I have some "encouragers" that are dear to me: Grainger Hines, "brother" R. W. Hampton, Wyatt McCrea, and Phil Roosevelt.

My dear friend Donita Sparks has shown such belief in me and support for my endeavors (including showing up at my door with soup and pie from the Methodist Church) that I cannot thank her enough.

Dena Anson finds treasures—whether nuggets of research or the odd diary at an estate sale—and her keen eye is a gift, as is her friendship.

Heather Silver Newell is simply one of the most incredible, resourceful women I have ever known and is helpful in hundreds of ways. I am in your debt.

Dr. Michelle Martin has been my "partner in historical crimes" for many years now and no matter what I need—friendship or footnotes—she is there night or day to offer her expertise and support. As a resource, she has no equal.

My colleagues in Western Writers of America encourage, critique, brainstorm, and offer the most excellent advice—Johnny D. Boggs, especially you.

Serving as the Garvey Texas Foundation Historian in Residence at the Fort Wallace Museum is a joy and an honor. Thanks to the Garvey Family for making this possible as well as the staff and my friends who keep this wonderful museum going. Our Guardians of Fort Wallace is such an amazing, hard-working, dedicated group and I am so proud to be able to research, to create programming and exhibits, and to connect the dots between Fort Wallace and the American West. Thanks to Lynn Kirkham, Dr. Jake Bauer, J. D. Perry, Christal Bohrer, Debra Fischer,

Darrius Bussen, Larry Eberle, Pam Whitson, Nancy Arendt, and Cecil and Jayne Pearce.

Over the years our circle has grown to include so many others who support the museum, and me, as friends and professionals: Dennis "Deb's Encyclopedia" Clark, for whom our Distinguished Lecture Series is named; Marla Matkin, educator and performer who constantly inspires me with her interpretations of the past; Michael Martin Murphey, songwriter, singer, historian, and missionary for the history of the American West; and Frank Goodrich, my "brother" who is always there for me and my crazy projects, and his wife, Judy.

Dear friends Dr. Andy and Carol Neumann Waskie have been more than generous with their time, home, and vast knowledge of history. I cannot thank them enough for sharing their home and adventures with me.

Ken Spurgeon and I have worked on so many projects that I can barely recall a time before that collaboration began. Always, he is a gentleman and a scholar, and I am so very proud to call him my friend and professional partner.

My sister, Denise Coalson, has been there for me more times than I can count (she got the math genes), and the value of her counsel and support cannot be overstated. She and Jayne Humphrey Pearce and Carol Neumann Waskie were my first readers and critics and devoted many hours to this manuscript. I am in their debt—literally, as my sister the bookkeeper constantly reminds me.

To Karen Knox, I am grateful to be your mother and to share in your triumphs and challenges; to my daughter Noel Coalson, I am in awe of your heart and spirit; to Becca Miller, the reason I came to Kansas—each of you has changed my life in rich and amazing ways. I love all of you and each of you.

Heartfelt thanks to Debra Murphy, my editor at TwoDot, for her infinite patience and professionalism, and to Sarah Parke, who first saw potential with this topic. Thanks also to Justin Rossi for his efforts in promoting this work. Special thanks to Cindy Johnson for lending her photography expertise.

Kitty Hamilton (Franks) deserves special recognition for taking Charles Curtis's unpublished manuscript and making it available to the public. Thank you, Kitty, for allowing me to use that work as a reference.

Prologue

I first became acquainted with Charley Curtis in Historic Topeka Cemetery, his final resting place. Sarah McNeive, the unofficial historian, was guiding me around the stones—some plain, some ornate, each holding a story.

There was Hib Case, whose stone said "Pioneer Lawyer," and Samuel Crawford, who was a governor and a general, with his plain, flat marble stone. There was his son-in-law, Arthur Capper, governor, US senator, also with the plain, flat marker. There was the Gage Memorial, a Union soldier atop a base several feet high, but it wasn't a memorial to Gage; it was a memorial to his comrades, men with whom he served during the Civil War. There was Judge John Guthrie, for whom Guthrie, Oklahoma, is named. Crane, Vail, Holliday, Farnsworth, Ross—a publishing company, the hospital, the Santa Fe Railroad, an author, another US senator—some names were familiar, having streets and businesses named for them. And some were new, like Charles Curtis.

"He was vice president under Herbert Hoover, a US senator, a congressman, Shawnee County Attorney," Sarah said. "A Kaw Indian." To be honest, I hadn't heard of them either. Having just moved to Kansas, I had a lot to learn.

The Kaw (the Kanza, or Kansa, or Kanzai), the tribe from whom the river takes its name (and the state takes its name from the river), no longer live in Kansas as a tribe. They were removed to present-day Oklahoma in 1873. Charles Curtis almost went with them; if he had, well, this would be a different story.

Vice President Charles Curtis in his office. His ornate chair, carved with his name and office, is one of the items he took with him when he retired. There is evidence of his Native heritage all around him—in gifts from tribal representatives and keepsakes.

Sarah continued, "Young Charley was a jockey, and there was a race-track on what is now the cemetery grounds. The jockeys stayed in the upstairs of the carriage house." The stone outbuilding still stood.

His presence was everywhere. His stately home still stood just a block from the Kansas Statehouse. It was a private museum purchased and preserved by Don and Nova Cottrell. I visited often, running my hand over the ornate wood of the handrail that Charles Curtis and his family had touched many times, gazing out the windows at the view of the capitol dome they would have enjoyed (minus the sculpture of the Kaw warrior, *Ad Astra*, that is perched there now). Kansas has since named a state office building for Curtis and erected a bronze sculpture on Kansas Avenue where other luminaries are enshrined. (I was invited to speak at the dedication of that monument.) Yet, most Kansans know nothing of his life, and for America, he is the answer to a trivia question.

There is so much more to his story.

Charley (he encouraged the familiar) was likeable. It was a trait that served him well as a politician. He remembered names, spouse's and children's names. (His half sister, Dolly, helped compile the famous black books he used as a reference.) He championed Prohibition and was reported to have been a teetotaler, but did not believe the law was just. He was a formidable poker player, maybe even a cheat if we are to believe Alice Roosevelt Longworth. In some of those heated games, he was prone to swear.

I like him.

I was impressed by his loyalty to his family, his work ethic, his ambi-tion, and his championing women's rights. Not only did he introduce the Equal Rights Amendment in the Senate, but he also practiced those equal rights by bringing Dolly to Washington to serve as his secretary when he was elected to Congress (only the second congressman to employ a woman). He had trusted Dolly with his campaign, calling upon her when she was young to join seasoned campaigners—*men*—on stage to represent him. Not many ambitious politicians at the time would have done the same.

Charley defended minorities in court and drafted an anti-lynching law. He fought for Native Americans to be recognized as American citizens with full voting rights. He had witnessed their rights being trampled his entire life. This is the most controversial aspect of his legacy. In the process of granting citizenship, tribal governments were dissolved. Charley valued American citizenship over tribal identity, there is no doubt. He believed, in light of his experiences, that this was the only way forward.

The author Elizabeth Gilbert wrote in *Eat, Pray, Love*, "There are only two questions that human beings have ever fought over, all through history. *How much do you love me?* And, *Who's in charge?* Everything else is somehow manageable. But these two questions of love and control undo us all, trip us up and cause war, grief, and suffering."[1]

Charley was born into a chaotic world, a world at war, a world where the person who loved him most, his mother, died and left him with only memories, a world where the entity in charge—of his life, of the government—constantly changed. His Native culture had been negotiating with the government for generations, but to what end? He had witnessed even the most powerful tribes conquered by rules, laws—federal law. It may have been the US Army's implementing policy or enforcing the rules, but the laws themselves came from the hallowed halls of Congress.

Ultimately, the federal government was in charge. In the years before he was born, in the violence of Bleeding Kansas, in the creation of the state, in the Civil War, in the Plains Indian Wars and Reconstruction—in every aspect of life as it related to him, the US government was present, as arbiter and benefactor. The lesson was clear: real power was in the hands of the federal government, so to have any real control, he must be a part of that government. And to be a part of that government, people must love him.

Or at least *like* him.

His smile won friends. His "gentle, ingratiating voice" put people at ease. His straightforward manner engendered trust. He was ambitious, and he shaped his mongrel background to suit his aspirations.

Perhaps Charley's greatest asset throughout his career was his younger half sister, Dolly, and the story of his achievements is equally her story. Dolly had a take-charge personality and the same boundless energy and positive attitude as her older brother. Her belief in him was absolute. Personally and professionally, he would rely on her until his dying day.

"He is the hero of one of the most romantic life histories in the epochal West," wrote reporter Joe Nickell, who was covering the Republican National Convention meeting in Kansas City in 1928. "Horatio Alger, writer of inspirational stories for boys—of how poor boys become rich and powerful—never in his wildest flights of fiction wrote anything as interesting and romantic as the true story of Charley Curtis's life."[2]

That much is true, but rarely, if ever, would the details of that inspirational life be reported fully or accurately. Much was made of Charley descending from both pilgrim and Indian, "uniquely American."

He was, indeed, "uniquely American." He and Hoover were the first men born west of the Mississippi River to assume the vice presidency and presidency. So many firsts. But the number one spot, the presidency, eluded him. His friend Will Rogers said the only reason the Republicans didn't nominate him in the top spot was because he was an Indian.

Just how much Indian was a matter of much discussion. "Half," "quarter," "one-eighth," but finally, just "Injun."

The "blood quantum" was used to discriminate against African American and Native American people, with one-sixteenth blood being the usual cutoff where one was no longer considered white. Charley was technically one-eighth Native, but half French-Kaw, which I believe is an important distinction. The French had intermarried for generations in his family and had become somewhat separate from the full-blood Kaws, but these were mostly internal issues. For the majority of Americans, a drop of Indian blood made you an Indian. It is remarkable that Charley was counted as white in census records, because other people with his racial status would not have been. Had the census taker marked him as Indian, he would not have been allowed to vote in most of the elections in which he was a candidate.

Yet, he would always be an Indian no matter what box the census taker checked or which world he decided to live in. Growing up around Topeka, he was "Injun Charley." When he raced horses, he was that "Indian boy." When he was in the US Senate, he was "the Indian."

The Indian was half of his identity. The other half he inherited from Captain Jack Curtis.

When someone is described as colorful, he may be interesting but probably not someone who would make a great father. Captain Jack was often absent, often drunk, often broke, and often married, and Charley was often asked about his father's escapades. But Jack Curtis was also bold—absolutely fearless. His life was punctuated by failures, but he never quit. He was the very symbol of nineteenth-century America, with his spirit of adventure and independence. Captain Jack was, by nature, a gambler, a risk taker, and while Charley guarded against the excesses that scarred his father's life, he must have also gleaned much that was good.

Charley's rise to success was as remarkable as that of Cherokee/Democrat/Oklahoman Will Rogers. Will never attempted to disguise his Cherokee ancestry and often commented on Charley's Native blood. Will eclipsed Charley in fame, but not by a lot at the time. They were the two most famous Indians in America: Will had achieved success in entertainment (though he was an astute businessman who parlayed his success into wealth and influence); Charley had come within a breath of the presidency.

Three times Charley appeared on the cover of *Time*. On December 20, 1926, he made the cover as Republican leader of the Senate. The second time he appeared on the cover was during the Republican National Convention on June 18, 1928, and the last time was while he was vice president on December 5, 1932.

The administration of Herbert Hoover has been inextricably linked to the Great Depression. Would Charley have led differently? There is no way to know, but just as Hoover's reputation has been somewhat rehabilitated over the past decade, so too should Charley's. He was a remarkable man, and understanding the world that created him and the legacy he left is a worthy pursuit. He deserves to be remembered, and we deserve to know who he was.

If Charley's legacy is "complicated," as the modern media has described it, it is because his life was complicated, his background was complicated. It is incredibly relevant today as people of mixed race navigate the world. Check the box "Black" and people ask, "Just how Black are you?" Check the box "Native" and people ask for tribal enrollment forms. People with mixed-race identity tried to "pass" as white in the past, and now people with no such ancestry are anxious to be the minority—"Wannabes" or "Pretendians."

In an interview with journalist/politician Richard B. Morrow in 1928, Charley was asked, "What will become of the Indian?" "They will vanish by and by into the white race," Charley answered. At the time, the outcome appeared inevitable.

The Kaw Nation has not ceased to exist. According to the tribal headquarters in Kaw City, Oklahoma, there are more than 3,800 enrolled members of the tribe today. But there are no full-bloods; the last person recognized as being full-blood, WWII veteran William Mehojah, passed away in 2000. The tribe has purchased some of its original homeland near Council Grove and holds ceremonies there each year in Allegawaho Park, named for the man who was chief when the Kaw were removed.

In 2023, the Sacred Red Rock, *In'zhúje'waxóbe*, was returned to the Kaw Nation from the city of Lawrence, Kansas. The twenty-eight-ton Siouxan quartzite boulder, which for centuries had rested in the confluence of the Kansas River and Shunganunga Creek in northeastern Kansas, had been moved to a city park in Lawrence in 1929 and a bronze plaque honoring the sacrifices of those early Kansas pioneers was bolted to it. When the boulder was moved from that location, the plaque was given to the Watkins Museum in Lawrence. A new home was designed for the sacred stone in Allegawaho Park, where it will once again occupy a place of reverence for the Kaw people.

The state of Kansas has tried to welcome the Kaw Nation back to its homeland. On June 13, 1998, Council Grove unveiled *The Guardian of the Grove*, an eight-foot-high bronze sculpture of a Kaw warrior, a "tribute to a Native American people who have refused to fade away into extinction." Situated on the path by the Neosho River, it is a counterpoint to the sculpture across the street, the *Madonna of the Trail*, representing the pioneer mother, babes in tow. There are twelve such statues spanning the country that were erected by the National Society of the Daughters of the Revolution in 1928–1929.

The final resting place of Charles and Annie Baird Curtis in Historic Topeka Cemetery. Charley's younger sister Elizabeth Curtis Layton Colvin and her husband are resting in the plot immediately to the left of the Curtis plot. She was his only full sibling.
COURTESY DR. MICHELLE MARTIN

The Kaw Mission State Historic Site in Council Grove interprets the story of the Kaws, and former site director Ron Parks and current director Mark Brooks have worked and continue to work with the tribe on projects that will benefit the community and the tribe.

In 2002, a bronze sculpture of a Kaw warrior, in readiness to release an arrow from his bow, was placed on top of the statehouse dome. The twenty-two-foot *Ad Astra* is aimed at the North Star, symbolic of the state's motto, *Ad Astra per Aspera*, "To the Stars through Difficulties."

Ken Bellmard, governmental affairs liaison for the tribe and a distant relative of Charley's, said that Charley "was a man of his times, and he did what he believed was best, for himself and for his family, and for his political party."

In the 1990s, the Historic Topeka Cemetery improved the Curtis gravesite. A flagpole was erected, and the large granite marker was

8

enhanced by the addition of the vice-presidential seal and the words "Shawnee County Attorney, Congressman, U.S. Senator, Senate Majority Leader." Above those were etched in granite, "Son of the Kanza Nation." No matter what world he was born into or world he chose, he would always be Kaw. He was born during their "darkest period," as Chief Allegawaho described it. That dark time of the Kaw, and the dark times of the nation, would shape Charley's perspective and guide his actions.

CHAPTER I

Roots and Branches 1791–1842

No voice can awake the dead; no power undo what is done.
—Thomas Jefferson

It may seem incongruous for a mixed-race boy in the nineteenth century to grow up to be an influential politician, to come within a breath of the presidency. But Charles Curtis's ancestors had been significant political and military leaders; they had met and made deals with presidents and others of high station in the government and army. The art of negotiation and the qualities of leadership were in his blood—his Indian blood.

In 1791, the November sun had not yet risen on the encampments along the Wabash River, Northwest Territory, but the soldiers had already paraded and had been quickly dismissed because of the cold. Some had kindled fires and were eating a meager breakfast. Their commanding officer was still abed. Suddenly, strange noises came from the woods around them. Horse-bells? Wolves? The noise was indistinct, confusing. Only a few realized it was the "war yell of Indians." It was likened to a swarm of bees, surrounding them all at once. One man recalled it was like a sudden thunderstorm. Major General Arthur St. Clair had no time to dress; he threw on a cloak and hat and left his tent to behold the all-out destruction before him.[1]

The dying and mutilated were a macabre tableau, recalled a survivor: "The freshly scalped heads were reeking with smoke, and in the heavy morning frost looked like so many pumpkins through a cornfield in December."[2]

The camp had become a killing field. All St. Clair could do was call for a retreat, a desperate scramble for survival. Those who huddled together only made for an easier target as they were picked off like a flock of turkeys.

Author Colin G. Calloway called it *The Victory with No Name*. It had no name because the burgeoning republic wanted to forget it. It was commonly called "St. Clair's Defeat," the "Battle on the Wabash," or, most dramatically, "The Battle of a Thousand Slain." The engagement was the result of President George Washington's sending his friend Major General St. Clair, veteran of battles at Trenton, Princeton, Ticonderoga, Brandywine Creek, and Yorktown, with around 1,400 soldiers to make Ohio safe for white settlement. This meant addressing the "Indian problem" by treaty or military action, usually meaning, of course, forced displacement. Sale of these lands was crucial to Alexander Hamilton's plan to pay the massive debts incurred during the American Revolution. There had been attacks and skirmishes; St. Clair's forces were attacked by a thousand warriors—a loose, and rare, coalition of Iroquois, Shawnee, Miami, Kickapoo, the Three Fires of Ojibwa, Ottawa, and Potawatomi.[3]

When the president heard the news, he remained calm in public, but in private he exploded. His ire, however, was directed more at St. Clair and less toward the enemy combatants. According to his secretary, he paced and fumed, hardly able to contain himself:

> It's all over!—St. Clair's defeated!—routed: the officers nearly all killed, the men by wholesale; the rout complete; too shocking to think of. . . . Yes, here on this very spot, I took leave of him; I wished him success and honor. "You have your instructions from the Secretary of War," said I. "I had a strict eye to them, and will add but one word, Beware of a Surprise!" He went off with that, my last warning, thrown into his ears. And yet! To suffer that army to be cut to pieces, hacked, butchered, tomahawked, by a surprise—the very thing I guarded him against—O God! O God! He's worse than a murderer! How can he answer it to his country! The blood of the slain is upon him—the curse of widows and orphans—the curse of heaven![4]

The defeat was a public relations nightmare, and the administration's PR machine began dissecting the battle, explaining how the US Army, which had just wrested independence from a world superpower, had been beaten—nearly annihilated—by the Indigenous population—savage, unsophisticated, simple people.

"It was the biggest victory Native Americans ever won and proportionately the biggest military disaster the United States ever suffered," wrote Calloway.[5] Nonetheless, President Washington chose to retaliate with diplomacy, inviting tribal representatives to the nation's capital, Philadelphia, in the hope of gaining their confidence and creating peace envoys among them. A pattern emerged—battles, treaties, delegations, promises—with each subsequent administration.

Charles Curtis's great-great-great-grandfather was a participant in this stinging victory, a participant on the winning side.

Osage warrior Iron Hawk, *Gra-to-Moh-se*, was not yet thirty years old when he went into battle against America, fighting alongside allies of various tribes. In the melee, the warrior attempted to scalp a fallen army officer, but the man's powdered wig came off in Iron Hawk's hands and the man escaped. The warrior was impressed with the power of the wig to protect the soldier and kept it, wearing it for ceremonial occasions and taking the name *Paw-Hiu-Skah*, or Pawhuska, meaning "White Hair," from this moment.

The Osage Nation split into factions, and Pawhuska was considered the chief of the Thorny-Valley people. Through his association with Pierre Chouteau, a member of the prominent French-Canadian fur-trading family, Pawhuska garnered an invitation to meet President Jefferson in 1804.

On July 12, Jefferson addressed his remarks to "My Children White Hairs, Chiefs & Warriors of the Osage Nation." "I receive you with great pleasure," wrote Jefferson. "I thank the Great Spirit who has inspired you with a desire to visit your new friends, & who has conducted you in safety to take us this day by the hand."[6]

The fatherly tone continues a few days later with a much more detailed address, again addressing them as "My Children" and explaining how the United States would be taking the place of France and Spain as

Osage Chief Pawhuska is the great-great-great-grandfather of Charles Curtis. The leader was invited to visit President Thomas Jefferson as part of a delegation to negotiate trade. He is believed to be buried near the site of Fort Osage (in western Missouri on the Missouri River), but there is no marked grave site.
COURTESY FORT OSAGE NATIONAL HISTORIC LANDMARK

their "neighbors, friends and fathers." Further, Jefferson stressed that he and his fellow Americans had been in North America for so long that they had no memory of their own arrival, an attempt to equate white Euro-Americans with Native Americans: "We are all now of one family, born in the same land, & bound to live as brothers; & the strangers from beyond the great water are gone from us." Then, the president got to the point: trade. With his most ingratiating tone, he wrote:

> The great Spirit has given you strength, and has given us strength; not that we might hurt one another, but to do each other all the good in our

power. Our dwellings indeed are very far apart; but not too far to carry on commerce & useful intercourse. You have furs and peltries which we want, and we have clothes and other useful things which you want. Let us employ ourselves then in mutually accommodating each other.[7]

Jefferson explained the importance of exploring the Louisiana Purchase to meet the nations that inhabited the land, land "which embraces all of the water of the Missisipi [sic] and Missouri," and to find "what number of peltries they could furnish," to discover what the tribes wanted in return, and to determine where trading posts would be established.[8]

The Louisiana Purchase nearly doubled the size of the nation, adding 828,000 square miles in the middle of the continent. To discover what lay in this vast territory and to create the maps necessary for future transactions, President Jefferson had sent "a beloved man, Capt Lewis, one of my own household to learn something of the people with whom we are now united, to let you know we were your friends, to invite you to come and see us, and to tell us how we can be useful to you."[9]

And finally, the plan:

We propose, my children, immediately to establish an Agent to reside with you, who will speak to you our words, and convey yours to us: who will be the guardian of our peace and friendship, convey truths from the one to the other, dissipate all falsehoods which might tend to alienate and divide us, and maintain a good understanding & friendship between us. As the distance is too great for you to come often and tell us your wants, you will tell them to him on the spot, and he will convey them to us in writing, so that we shall be sure that they come from you. Through the intervention of such an Agent we shall hope that our friendship will forever be preserved. No wrong will ever be done you by our nation, and we trust that you will do none to us. . . .

My children. These are my words. Carry them to your nation. Keep them in your memories, and our friendship in your hearts. And may the Great Spirit look down upon us, & cover us with the mantle of his love.[10]

The agent was William Clark. As brigadier general of the militia in the Louisiana District and US Agent for Indian Affairs (a combination of duties that speaks volumes about intent), Clark selected the site for Fort Osage. He had noted the location on the way up the Missouri River four years earlier; high banks on the north side of the river offered security and protection from flooding. Fort Osage (then called Fort Clark) was built thirty miles east of the river's confluence with the Kansas River.

The fort was built on the factory model, as a trading post. It was intended to create a mutually beneficial relationship with the Osage and maintain enough military presence to keep Spain and France at bay. George Sibley was the "factor," the man responsible for the trading and keeping the books.

By 1808, the Osage had become accustomed to trade items and had incorporated them into their daily lives as well as their clothing. Beaver pelts and other hides were traded for knives, pipes, tobacco pouches, mirrors, and woolen sashes. Cloth, beads, and tools became highly desirable items for the Osage. For a short time, the plan worked—trade did flourish and it did benefit the Natives and the government. But settlement kept pushing westward, and private trades lobbied to end the factory-forts.[11]

Pawhuska's daughter married the Kaw chief White Plume. The two daughters from this union married the sons of French fur trader Louis Gonville. Like so many other tribes, the Kaw were growing increasingly dependent on this trade for everyday items but also for guns and ammunition for hunting, so maintaining alliances with these traders was important for the well-being of the community.

Like his father-in-law years before, White Plume was asked to join a delegation to Washington. In 1821, the entourage met President James Monroe as well as other dignitaries and performed war dances on the White House lawn. They also visited Philadelphia, Baltimore, and New York City. The eminent artist Charles Bird King painted a portrait of White Plume. According to the US government, White Plume was the chief of the Kaw. But he wasn't. He had little or no control over other villages. In truth, the tribe was fracturing. Diminished by disease in the prior decades, the Kaw were struggling to maintain their customs and identity. Increasing tensions between the full-bloods and the French Kaw further splintered the tribe.

Another event in 1821 would have a lasting impact on the fate of the Kaw Nation. When Missouri became a state and Mexico gained its independence from Spain, a bankrupt entrepreneur made the trek from Missouri to Santa Fe, essentially following pieces of old trails slicing diagonally across Kansas. When he returned with a handsome profit in silver, the Santa Fe Trail was born, and for six decades traders and troops rolled their wagons back and forth along the route, through the lands of many Native tribes. The United States did negotiate treaties with the Kaw and Osage in 1825, which gave US citizens the right to travel across the Native lands.

White Plume also signed a treaty in 1825 ceding millions of acres of land to the United States; in reality, the land was no longer controlled by the Kaw Tribe since there had been so much encroachment by whites and other tribes. The trip to Washington had its desired effect on White Plume. The only way to survive was to find a way to work with the whites. The old conservative chiefs did not agree, and the fact that White Plume's granddaughters, mixed bloods married to Frenchmen, were each granted a square mile of land on the north side of the Kansas River did little to heal the resentment.

White Plume's ceding of so much land had paved the way for Indian removal from the East. Former Kaw lands would become home to Shawnee, Wyandotte, Potawatomi, Delaware, Iowa, Sac and Fox, Kickapoo, and other tribes relocated from their homelands. No thought was given to the disparate cultures, the varying customs, the different languages, the troubles that would be caused by putting these diverse tribes together on another tribe's land. Furthermore, none of these tribes were given a choice. The Wyandotte had already been moved to Ohio and had thriving businesses and farms. When the government realized that it had agreed to compensate them for the property, it removed the people first, let the homes and stores and farms go to ruin, then valued the property and paid them a sum greatly reduced from that they had fairly expected.

So, it would seem to many people that White Plume's grandchildren had fared better than anyone in their government deals, and the Frenchmen who had married them had chosen well. Years later, when newspapers described Charles Curtis's background, his grandmother,

Julie Gonville Pappan, pictured here with her granddaughter, Belle, was the
French-Kaw grandmother of Charles Curtis and the granddaughter of the Kaw chief
White Plume. As a child, Charles lived with Julie and Louis Pappan on the Kaw
Reservation near Council Grove, Kansas.

Julie Gonville Pappan, was presented as an "Indian Princess," an heiress. As the granddaughter of White Plume and the great-granddaughter of Pawhuska, she may have had some status and she did inherit a big chunk of land, but her life was hardly that of a royal.

Julie's husband and his brothers, of French-Canadian descent, may have fallen in love with her and her sisters—each of the brothers married one of Louis Gonville's daughters—but maybe the marriages between the Gonville sisters and the Pappan brothers were political arrangements, practical liaisons to benefit all involved. Julie's sisters inherited land too, and the Gonville-Pappans moved to those lovely, wooded tracts of land, settling side by side along the river that would become their livelihood and their downfall.

In 1842, the Pappan brothers started a ferry operation, quite a lucrative, if challenging, enterprise. The ferry served traffic between Fort Leavenworth and the southwest—soldiers, trappers, traders, government officials. Business was growing but the Kansas River flooded in 1844, washing away cabins, boats, and their business. The families returned to Kansas City for a time, but returned and were back in business by 1846. The ferry flourished as traffic along the Oregon Trail and California Road increased. A traveler wrote in 1849 that using two boats the ferry carried from sixty-five to seventy wagons per day at $1 per wagon.[12] By comparison, a blacksmith in the same era might make $2 a day.

All those wagons were evidence of western migration, and it was ramping up. The 1849 gold rush in California had people in eastern cities tossing their homes and families aside for the opportunity to strike it rich. Merchants selling picks and pans made more money than gold-seekers, but the hordes kept coming. Soon, the idea of Kansas's being set aside as an Indian Territory would be abandoned and it would be open for settlement. The area south of Kansas that nobody wanted would serve as the perfect location to locate all the tribes that needed to be moved, eventually.

As Congress talked about western expansion and railroads, the nation looked greedily toward the land of the Kaw.

CHAPTER 2

Gold-Seekers, Dreamers, and Ferryboat Men 1855–1863

I believe man will not merely endure, he will prevail . . . because he has a spirit capable of compassion and sacrifice and endurance.
—WILLIAM FAULKNER

ORAN A. "JACK" CURTIS,[1] THE HARDY PIONEER, THE WANDERER, THE fortune seeker, had left western Indiana heading for the gold fields of California. That's one story. Another goes that he divorced his wife and joined a circus wagon train (this is what Charley said). Maybe he went to Iowa for a short time. Some said his aim was Kansas Territory all along, that he planned to seek his fortune and throw in his lot with the Free-State folks all at once. Whatever circuitous path he took, he landed on the north side of the Kansas River, hired by the Pappans to run the ferry.

Jack built a cabin not far from the Pappans and cultivated about five acres of ground. The Territory was ripe with opportunity, and he was not the only person lured by the prospects. Missourians had been eyeing the ground just across the way for decades, waiting for it to open for white settlement. The fact that it had been set aside as "Indian Territory" and tribes from the East relocated a generation before made no difference. The holdup, ironically, was the people of another color. Would slavery be allowed in this new territory? Not under the laws of the time.

The Missouri Compromise of 1820 admitted the states of Missouri and Maine into the Union; Missouri came in as slave state and Maine as a free state. The compromise was aimed at maintaining the balance of power in Congress equally between slave and free state representatives. The bill also set the future boundaries: any state above the 36 degree 30☒ parallel would come in as a free state, below would be slave. Missouri was above the parallel, but it got a pass.

As talk of a transcontinental railroad increased and hungry eyes looked toward Kansas, it was not the fact that it had already been designated as an Indian Territory that posed problems; it was the fact that under the Missouri Compromise, it would enter the Union as a free state. Missouri slave holders were especially concerned that a free state next door would create problems. After months of debate, there was a new compromise, and it stank to high heaven.

The Kansas-Nebraska Act was viewed as a pro-slavery measure, signed by the wishy-washy President Franklin Pierce and urged by a Congress fearful of tackling the issue head-on. Built into the legislation was the mechanism to decide the issue: popular sovereignty. The voters of the Kansas Territory themselves would decide.

How very democratic.

Abolitionists were outraged. The outcome was a foregone conclusion because those voting would be from the slave state of Missouri. Since the founding of the colonies, the formula had been that the territories to the west took on the culture of its mother colony or state. Virginia, a slave state, had settled Kentucky, a slave state. Kentucky had settled Missouri, and Missouri would settle Kansas. The fate of Kansas was sealed.

New England abolitionists organized settlers of their own, forming groups like the New England Emigrant Aid Society, and sent them to outvote the pro-slavery Missourians. For Missouri, this was tantamount to a declaration of war. The fate of Kansas was indeed sealed; it would be a battleground for ten years, and the very soul of the nation rested on the outcome.

Finally, the day came on May 30, 1854, and settlers were waiting to spring. In fact, William F. "Buffalo Bill" Cody's family had come from Iowa and picked out lush grassy hills near Fort Leavenworth. They had hastily built a cabin and cut trees in anticipation of filing their claim. Cody also observed the eagerness of the Missourians to claim land in Kansas:

> [They] would come laden with bottles of whisky, and after drinking the liquor would drive the bottles into the ground to mark their land claims, not waiting to put up any buildings. . . .
>
> [T]he western boundary of Missouri was ablaze with the camp fires of intending settlers. Thousands of families were sheltered under the canvas of their ox wagons, impatiently awaiting the signal from the Nation announcing the opening of the territorial doors to the brawny immigrants, and when the news was heralded the waiting host poured over the boundary line and fairly deluged the new public domain.[2]

Jack Curtis rode that wave of immigration and then he profited from the throngs that kept coming. He may have even passed the Codys along the way as he wound his way into the Territory from Indiana.

Kansas was sprouting towns all along the streams and trails of the eastern counties and eventually the far-flung Rocky Mountains, as gold and silver were discovered. Across the river from Jack's cabin, the town of Topeka had been established in December 1854. It wasn't much to speak of then, but men like Pennsylvanian Cyrus K. Holliday came with pockets of cash and a vision of steel rails crossing the prairies, and an impressive statehouse on the high ground above the river crossing. It took quite the imagination to picture a city rising from what most considered a howling wilderness.

Holliday, along with other men from the New England Emigrant Aid Society, huddled in a shabby cabin made from the trunks of small, crooked trees with brush and prairie grass as a roof and declared a town into existence. They went to work surveying with a 50-cent compass and the pieces of rope that had bound their belongings.

The privation experienced by those early settlers is evidenced by a letter that Holliday wrote his wife waiting in Pennsylvania:

> [I]f you know the inconveniences under which I write you would almost excuse me from writing at all—I am now better situated for

CONFERENCE OF KAW INDIANS (KANSAS) WITH THE UNITED STATES' COMMISSIONER OF INDIAN AFFAIRS.—SEE PRECEDING PAGE.

Europe was fascinated by the Native Americans in North America. While Kansas was consumed by the issues and violence of Bleeding Kansas during the Territorial period, the Kaw Nation was still trying to negotiate for lands and its very existence. This illustration of Kaw delegates meeting with the Commissioner of Indian Affairs appeared in the *London News* in 1857.
COURTESY LIBRARY OF CONGRESS

> writing than I have been in, perhaps, any other occasion; and I am now sitting upon a trunk with a box . . . before me as my desk—at this moment the Minister who has just preached for us—and who is lying upon my bed, which consists of a handful of hay and a Buffalo Robe, by accident, has almost kicked my desk over—and while writing the last line I have removed twice—once to get out of our cooks way—and once to get nearer the door for light—our cabin having no windows in it.[3]

Politicians and speculators set their sights on the plains. Missouri Senator Thomas Hart Benton addressed a crowd in Maryland touting the bounty of Kansas and the coming of the railroads that would bring prosperity.

He said immigrants would be flocking to the center of the country where the "soil was rich as Egypt!" But the ultimate reason to settle Kansas, exhorted Benton, was the Pacific Railroad:

> The road will be made, and soon, and by individual enterprize. The age is progressive and utilitarian. It abounds with talent, seeking employment, and with capital, seeking investment. The temptation is irresistible. To reach the golden California—to put the population of the Atlantic, the Pacific, and the Mississippi Valley, into direct communion—to connect Europe and Asia through our America—and to own a road of our own to the East Indies: such is the grandeur of the enterprize! And the time has arrived to begin it. . . . The world is in motion, following the track of the sun to its dip in the western ocean. Westward the torrents of emigration direct their course; and soon the country between Missouri and California is to show the most rapid expansion of the human race that the ages of man have ever beheld.[4]

The world was most certainly in motion and at an unprecedented speed. The building of railroads captured the public's imagination and the ambition of investors. The fortunes that would be made and lost during the last half of the nineteenth century were equally unprecedented. Perhaps at no time in the nation's history has the American Dream been more possible—for paupers to become millionaires, for commoners to become pillars of society. It was the golden age of speculation and con games, of sideshows and spectacles. Kansas would have its share of all of them.

Settlers flocked to the Territory, always good news for the ferry business and perhaps behind the Pappans' motivation to hire Jack Curtis. Fortunately for Holliday and other newcomers, the winter of 1854–1855 was mild, perhaps lulling folks into believing the climate of Kansas would be welcoming.

Among the new arrivals were John and Mary Jane Ritchie from Indiana, with their small children, Hale and Mary. Their first home was a dugout in the bank of Shunganunga Creek, a hole carved into the ground with a lean-to built of lumber scraps to protect it. It was damp and cold, and their baby girl became ill and died that fall. Winter would be even worse, and Mary recalled that water froze in the glass on the table and bread had to be thawed to be sliced. Temperatures fell to 24 degrees below zero in December.[5]

Spring 1856 brought warmer temperatures but higher tempers. Jack Curtis had arrived just in time for the most violent year of what would become known as "Bleeding Kansas." As Cody recalled, "The Kansas troubles reached their highest pitch in the spring of 1856."[6]

The patriarch of the Cody clan, Isaac Cody, was an outspoken abolitionist and participated in establishing new communities in the Territory. He had secured a lucrative contract providing hay for the horses and mules of the post at Leavenworth. On his return one day, he was attacked by pro-slavery Missourians. He never fully recovered, and border ruffians often came to the Cody home to find him and finish him. Young Willie, as Bill was referred to when he was a boy, described how his father would hide in the woods until he felt it was safe to return home.[7]

Located along one of the main thoroughfares, Jack may not have taken an active part, but the climate of fear and uncertainty affected everyone in the Territory and he would have observed the comings and goings of all the players in this grand drama. In time, he would be in the thick of the conflict.

Towns and neighborhoods assumed political identities as pro- or anti-slavery. Generally, Atchison, Leavenworth, and Lecompton had Southern sympathies, while Lawrence and Topeka were abolitionist strongholds. The federal government itself was in the hands of a Northern Democrat, President Franklin Pierce, who saw abolishing slavery as a threat to the nation's unity. Having lost his only son in an accident between his election and assuming office, Pierce seemed unable or unwilling to fully deal with the demands of the presidency and relied heavily upon his Secretary of War, the former Mississippi senator and Mexican War hero Jefferson Davis.

It was Davis (who soon would become the president of the seceded states) who gave orders to his old friend Colonel E. V. Sumner and other officers in the Territory. Colonel Sumner commanded Fort Leavenworth, the oldest fort west of the Mississippi River and headquarters for soldiers protecting much of the Great Plains. Events in the spring and summer of 1856 kept Colonel Sumner and his men scurrying to deal with the conflicts, though they were rarely in the middle of it. Their role appears to have been more referee than protector, pulling the combatants apart and sending them back to their respective corners. Colonel Sumner, a Unionist and an abolitionist in principle, struggled to follow orders and keep the peace, all the while following his own conscience.

It was a Herculean task.

A study of the US Army officers who served in the Kansas Territory is a who's who of Civil War officers, but sadly on different sides. Lieutenant James E. B. Stuart, Sumner's adjutant, would become a Confederate major general, commanding the First Virginia Cavalry in the Army of Northern Virginia. Major John Sedgwick, a veteran of the Mexican War, served under Sumner in Kansas and went on to become a major general in the Union Army during the Civil War. Stuart and Sedgwick would die only two days apart during battles in Virginia. Bleeding Kansas was a proving ground for the devastating war to come.

After decidedly compromised Territorial elections, the legislature had a pro-slavery agenda. (The election fraud was overwhelming, with more votes cast than eligible voters in the state.) The Free-State faction, refusing to accept defeat, formed their own legislative body, which was to meet at Topeka in Constitution Hall in early July. The first six months of the year were marked by violence heretofore unimagined in civil society. In May, Missouri's US senator David Rice Atchison had led a mob in the destruction of Lawrence, the home of many of the state's most ardent abolitionists. Spurred by the attack (and perhaps the news that Massachusetts Senator Charles Sumner had been beaten nearly to death on the floor of the Senate by South Carolina Congressman Preston Brooks), noted abolitionist John Brown went on a rampage of his own.

Brown had made no secret of his hatred of slavery and those who defended it. Members of his family had moved to Kansas to secure its status as a free state, but as the cause became increasingly doomed, they had written to Brown to come join them in the effort. He and his sons were encamped south of Lawrence, near Baldwin City. As it happened, there were Southerners who had settled in the neighborhood, families of little means who were not slave owners. "I came to the territory to secure a home for my family, not for political purposes," said James Doyle. "I wish nothing to do with politics."[8] But despite their wishing to remain neutral, Doyle and his neighbors would be made examples.

His wife, Mahala, recalled:

> [A]bout eleven o'clock at night, after we had all retired . . . we heard some persons come into the yard and rap at the door and call for . . . my husband. . . . [M]y husband, opened the door, and several came into the house, and said they were from the army. . . . They told my husband that he and the boys must surrender, they were their prisoners. . . . They first took my husband out of the house, then they took two of my sons—the two oldest ones, William and Drury—out, and then took [them] . . . away. My son John was spared, because I asked them in tears to spare him.[9]

As the men were led into the darkness, Mrs. Doyle heard two gunshots and then a whoop. The widows found the mutilated corpses of their loved ones the next day, and the terrorist act had the desired effect. Southerners left the Pottawatomie Valley.

Just days later, John Brown led forces against Missourians at the Black Jack campground on the Santa Fe Trail near Baldwin City. Brown captured several of the Missourians and held them prisoner in his camp until Colonel Sumner and his troops arrived to release them. Brown had won what many people considered the first battle of the Civil War.

The Territory was a powder keg, and following these events even the *London Times* proclaimed, "War in Kansas!"

The Free-State government was meeting in Topeka and among the delegates was Isaac Cody, the delegate from Grasshopper Falls. His son, Willie, may have been in tow.[10] They very likely used the ferry operated by Jack Curtis to cross the river.

President Pierce had ordered the extralegal body to be disbanded. Colonel Sumner arrived on July 3 and his troops camped on the edge of town. On the morning of July 4, the colonel ordered the cannon to be fired in salute to the nation's eightieth birthday. Not only was the Free-State Legislature in session, but the Free-State Militia had also assembled and were well-armed with new Sharps rifles. (Perhaps the firing of the cannon was more of a psychological ploy than a patriotic salute—a loud reminder of the might of the US Army.) Temperatures reached 100 degrees by noon and tensions were high.

Colonel Sumner assembled his troops on Kansas Avenue and ordered the cannon match lit in readiness to fire the weapon. He strode into the chamber and informed those assembled that he had been ordered to disperse the gathering. It was the most painful duty of his life, he said, but he would use every tool at his disposal to carry out his orders. His reputation was well known, and the group left without incident.

Jack would have heard the cannon boom from his cabin. With so many people coming in and out of the city, the ferry must have been operating overtime. We have no record of Jack's activities, but it is likely that he was transporting passengers of every political persuasion across the Kansas River. Once, reported a local paper, his passengers were legislators, and the ice was so thick that "Capt. Curtis had to beat his way across." The officials themselves were called in to serve and with "poles, hooks and axes, the ice was broken clear across, security for the boat had to be given before the captain could take the august body onboard." The legislators congratulated themselves upon successfully crossing the river, "rivaling Washington in his perilous crossing of the Delaware." Another account tells of his transporting John Brown with slaves escaping from Missouri.[11]

These stories may be apocryphal; at the very least the writer was confused. The article described the ice-breaking incident as the same time the Free-State Legislature was dismissed; since that event occurred in July, the legislators could not have been breaking ice to get there. Also, the federally recognized government was in Lecompton then, not Topeka. As for transporting John Brown with his escaping slaves, it is possible.

With the help of John and Mary Jane Ritchie and other Topeka abolitionists, Brown was hiding twelve slaves stolen from Missouri, among them a newborn baby. Clothes and provisions were collected in secret until at last it was determined they must leave. This was January 1859. They crossed the Kansas River at night leaving the Ritchie home; Captain Jack's ferry would have been the most direct and the family's politics were also known. Thus, it is very likely that it was Captain Jack who escorted John Brown and his charges across the river as they moved northward.[12]

Whether Jack came to Kansas with abolitionist ideals or not, his parents certainly did. They left Indiana at his urging and settled not far from him, purchasing a large tract of land on the north side of the Kansas River. William and Permelia Curtis, both descended from the earliest settlers in New England, were aligned with the newly established Republican Party and were staunch in their abolitionist beliefs. They became anchors in the community.

The Curtises were everywhere. Jack left his wife, Isabel, and their three surviving children (including a newborn) in Indiana, but she soon relocated to the community where the other Curtises lived. Jack and Isabel divorced in 1858 and she remarried soon after, but she would remain near her in-laws for the rest of her life.

On May 1, 1859, the thirty-year-old Jack married nineteen-year-old Helen Pappan, the only daughter and eldest child of Julie and Louis Pappan. The nuptials were performed at Immaculate Conception Church in St. Mary's, about twenty-five miles to the west. Helen had some education from the Catholic mission at St. Mary's, and Jack had some ambition and the common sense required to survive the frontier. The couple settled in Jack's cabin and life was promising despite the unrest in the Territory. An advertisement in the local paper on December 1 read:

TOPEKA FERRY
O.A. CURTIS, Proprietor
This Ferry is now prepared for THE SEASON.
Boats in readiness Night and Day!!!!

This first class Ferry, across the Kansas River, is again in the hands of the subscriber, who is making quick trips with the greatest of safety. My boats are good and hands experienced. This is certainly the best and most reliable Ferry on the River. It is on the Route from Leavenworth to Topeka, Santa Fe, and the Gold Miles, and over which Government trains invariably pass.[13]

Jack's 1859 charter gave him right-of-way on the river for four miles. A newspaper reporter recalled:

The first boat built was fifty feet long, which was soon found to be too small for the increased travel, and another boat, seventy-five feet in length, was built. A rope cable was stretched across the river, and the flat boat, being fitted with lee-board and center wheel, Capt. Curtis was ready for the hundreds and thousands who were to become his customers. The tollage averaged about $50 daily, some days going as low as $5, while it ran up, on others, to $280. Many times Capt. Curtis had to go to his house and empty his pouches of silver for fear that an accident or a capsize might cause the weight in his pocket to carry him to the bottom of the river.[14]

The reporter shared another incident demonstrating how profitable the ferry business was. In 1858, a "traveling beat," a deadbeat, had showed up at the ferry and the smallest denomination he had to pay the 10-cent toll was a $50 gold piece, assuming that the ferry operator would not be able to make change. The "traveling beat" had hoodwinked many other toll keepers out of their fare because they had not enough on hand to break the gold piece. But he met his match in Jack Curtis:

But "Capt. Curtis" was not commanding officer of this ferry to no purpose. His cabin was a regular government mint, where silver, if not coined, was kept in quantities to suit such millionaires as choose to walk the trackless plains. Investigating the resources of the family crocking, it did not take long for the Captain to fish out $49.90 which was carried down to the tramp who had fondly imagined he could beat the ferry out of ten cents. The load of silver appalled him.[15]

The customer offered Jack $2.50 to have his gold coin returned, earning Jack the highest fee anyone had heard of for transporting one person over the river.[16]

The lucrative ferry business would seem to provide a comfortable home when Jack and Helen welcomed a little boy, Charles Brent, "Charley," on January 25, 1860, and two years later, a little girl, Elizabeth, "Libby."

The Territory was growing rapidly and its population supported statehood, but it came with a price. Abraham Lincoln, a Republican outsider, was elected president in November 1860. The crevices in the country became canyons. Kansas was admitted to the Union as a free state on January 29, 1861, just four days after Charley's first birthday. But as Kansas came in, other states seceded. The country reeled toward war, and the first shots were fired in April in South Carolina. President Lincoln issued a call for 75,000 troops to quash the rebellion. Jack did not answer the call. His life was going well; there was no need to rock the boat.

Charley was christened in the same church where his parents had married, by the same priest. He could not remember, but Charley was told that his mother taught him to swim in the Kansas River and to ride a horse. He could not remember because he was only three years old when she passed away from black fever in April 1863.[17]

Jack's sister, however, said that Helen died of a broken heart as "her husband had conducted himself so shamefully." Emma Curtis La Tourette described her oldest brother as the "ne'er-do-well" of the family. He was known as a "holy terror," a combination of "bad man, broncho buster and fire eater. He made short work of his wife's estate," Emma confided to neighbor James E. Safford.[18]

Charley and his infant sister went to live with Grandfather and Grandmother Curtis at the Curtis House, a hotel anchoring the businesses in North Topeka. Sister Emma said that Jack had wrecked their parents' finances as well, "reducing his father to very straightened circumstances."[19]

"He was a frightful handicap to his family," Safford wrote of his observations and conversations with Emma, "especially his children, who were accustomed to hide themselves in fear and trembling whenever he made his infrequent visits to the house on the Kaw river." At some point, Libby went to live with her Aunt Emma, according to Safford.[20]

Jack was lost following Helen's death, whether from a combination of guilt and grief who can know? As is often the case, he quickly remarried to fill the void, and perhaps with the thought of regaining his children. He married Rachel Funk in late July. Then in August, the unthinkable happened. One word spoke terror along the Kansas border: Quantrill.

CHAPTER 3

Copperheads, Bushwhackers, and Jayhawkers 1863–1866

It was not well to drive men into final corners; at those moments they could all develop teeth and claws.

—STEPHEN CRANE

ABOUT TEN O'CLOCK IN THE MORNING ON AUGUST 21, 1863, TERRIBLE rumors began reaching Topeka: "Missouri Bushwhackers were in Lawrence enacting their hellish deeds of robbing, murdering and burning."[1]

Topeka's mayor sent messengers to investigate, and they returned around dark to confirm the news of the raid. A force of five hundred men had arrived at dawn and taken the sleepy town completely by surprise. "The first notice of their approach was a furious charge through the streets, in which they indiscriminately shot down every one in their way without respect to age. . . . The work of their slaughter continued until 9 o'clock, A.M., when the bushwhackers left town, having left the whole business district in ashes."[2]

The mayor was sending aid to Lawrence as well as calling into service the local military. But one of the first people to respond to news of the raid was Jack Curtis: "We take pride in calling attention to O. A. Curtis and his company of cavalry from Soldier Township and the southern portion of Jackson county which have been recruited, mounted, and armed in the space of a very few hours, and are now at this point ready to march towards the foe, whenever and wherever they may show themselves."[3]

As outlandish as the initial reports from Lawrence were, the reality was far more horrific. Confederate guerrilla William Clarke Quantrill, schoolteacher turned bushwhacker, had led a force of 350 to 450 men, some battle-wizened veterans, some angry farmers, into the second-largest town in Kansas and laid waste. They had carried "death lists," names of the leading abolitionists they would target. At the top of the list, Senator/General Jim Lane. But Lane heard the shots and escaped into a corn-field. Former governor Charles Robinson had awakened early and was at his barn on one of the highest points in the city. He could only watch helplessly as his town was burned and his neighbors murdered. The final tally was two hundred men and boys killed. A column of black smoke in the windless summer sky could be seen in thirty-eight counties on the Kansas-Missouri border. More than two hundred homes and businesses were destroyed.[4]

The impact of Quantrill's raid cannot be overstated. It is the nature of a terrorist act to result in fear and paranoia. This was achieved in spades. While the communities hugging the Missouri line had been vulnerable and were plundered and pillaged sporadically during the preceding years, for the guerillas to stage an attack so far into Kansas was thought impos-sible. They had passed near Union troops, marching through towns where they were taken for Union soldiers themselves. The Missourians had traveled in military formation, four abreast, with those in front and rear wearing blue uniform jackets over their brightly colored guerilla shirts. If this could happen in Lawrence, no place in Kansas would be safe.

As the details of the raid became known, no exaggeration was needed to instill fear or fuel the fire of retribution. Quantrill's men had strict orders that no woman or child be harmed (there was a boy of twelve killed, wearing a Union jacket). These orders were followed, but the harm to those left behind was worse than death. Bodies lay roasting in the street, literally being pulled apart as they were moved. The town ran out of coffins—there were nearly none to be had with the businesses destroyed. The grim vision of lanterns leading to Pioneer Cemetery on the hilltop above the town, bodies laid out on boards, or in one instance, a widow carrying the remains of her husband in a bucket—these images would haunt Lawrence for generations to come, and it would galvanize Kansans into action.[5]

Another call went out for volunteers to protect the state. At a meeting in the Methodist church in Topeka soon after the raid, Colonel Charles Jennison and Captain George Hoyt were invited to speak. The colorful Jennison had already made a name for himself in his conduct of the war. "Jennison's Jayhawkers" became infamous for their taking advantage of the situation on the border to loot and plunder western Missouri, and some thought provoking the attack on Lawrence. Jennison, however, was ill and unable to attend. It fell to his captain to excite the crowd, and he did. An experienced lawyer, Captain Hoyt had represented John Brown during his 1859 trial for treason following the failed raid at Harpers Ferry. Hoyt had earned credibility as a champion of the Union and abolitionist causes. He boomed at his audience:

> The massacre at Lawrence calls for retribution, and we propose to mete it out, through an organized regiment, under the old Jayhawker himself. The men composing this regiment will not stay their hands until retribution is complete. The first gun against Sumter was not fired by the rebels, but from the little howitzer planted in front of the Free State Hotel at Lawrence in '56, in defence [sic] of freedom, and in opposition to the aggressions of the slave powers.[6]

Captain Hoyt was referring to the attack led by Senator Atchison on Lawrence. During the attack, the Free State Hotel (as its name would indicate, home to many abolitionists and their meeting place) was burned to the ground by the pro-slavery county sheriff. The hotel was rebuilt as the Eldridge and continued to be the center of the abolitionist movement. When Quantrill attacked the town in 1863, the hotel was again destroyed. There had always been talk of spies in the Territory and the state, those who gathered information on the pretext of doing business and carried the intelligence back to Missouri, but following the events in Lawrence the need to identify these traitors became urgent. Captain Hoyt continued:

> There are copperheads and Southern sympathizers in Shawnee county.
> They infest the valley of the Kaw from Wyandotte to the Blue [River],
> and are thicker on the Wakarusa [River] than anywhere else. Will you
> have these men among you give information to Quantrill? It is worse
> than folly to attempt to guard your town with these men in it. If you
> don't like to undertake the job yourselves, send down to Leavenworth
> for me. and I will come up with a delegation of Jayhawkers, and we will
> quietly dispose of them.[7]

Another in the crowd urged all true Union men "who were foot-loose
and able-bodied" to enlist, but only after they had "killed every Copper-
head in the county."[8]

Since Jack had so readily responded, it begs the question, was he "foot-
loose"? He and Rachel had only been married three and a half weeks, and
he would rarely, if ever, be at home in the coming months. Whether his
enlistment hastened his marriage's demise or was a result of a crumbling
relationship, he and Rachel officially divorced in December 1864.

Jack was made captain of the 15th Kansas Volunteer Cavalry and
actively recruited his neighbors, including at least one French-Kaw
brother-in-law, Louis Pappan, and other Kaws, Joe Bellmard and Henry
Pappan, who were only sixteen years old.[9] Since arriving in Kansas, he
had often been referred to as "Ferryboat Jack," but from this time forward, he would be Captain Jack and the newspapers reported on his
exploits, even before he was in the field:

> Just previous to Capt. Curtis and his recruits for Jennison's regiment
> leaving this city on Monday, they made a dash into Harrison's saloon
> for Jack Thompson of Indianola, but he was not there. The boys said he
> had got to enlist or be hung. In the temper they were in we presume
> they would have carried out their threat. When his recruits were assem-
> bled in the street, Capt. Jack rode out in front and addressed them,
> "Now, gentlemen, I want you to follow me. Ther's no place where Jack
> Curtis dassent go."[10]

Following Quantrill's raid, Brigadier General Thomas Ewing Jr., in
charge of guarding the border, was pressured to act. Ewing was the foster

Captain Oran A. "Captain Jack" Curtis, Company 5, 15th Kansas Cavalry, was the father of Charles Curtis. His colorful life was sometimes an embarrassment to the family. He worked as a ferryboat operator, deputy, fisherman, farmer, and soldier.

brother and brother-in-law of General William T. Sherman, who was making a name for himself at that moment on the southern battlefields. In Missouri, Ewing would become as infamous as Sherman in the South after he issued General Order No. 11.

It is the nature of guerilla warfare that the soldier blends into the background, emerging to fight, returning to an ordinary life—hidden, as it were, in plain sight. General Ewing was tired of it. If the people were going to protect these brigands, then he would make war on the people, not unlike General Sherman's "March to the Sea." Both were aimed at destroying the material support for the rebels. In short, residents of three and a half Missouri counties bordering Kansas would be depopulated, except for cities and towns under martial law. Roughly twenty thousand residents were to be out of their homes in fifteen days. The enforcement was draconian.

As Union soldiers scoured the Missouri countryside, the order was interpreted as giving them a free hand upon the population. Those not already out of their homes were forced out and the houses and barns burned. One single squad of men burned 110 houses, admitted one officer. Two weeks after the order had been issued, "[t]he border counties of Missouri have almost as desolate an appearance as before the soil was trod by the white man," reported a Kansas soldier. "Not a man, woman or child is to be seen in the country to which Order No. 11 applies. . . . Chimneys mark the spot where once stood costly farm houses."[11]

Somehow, despite his service in the 15th Kansas Volunteer Cavalry, Captain Jack managed to launch "two large Ferry Boats at Topeka, capable of holding one six mule team or wagon with six yoke of oxen, and crosses New Mexico wagons for only fifty cents for crossing. The landings are good, and a train of wagons can be put over in a very short time. New Mexico merchants call it twenty miles nearer to this city by that route than to Kansas City."[12] It would seem that Captain Jack's entrepreneurial drive was not dampened by the border war.

Tensions once again were at an all-time high when Confederate General Sterling Price invaded Missouri and turned his thousands of troops toward Kansas. Price was repulsed at Kansas City and again at

Mine Creek, near Fort Scott in southeastern Kansas, but the threat had been very real.

While on the battlefield, Colonel Samuel Crawford was nominated as the Republican candidate for governor in Kansas. He had been a member of the first Kansas State Legislature but had resigned his seat to join the army when Lincoln issued his original call for volunteers in 1861. One of the greatest fears in that 1864 election was that the Kansas troops answering the call would not be home to vote in November. Crawford received a promotion and was elected to become the third governor of Kansas. He finished the war in the governor's office and would forever boast of being one of the "War Governors."[13]

Price's raid had begun in late August, and attention was drawn from the western reaches of Missouri to the eastern half of the state as he looked toward St. Louis. While troops were engaging Price's forces in that area, once again the border with Kansas became more dangerous, no matter what side of the fight. In the field, Captain Jack was ferocious in rooting out the enemy, as evidenced by an account from Mound City's *Border Sentinel* on September 2, 1864. This would lead one to believe that he had taken to heart the words of George Hoyt. The headline read "Two Bushwhackers Killed":

> Capt. Curtis left this post in search of bushwhackers living in Kansas, and engaged in giving information and aid to the bushwhackers of Missouri, and stealing and running off stolen horses. The information upon which this scout moved was given in a confession of this man Davis, who stated that there was an organization of thieves and bushwhackers extending along the eastern border of Kansas, from the South to the North of the State, and also back into the State.[14]

The guide proved to be worthless, and Captain Jack turned back. On his return, however, he found a man named Ellis, who admitted that he fed Quantrill and his men when they made the raid on Lawrence. The man claimed to know the names of one hundred Missouri bushwhackers but refused to give them up. He was taken prisoner and attempted to escape once they reached the timber of the Marais des Cygnes River. He was shot. In the meantime, the useless guide, Davis, had confessed that he was a deserter from the 14th Kansas Volunteer Cavalry and that he had been involved in stealing horses. The article concluded:

> Curtis thought, and rightly, too, that he was of no use to the government in particular or to mankind in general so he hung him until he was dead. This ended his treacherous existence. So, two more of the enemies of human-kind have gone to account for their misdeeds. There can be no question as to the justice of killing these two men. By their own admissions they had forfeited their lives, and utterly refused any information that would lead to the punishment of those with whom they were confederated to murder and steal. This is some more work in the right direction. We hope Capt. Jack Curtis may be sent out often, and double the number of these devils killed each time.[15]

"Devil" is such a subjective word.

The savagery was not limited to the eastern part of Kansas. General Price's raid in Missouri had drawn attention to the eastern border of the state, while leaving a void in the western reaches. Colonel John Chivington took advantage of that lack of oversight. On November 29, 1864, Chivington led the more than seven hundred US volunteers in an attack upon a village of five hundred Cheyenne and Arapaho, mostly families, in eastern Colorado Territory:

> Using small-arms and howitzer fire, the troops drove the people out of their camp. While many managed to escape the initial onslaught, others, particularly noncombatant women, children, and the elderly, fled into and up the bottom of the dry streambed. The soldiers followed, shooting at them as they struggled through the sandy earth. At a point several yards above the village, the people frantically excavated pits and trenches along either side of the streambed to protect themselves. Some attempted to fight back with whatever weapons they had managed to retrieve from the camp, and at several places along Sand Creek, the soldiers shot into them from opposite banks and presently brought forward the howitzers to blast them from their scant defenses. Over the course of seven hours, the troops succeeded in killing at least 150 Cheyennes and Arapahos, mostly the old, the young, and the weak.

During the afternoon and following day, the soldiers wandered over the field, committing atrocities on the dead, before departing the scene on December 1.[16]

The wanton brutality of the attack beggars belief. Historian Louis Kraft, writing in *Sand Creek and the Tragic End of a Lifeway*, shared the experience of a corporal who participated in the massacre. Wandering about the encampment afterward he saw "a little boy covered up among the Indians in a trench, still alive" and he saw a major "take out his pistol and blow off the top of his head." He watched the plundering of the bodies for rings and trinkets, cutting off body parts to get ornaments, a woman with her head smashed in. The soldiers dug up bodies buried the night before and scalped and robbed them.[17]

Some of the soldiers with Chivington refused to participate, and there were ample witnesses to the atrocities. He resigned from the army and even though he faced court-martial, the Civil War amnesty kept Chivington from facing justice. Even as the horrific details emerged, however, Chivington had his supporters. In January following the attack, the *Nebraska City News* reported:

We are credibly informed that the Indians recently captured, killed and scalped an "American citizen of African descent" near Julesburg in this Territory. Heretofore they have only murdered common white folks and "the Government" has treated them ever so tenderly. In fact, Col. Chivington has been arrested for *abolishing* a few Indians and *confiscating* their ponies and other traps and calamities; but now that the red-skins have actually killed a nigger, we think Abraham will see palitating circumstances in Chivington's case, and release him and order the aboriginees to receive a tremendous threshing.

"The Government" will soon teach Mr. Indian that, though he has, during the past few months, slain with impunity several hundred white persons—killing a nigger is a serious crime add not to be passed over with indulgence.[18]

Here was a country at war to end slavery, but it would take more than legislation to change hearts. A dream of equality between the races evaporated in the light of reality.

In January 1865, Barnesville, Bourbon County, Kansas, was raided by a gang of guerrillas who quickly crossed the nearby border back into Missouri. Historian Thomas Goodrich wrote in *Black Flag*, "In response, a band of Unionist regulators scoured the land about the stricken town, menacing and murdering settlers of questionable loyalty. The leader of the group was Jack Curtis, a Jayhawker who spent much of his time 'in search of bushwhackers living in Kansas.'" A likely suspect was caught and, in an attempt to escape, was shot and killed.[19]

In February, Captain Jack was among the "festive crowd" gathered at the Michigan House Hotel in Leavenworth with other members of his regiment, with their leader as the guest of honor. Newspapers reported their purpose was to "do honor to that gallant heart, that tried, true and fearless soldier, that original champion of human freedom, Col. Charles Jennison, 15th Kansas Volunteer Cavalry." Not everyone would have recognized Colonel Jennison from that description. He had faced one court-martial already and was scheduled for another one for war crimes, but for the time being, he was available to attend the gala.

Captain Jack presented his commander with a pair of ivory-handled Colt revolvers (burnished with silver and gold) as a small token of his respect. He alluded to the legal proceedings when he said that although the colonel was now "under a cloud" he would come out "all right," and if Jennison were forced "through injustice and persecution" to leave the regiment, he would resign as well.[20]

Colonel Jennison received the gift graciously and praised his fellow soldier, "a true and tried friend." The colonel then described some of the captain's exploits. "It may not be generally known," said the colonel, "but it is a fact, that Capt. Curtis fired the first gun at Lexington [Missouri], while at the same time some of my traducers, and the slanderers of the 15th, did not come to time for six hours afterwards."[21]

The account said the revolvers had cost $150. One cannot help but question what that amount of money would have meant to Captain Jack's children, or to his parents who were raising them.

Captain Jack's zeal in prosecuting the war on bushwhackers, as well as that of his comrades, did not go unnoticed. General James Blunt ordered an inquiry into the regimental activities, and several courts-martial ensued. The overzealous Captain Jack faced a tribunal in 1865 at Leavenworth, charged with murder for the hanging of three citizens near Cane Hill, Arkansas, on November 12, 1864. He was also charged with defrauding the government by using confiscated goods and wagons for himself. He was found guilty and sentenced to a year's hard labor in a Missouri prison. He was pardoned after a month behind bars.

In 1866, the *Topeka Weekly Leader* serialized the transcripts of the court-martial. For weeks, Topekans could read verbatim the words of every witness for the prosecution and the defense. It likely sold a lot of papers. But at the end of the series, the editor wrote, "Many persons have read these proceedings, and unanimously the verdict is that there is nothing in the testimony to convict the defendant. The publication of this testimony has done much to take all blame from the shoulders of Capt. Curtis."[22]

"Capt. Curtis acted under the orders of his superiors," the *Leader* concluded, "and when detailed for special duty he followed those orders to the letter as any other efficient officer, with the good of the service and country at heart, would have done."[23]

Nonetheless, the conversations around the Curtis dinner table must have been disturbing to young Charley. News of the war was impossible to avoid, especially for those living along the main routes of travel like the Curtises. The youngster had seen returning veterans as well as coffins coming into town. The very real threat of attack cast gloom over every Kansas community, and Topeka's role as the state capital now made it a target. There were attempts to fortify the city in the wake of the events at Lawrence, but those across the river in North Topeka would have been left to look after themselves. Then, too, news of Captain Jack's court-martial and imprisonment had to have been concerning at worst and embarrassing at best.

Another event in 1865 had a profound impact on Charley's life. His maternal grandparents, Louis and Julie Pappan, sold their remaining land to Grandfather Curtis and left North Topeka for the Kaw Reservation at Council Grove, some sixty miles south. While he was living with his paternal grandparents, his mother's family was nearby and no doubt Charley was back and forth between the households.

Having been pardoned and released from prison, having had the court of public opinion turned to his side by the newspaper, in May 1866 Captain Jack went into the grocery business. "The Capt. generally runs things heavy on anything he undertakes," read the notice.[24] Apparently, that was a compliment to his wholehearted commitment. He was an active citizen, serving on a grand jury that fall and withdrawing his previously announced candidacy for the legislature.[25]

Whatever he was doing, it seemed that his parents were experiencing hard times. That may have influenced Grandmother and Grandfather Curtis's decision to send Charley to live with the Pappans. He would make his home with the Kaws, leaving behind his sister Libby and the old familiar neighborhood.

CHAPTER 4

A Bowl of Corn,
a Piece of Ground 1866–1868

*There is a sacredness in tears. They are not the mark of weakness,
but of power. They speak more eloquently than ten thousand tongues.
They are messengers of overwhelming grief, of deep contrition, and of
unspeakable love.*

—WASHINGTON IRVING

WHEN SIX-YEAR-OLD CHARLEY ARRIVED ON THE KAW RESERVATION,
he saw scenes that he would never forget. Unlike his French-Kaw family,
the full-blood Kaw were not Catholic and they were traditional in their
ways. He knew the language and he visited the "lodges, wigwams, tee-
pees, and the Indian villages, watched the dances, attended the council
meetings, and was always on hand at the feasts."[1]
And he witnessed the burials:

I saw the full bloods bury their dead. Sometimes they were placed on
the side of a hill and great rock piled on them, their ponies were killed
and placed on the graves. Some were buried in the ground . . . and
their ponies, tomahawks and trinkets were buried with them. . . . [T]
he relatives of the dead would mourn their departed one for days and
their moaning, wailing and chanting was sad indeed; it seems that even
now I can hear some of the wailing that went up in the early morning

from those poor people whose loved one had been taken and they are the saddest memories of my recollection.[2]

A traveler passing through the reservation confirmed Charley's descriptions as they observed a recent grave:

Two ponies, the property of the dead man, had been slain, and their bodies left on the grave; and over the spot a United States flag was flying. Upon the flag-staff were tied ears of corn, wampum, and some broken arrows, while other articles which the dead man might be supposed to require on his journey to the "happy hunting grounds" were buried with him.[3]

This *Harper's Weekly* illustration was sketched by James Kidd in 1868. The Kaw burying their dead was one of the customs Charley recalled from his time on the reservation. The sounds of mourning from those who lost their loved ones was the saddest memory of his childhood.
COURTESY DEBRA GOODRICH

Charley recalled the "squaw corn, it was sweet and the grains, highly colored,"[4] and drying great quantities for fall and winter. Corn for soup, corn for meal, corn for hominy—corn was such an essential part of sustenance that it had its own story of how it came to be. A Kaw chief, Rattlesnake, told the story to the "White Prophet," Pere Marquette, and it has been shared by Henry Wadsworth Longfellow and by chronicler of the frontier Henry Inman, who wrote the account in a book called *The Ranche on the Oxhide.*

The tale was thus: It came to pass that a Great Chief had so many children that it was difficult to feed them all, but he provided enough to raise them through his skillful hunting.

> In those days the red men all lived in peace and friendship. There was no war, and no scalplocks hung from the doors of the lodges. The eldest son had the fear of the Great Spirit in his heart, and, like his father, he toiled patiently in the chase that he might assist in procuring food for his brothers and sisters.[5]

When a boy reached manhood he went alone into the forest, fasting and thinking intently on the request he had of the Great Spirit. And so it was the chief's eldest son went into the woods and prayed for a food to sustain his people when the hunts were not successful. That night, he had a vision:

> He saw a magnificently attired youth coming toward him. He was clad in robes of green and green plumes hung gracefully about his comely countenance.
>
> "My dear young friend," said the stranger, "the Great Spirit has heard your prayer, but the boon you ask is a great boon; and you must pass through a heavy trial of suffering and patience before you will see the realization of your wish. You must first try your strength with me."[6]

And so, in the manner of Jacob's wrestling with the angel from the Bible, the young man wrestled with the stranger who was "endowed with muscles like the oak, and he had the wind of a wolf, that never was exhausted by effort." They wrestled and wrestled, until the stranger said they would

47

resume the next night. Again, the stranger admonished the young warrior to refrain from eating and drinking, and though tempted, he did as he was told. And the stranger took flight, his green and yellow vestments "expanding like wings."[7]

The next night, the young warrior was even stronger. When morning came, the stranger told him that upon their next trial, the warrior would be the victor and the stranger would die. His instructions were specific:

> Strip me of my yellow garments and bury me in soft and newmade earth. Visit my grave week by week, for in a little time I shall return to life in the form of a plant, which you will readily recognize by its resemblance to me. Let no weeds or grass be near me to keep the dew and sunshine from my green leaves.[8]

The stranger instructed the warrior how to harvest and cook the substance, and said, "There shall be no more hunger upon the earth excepting among those who have a lazy spirit, or whom the Bad Manitou claims as his own." The warrior did as he was told, and knew that Manitou had heard his prayer, and that the grain was the body of his friend.[9]

Corn was the most important crop raised by the Kaws, and Charley recalled, "We raised it in great quantities and dried much of it in the summer and fall for winter use."[10]

"I helped jerk the buffalo meat the members of the tribe would bring in from their hunting trips," he wrote. "We would jerk it and place the strips across a long pole to dry."[11]

The buffalo—bison—was the other essential ingredient to survival not only for the Kaws but for all the Plains Tribes. The buffalo was the cornerstone of the Natives' livelihood and would make a decent living for others too, like Bill Cody.

In October 1867, Cody was offered $500 a month (a private in the army at that time made less than $15 a month) to furnish buffalo meat to feed the men building the Kansas Pacific Railroad across Kansas. They required twelve buffaloes a day, taking only the hind quarters and the hump. He claimed to have killed nearly 4,300 of the beasts by the time his contract ended in May.[12] That was a drop in the bucket to the vast numbers of bison on the Plains. But their days were numbered.

The bison, commonly referred to as the buffalo, was the foundation of the economy and cultural focus of the Plains Tribes, providing food, shelter, and tools. Historian Towana Spivey, in estimating exactly how many of the animals once inhabited the content, said, "In numbers, numberless."
COURTESY DR. MICHELLE MARTIN

Increasingly, the competition for the bison diminished the immense herds. They were harvested not only to feed the railroad workers, but also for their hides—leather for belts on the machinery that fueled the Industrial Revolution. And they were harvested for pleasure and for the delicacy of the tongue to be served in fancy restaurants. Excursions brought indiscriminate hunters to the American West and as the lumbering herds blocked the tracks, they were shot from the windows of the train cars. And they were shot to destroy the economy of the Plains Tribes. Their fate was intertwined, so dependent were the tribes on the buffalo.

While men in Congress debated the "Indian problem," Charley watched it play out. The problem was not where to put them, in his young mind. Everything was diminished, the adjective of the era as it applied to the tribe. The tribe was diminished from disease. The land was diminished through continual negotiation with the government. Their hope was diminished by circumstance.

The problem, as Charley observed, was that they were starving and the old ways of providing were not working.

In the post–Civil War years, the US Congress had some big issues to tackle: Reconstruction and civil rights in the South were hotly debated. The Reconstruction Amendments—the Thirteenth, Fourteenth, and Fifteenth Amendments to the Constitution—were passed during this period. The Thirteenth Amendment abolished slavery and was ratified December 6, 1865; the Fourteenth Amendment addressed citizenship and "equal protection" under the law; the Fifteenth Amendment prohibited the federal or states' governments from denying or abridging the right to vote on account of race, color, or previous condition of servitude.

In the midst of these amendments, Congress passed the Civil Rights Act of 1866, which reinforced the definition of citizenship and voting rights. The legislation passed the Senate and House but was vetoed by President Johnson. Congress overrode the veto, and the Civil Rights Act went into effect on April 9, 1866. These measures were deemed necessary to protect African Americans in the South. As Reconstruction failed miserably, state and local governments found ways around the laws—poll taxes, literacy tests, and any number of qualifications designed to disenfranchise whomever was deemed undesirable.

These measures, however bold, did nothing for Native Americans. The "Indian problem" plagued lawmakers even as they discussed equal protection and securing rights. Throughout the nation's history, the Native Americans, the civilizations that populated this continent for thousands of years before the arrival of white Europeans, were not recognized as having rights. "Life, liberty, and the pursuit of happiness" applied to everyone but the Indians who, just like the buffalo, were still an obstacle in the way of progress.

Senator John Sherman of Ohio, in discussing appropriations to the tribes early in 1867, called the treaty system "a farce."[13] Reporting on a later session of Congress, the *Philadelphia Inquirer* quoted Senator Sherman as saying the "only true solution was to absorb the Indians in the general population."

Senator Sherman's older brother, Lieutenant General William T. Sherman, had gained fame and promotion prosecuting the Civil War. Having dealt the death blows to the institution of slavery, the venerable general was tasked with taming the West, rounding up the "wild, savage" Indians and restricting them to reservations and keeping them well away from conflict with white settlers. Senator Sherman and his brother were coldly practical in their approach to the issues of westward expansion. The senator was direct in his remarks to colleagues:

> The Indian could no longer pursue the chase. He must either adapt himself to the usages of civilized life, or be fed and kept by the bounty of the government. White settlements were now scattered over all the territory formerly belonging to the Indian as hunting grounds. Treaties would not be observed; the Pacific Railroad was being built through lands held by treaty by the Indians and this was a violation of the treaty. So it would be with other treaties, it would be impossible to keep white settlers out of any portion of the Western Territories and the Indians must either adapt themselves to civilized life, or be killed off by the white settlers.[14]

Adapt or *die*.

For some Americans, adapting was not even an option. The *Philadelphia Evening Telegraph* published a report from the West characterizing the conditions:

> The fiery letter of our Montana correspondent upon the Indian question is a true picture, not so much of the atrocities of the Indians as of the sentiment of the people of our Territories in favor of exterminating the red race.

"They must leave the Plains or die," says our correspondent.[15]

The correspondent had observed that complaints about the tribes were mostly hearsay, second- and third-hand accounts that were often exaggerated, fueling the justification for eradicating the "red race":

We publish it to show how impossible it is to preserve peace with the Indians so long as the whites are imbued with the faith in extermination and massacre of which our correspondent's letter is so faithful an illustration.

There are two difficulties in the way of the extermination policy, viz: it is impossible, and disgustingly unjust, as all our army officers who have been called on to carry it out soon learn. Impossible, as it would be, by a fire of artillery to exterminate the mosquito in a swamp. Unjust, because investigation shows that at least half the Indian difficulties arise from violation of our treaties, or by starvation and suffering in consequence of the advances of the white race Westward.[16]

Even as they decried the policy of extermination, the moral issue was second to the practical matter of achieving it.

Charley's seventh birthday occurred in the midst of growing tensions on the Plains. The heroes of the Civil War's Union Army put their strength and confidence into fighting a new enemy in the West. The year 1867 was a flashpoint on the High Plains of western Kansas. From Fort Riley, fifty miles north of the Kaw Reservation, the newspapers reported:

Generals Sherman and Hancock have returned from the much talked-of and highly exciting Indian Campaign, after a month or more spent in counselling with the Indians, and several stampede and violations of faith on their part. Generals Sherman and Hancock declared war to the knife. Major-Generals Smith and Custar [sic], in command of the cavalry of General Hancock's forces, have started on the scout towards the Platte, thence south of that stream westward in the direction of Fort Sedgwick, afterwards down to the Smoky Hill, in search of Sioux and Cheyenne. . . . The military operations will be continued during the summer, and a war of extermination carried on.[17]

Extermination may have never become "official" policy, but it was in the official discussion.

While generals were studying maps of the area between the Platte and Arkansas Rivers and devising strategies for keeping certain tribes out of it, fifty miles away the Kaw were fighting to stay in Kansas. With increased traffic on the Santa Fe Trail, the rough frontier town of Council Grove was eyeing the ground occupied by the Kaw Nation, already a fraction of what they had been promised in every treaty to that moment. Every white visitor—lawyer, government official, missionary—posed a threat to their remaining on the land, and an even greater threat to their maintaining any semblance of their culture and customs. For example, when the Kaws initially refused the use of liquor, the whiskey peddlers came closer and closer and became more insistent, diminishing the morale of the tribe, making the "drunken Indian" stereotype a sad reality in some cases. Every circumstance pointed to the distinct possibility that the red man would cease to exist.[18]

The anxiety of the adults on the reservation must have been palpable, but as a child, Charley was free from responsibility and reveled in the freedom the place offered a boy. He could hunt, ride, fish, and swim with the lads his age. He became proficient with a bow. For amusement, white visitors from nearby Council Grove or those passing through on the Santa Fe Trail would place nickels in a notch at the end of a stick as a target. If the boy's arrow hit the nickel, he kept the coin. Charley recalled that he got pretty good at hitting nickels. The Emporia newspaper reported that another Kanza lad had impressively shot a nickel with his bow and arrow from sixty-five feet away.[19] There would have been ample opportunities for the boys to compete against one another whether with their bows, running, or hunting.

Charley said he attended the Quaker Mission School near the reservation, but it is not likely he was in class very often. He spoke French and Kaw and made no mention of any animosity between the French-Kaw and full-bloods, though his grandparents' home was on an allotment and not in one of the villages. He recalled the government cattle issue as thrilling:

> I attended but two—they were very exciting. The Texas steers with their great longhorns were placed in what was known as the issue pen, those that were to be killed at the time were turned out and as each steer passed through the gate a number of young bucks or young Indians on their ponies would start after it and it would only be a few minutes until it was down, killed, skinned and ready for the knife.[20]

53

It would have been the closest vision he had of a buffalo hunt. Other observers would say it was a sad thing to witness the horsemen who had once ridden into buffalo herds reduced to taking down a cow in such a decidedly domestic setting.

There must have been great excitement on the reservation in January 1867 when Chiefs Allegawaho, Fool Chief, and Watianga, along with interpreters Joseph James and Thomas Huffaker, joined a delegation of several tribal representatives bound for the nation's capital. They would meet with Commissioner of Indian Affairs Lewis V. Bogy so that they might be convinced how much better off they would be upon moving to the Indian Territory south of Kansas. At first, the government appeared to give them a choice—become US citizens or move to the Indian Territory to continue living as Indians. But Commissioner Bogy finally presented the ultimatum—move.

The treaty was signed on February 13, 1867. The Kaw agreed to turn over their already diminished reservation to the federal government for $100,000 with the remaining trust lands to be sold. The income from that sale would pay debts owed by the Kaws. There would be a new reservation in the Indian Territory with some features like a blacksmith shop, a trade school, livestock, implements, and housing for the agent and a doctor. A perpetual annuity of $10,000 would be paid in consideration of lands previously ceded to the government. In addition, Allegawaho, Fool Chief, Watianga, and Joseph James would be granted 320 acres on the reservation.[21]

The Kaws' debts were huge. Claims from traders, the bill for building those "commodious stone houses" and the school, and treaty obligations that forced the Kaw to pay the squatters on the reservation for the improvements they had made while living there illegally—all of these were billed to the tribe. There were depredation claims to be paid, plus the costs related to the sale of their lands, including appraisal and advertising. Everyone was making money and charging it to the Kaws' tab.[22]

Jack Curtis also went along on this trip to Washington, to look after the Kaws' interests. When famed photographer Alexander Gardner took a photo of the assembled delegation and government officials, Captain Jack was right in the middle. Commissioner Bogy had raised his arm at that moment, however, partially hiding Jack's face.[23] Since he was present on this trip, it is reasonable to infer that he visited the reservation while Charley lived there.

Allegawaho and Ojibwa leader Hole in the Day had a photo taken on a balcony of the White House with Commissioner Bogy, Secretary of the Interior Orville Browning, and President Andrew Johnson. For all the high-level discussions, the Native Americans achieved no more than any of their predecessors who visited the previous administrations. As it were, the Kaw representatives had an expense-paid trip to see the capital, and it is likely that too was eventually charged to their bill. The *National Republican* reported that on January 25, 1867, "Col. Thomas Murphy left Kansas city today, with sixty-six delegates, representatives of thirteen tribes of Kansas Indians, to make treaties for the cession of their land in this State."[24]

The timing for sympathy could not have been worse. While newspapers reported the details of the delegation's trip, the details of the Fetterman Massacre at Fort Phil Kearney the previous month grabbed more attention. Captain William Fetterman and his command, eighty men, were killed by a force of Lakota, Cheyenne, and Arapaho warriors. At the same time, General Winfield Hancock was responding to troubles along the Solomon River in north-central Kansas by assuring Governor Crawford that he would send one hundred soldiers from Fort Ellsworth to the area. No matter what rosy lens Charley looked through, the situation facing all the tribes was dire. No amount of negotiation could stem the tide against the Native American.

Allegawaho had emerged as the principal chief of the Kaws. He was tall, well over six feet, and straight. He took his name from a Pawnee warrior he killed in battle. In Pawnee, *Allegawaho* means "Big Elk." He was described as sober and unfailingly honest. His concern for his people was never in doubt, and he would do all in his power to secure their future. But he must have despaired at what that future would hold.

Whether in interviews or in penning his memoirs (unpublished until 2019), Charley never portrayed his circumstances as difficult or challenging. He reminisced through rose-colored glasses, shielded from the harshness of life by the love of his Grandmother Pappan. Perhaps

A delegation of tribes from Kansas with President Johnson and other officials in
Washington, DC. Pictured here are Mut-tut-tah, Councilman; H. W. Martin, US
Agent; Man-ah-to-wah, Councilman; Charles E. Mix, Chief Clerk of the Indian
Bureau; William Whistler; Antoine Gokey, US Interpreter; No-quah-ho-ko, Second
Chief Sacs; Keokuk, Principal Chief of Sacs; Captain O. A. "Jack" Curtis; Che-ko-
skuk, Principal Chief Foxes; Lewis V. Bogy, Commissioner of Indian Affairs; F. R.
Page, US Agent; Al-le-ga-wa-ho, Head Chief of Kaws; Joseph James, US Inter-
preter; Kah-he-ga-wa-ti-an-gah, Brave and Chief of Kaws; T. S. Huffaker, Special
Interpreter; and Wah-ti-an-gah, Brave and Chief of Kaws.
COURTESY KANSAS STATE HISTORICAL SOCIETY

that was how he truly remembered those days, or he had simply chosen
to spin the narrative that cast his life in the most palatable light. He was
ever loyal to his family. He never dwelt on the sadness of his mother's
death, or the embarrassment of his father's court-martial and imprisonment (which he did not mention at all). His description of his time on
the reservation is idyllic; he wrote of gathering wild grapes and drying
them by the bushel, of gathering the nuts from the woods—walnuts,

hazelnuts, and hickory nuts. He said that he saw the dances, but he did not describe the scalp dance that he must surely have witnessed after an annual buffalo hunt resulted in a deadly conflict with the Cheyennes.[25]

The buffalo hunts of the mid-1860s had been successful, and as the Kaw readied to head west in the fall of 1867, they must have had expectations for another bountiful harvest. Most of the tribe, including women and children, went on these hunts. Indian Agent E. S. Stover, formerly a major in the 2nd Kansas Cavalry, reported to the Commissioner of Indian Affairs in 1868:

> The past year has been one of hardships, suffering, and disaster to the Kaw Indians. As they depend principally upon the chase for their subsistence, and have been wholly deprived the privilege of the buffalo range by the Cheyenne and Arapaho Indians, you can well imagine what their condition has been and now is.[26]

The Kaw Nation was being increasingly squeezed. Between the emigrant tribes and white settlement to the east and the Plains Tribes to the west, the Kaws' access to viable hunting grounds was as diminished as every other aspect of their lives. They had left for the hunt around October 10 and traveled about 150 miles slightly southwest of the reservation when they encountered members of the Arapaho Tribe. The report continued:

> [W]hile the Kaws were entertaining them, another party of the same tribe stole and drove off 34 Kaw ponies, which much disabled them, as they were very short of transportation and ponies for hunting purposes. They proceeded to the vicinity of Fort Zarah, but could not do much towards securing meat and robes, as they dared not range far from their camp for fear of an attack from the Cheyennes, who were reported not far distant.
>
> On about the 1st of December, while the Kaws were encamped on Plumb Creek, near Zarah, a party of Cheyenne warriors came to their camp and pretended to be friendly, and said they desired to talk about the difficulties existing between the tribes. They remained several hours and were treated kindly by the Kaws, but upon their departure, when a

few hundred yards from camp, they came upon a Kaw herding horses and deliberately shot and scalped him, and then formed for battle.[27]

The Kaws charged the Cheyennes and a four-hour skirmish ensued. Several warriors were wounded on both sides. Two Kaw warriors were killed, but there were fourteen Cheyenne warriors dead. Many of the horses were killed. While the Kaw temporarily had the upper hand, they knew the Cheyennes would return in full force, and they could not repel such an attack. Instead, they headed for home.[28]

Having lost many of their horses and with their hunt interrupted, they were left unprepared for the coming winter or the journey home to the reservation. They camped south of the Kaw River, near Junction City, and were often seen begging for food or money. They performed "war dances" at their camp and sold pieces of the Cheyenne scalps they had taken. They were, quite simply, destitute. Many souls perished on the way home, and many died afterwards, most of them women and children.[29] According to historian Ron Parks:

> These Kanza dead have no grave markers. Their lives were as evanescent as wind-driven cloud shadows drifting across the plains. We know they were disproportionately young and female, but we don't know their names. They are historical nonentities. During a few cold days in December 1867, they became too weak to go farther, dropped to the ground, then died—sixty-one of them—on the Kansas prairie.[30]

Despite the tragedy, the Kaws celebrated their hard-won victory over the Cheyennes soon after reaching home. The Reverend Joab Spencer witnessed the event:

> When I reached the village the dance was in progress. The scalps recently secured were hung on a pole erected in the midst of the village. Only men dance among the Indians. The dancers arranged themselves in a straight line, or in a circle, one just behind the other, assuming a stooping position with the knees bent forward enough to balance the body. The dance consisted of a kind of shuffling moving and a spring up of a few inches from the ground. This gave them a

bobbing-up-and-down notion, but did not move them from their position. An onlooker would see a line of men shuffling and jumping but not changing place. Their dances were very serious affairs and continued far into the night. The dancers had a grave and serious look, and seemed to give close attention to their work. If a dancer tired he would step out of line. If another wished to join, he stepped into line at any time. How men could endure such exercise for hours without recess, is hard to understand. This dance, as well as all others, was a religious ceremony, and was really a thanksgiving service for their late victory, which they regarded as proof that the Great Spirit was not angry, but pleased with them.[31]

Charley would have felt the loss of those who did not return—cousins, playmates—and witnessed the grief of the survivors. He would almost certainly have witnessed the scalp dance, being the most important ceremony on the reservation for months. He was a very bright boy, and he had the perspective of living in two worlds. It would not be a leap to believe that despite his painting a positive picture, he understood the situation facing the Kaws.

Charley recalled that the following summer he and some other boys were playing on the creek bank when they heard the singing of war songs. Investigating, they found several members of the tribe,

their faces and bodies covered with war paint, bear claws around their necks, riding their ponies in single file and equipped with bows, arrows, and other weapons. I asked one of the warriors at the head of the line what the trouble was and he told me the Cheyenne were coming to fight the Kaw and they were going to meet them. . . . [He] asked us to go up the creek and inform those who lived on their separate allotments. . . . [W]e proceeded to notify my grandparents and others.[32]

The Cheyennes had been anxious to avenge the deaths of their warriors, but the Kaws had been confined to their reservation as a result of the unrest, presumably for their own protection. Thus, the tribes were not likely to encounter one another on the open plains:

[A]s the Cheyennes could reach them in no other way, they, together with the Arapahoes, numbering about 400 in all, made a raid into the settlements, and on the 3d of June about 100 warriors, well-armed and mounted, made their appearance upon the reservation and attacked the Kaws at their agency.[33]

Charley often described the incident:

It was not long after that that we were given orders to go up to the Mission, or trading post, and the older men, women and children were gathered into an old unused barn. They had with them their bows and arrows, shotguns, rifles and old muskets. Shortly after the Kaw and Cheyenne appeared near the village the war parties were fighting in circles, in Indian fashion. I remember some of the older men in our place of refuge shot through the holes and cracks in the walls.[34]

In his memoir and numerous interviews over the years, Charley described how he was sent to Topeka to alert the authorities of the attack. In his telling, he made the trek alone, but Governor Samuel Crawford recalled it differently:

When the battle began in the morning, Major Stover started a messenger to me at Topeka, sixty miles distant, with a note saying that the Kaws had been attacked by the Cheyennes, and a battle royal was raging: but he would "hold the fort" until I arrived with reinforcements. The messenger (Joe Jim) arrived in Topeka about 7 P.M. and related his blood-curdling and hair-raising story.[35]

According to Charley:

I volunteered to make the trip. When we heard the Cheyenne were coming, the horses and ponies were driven to pasture, some distance from my grandparents' home, so there was no horse or pony for me to ride. I, therefore, started out on foot, traveling during the night as rapidly as I could and notifying the campers whom I passed on the way and what few settlers there were (there being but few, and those on the creek) about the coming of the Cheyenne.

It was a very exciting time for the others as well as for me, but being accustomed to frontier life, I did not mind the trip. I had been over the road many times and even had I not known it, I could not have missed it as it was the main highway (a part of the way was the old Santa Fe trail) and well marked by camping places, the remains of broken down wagons and the bones of horses and oxen which had died as a result of the hard journeys they had been forced to make over the plains.

I arrived in Topeka, I think about noon of the next day. I told the story to my father and grandfather, and remember they went over to the State House and by night we had word that the Cheyenne were not coming on but were returning to their reservation.[36]

Stover reported:

[The Cheyennes] were readily repulsed, and after a few hours' skirmishing were driven from the reservation without loss of life to either party. One Kaw, three Cheyennes, and a few horses wounded; two Indian houses burned and several others robbed, together with several houses belonging to whites plundered of everything, was about the amount of damage from the raid. The Indians left the settlement the next day and have not troubled it since, except by keeping the Kaws in constant guard by their threat to attack again in large force.[37]

In 1922, Charley wrote a letter to Mrs. Lalla Maloy Brigham, who had penned an account of the raid and sent it to him for review. In his reply to her, he clarified his participation and explained that after informing his grandparents and others on allotments of the attack, he remained in the barn with the other tribal members. "As soon as the raid was over," he wrote, "I left for Topeka. I traveled all night and reached Topeka the next day."[38]

The raid ultimately had a more adverse effect on the Cheyennes than on the Kaws. Governor Crawford was enraged and rushed to the scene:

The only available troops I had within easy reach, were Thaddeus H. Walker, Geo. H. Hoyt, and Colonel J. W. Forsyth of Sheridan's staff. On reading Stover's note, I announced to these gentlemen that I was going to the front, whereupon they each tendered their services and said they would also go. In a few minutes were off to the war behind two dashing teams that made the run of sixty miles by the light of a full moon, and reached the field just as the sun was making its appearance over the eastern hills.[39]

When the governor and his officers arrived, the Cheyennes were already heading westward on the Santa Fe Trail and the excitement was over. But Crawford's anger was far from appeased. He had word of other raids by the Cheyennes along the Kansas Pacific Railroad in the vicinity of Fort Wallace and along the Smoky Hill Trail.[40]

Crawford speculated that the reason there were not more warriors with Tall Bull was that they were waiting at Forts Larned and Dodge for the distribution of arms and ammunition from the government or the traders. As tensions on the Plains increased, so had Crawford's pleas for increased protection for settlers. He petitioned President Andrew Johnson and General Phillip Sheridan. He urged them not to release promised arms, which the tribes arguably needed for hunting, because they were being used to terrorize the countryside instead. The raid on the Kaw proved his point and provided the evidence he needed to bolster his argument.

"Had it not been for the Council Grove raid, the guns, pistols, and fixed ammunition, which had been sent to Larned for them, would have been distributed in May," Crawford wrote.[41]

"After the Cheyenne raid," said Charley, "my folks at Topeka would not let me return to the Kaw Reservation."[42]

On September 1, 1868, the Surgeon General's Office of the War Department issued a memorandum to the Army's medical officers:

[A] craniological collection was commenced last year at the Army Medical Museum, and that it already includes 153 specimens of skulls. The chief purpose . . . is to aid in the progress of anthropological science by obtaining measurements of a large number of skulls of the aboriginal races of North America. Medical Officers stationed in the Indian country or in the vicinity of ancient Indian mounds or cemeteries in the Mississippi valley or the Atlantic region have peculiar facilities for promoting this undertaking. They have already enriched the Mortonian and other magnificent craniological cabinets by their contributions, and it is hoped they will evince even greater zeal in collecting for their own Museum.

A list of the crania now in possession of the Museum will soon be published. . . . It is sufficient here to state that 47 of the 143 specimens are Indian crania from the following tribes: Tsuktshi, 1; Flathead, Chenook, Selipsh, Nisqually, 13; Californian, 2; Piegan, Spokane, Mandan, 3; Arickaree, Gros Ventre, 2; Sioux, Kaw, Minataree, Menominee, 6; Cheyenne, Kiowa, Arraphahoe, Wichita, 10; Navajo and Apache, 5; doubtful or mixed breeds, 5.[43]

Since these crania were readily identifiable by tribe, they had likely not been dead very long. They would have been found in places where the evidence of battle or sacred burial was evident, thus enabling them to be connected to their people. The skulls of the Kaw were possibly those of people Charley knew.

The directive went on to list the officers who had so proudly collected these specimens: Brevet Lt. Cols. J. Cooper McKee, D. C. Peters, C. C. Gray, F. L. Town; Surgeon B. E. Fryer; Brevet Majs. J. F. Weeds, W. H. Forwood; Acting Assistant Surgeons W. Matthews and G. H. Oliver; Dr. George Suckley; Mr. George Gibbs; Lt. (now Brevet Maj. Gen.) G. K. Warren; and Mr. Lloyd Brooke. (Forwood served at several frontier forts and went on to become Surgeon General of the Army.) There had just arrived a shipment with an "interesting series of crania" from ancient mounds near Fort Wadsworth in the Dakota Territory, discovered by Acting Assistant Surgeon A. I. Comfort. Additionally, the medical directors of the Department of Columbia and the District of Texas procured some crania. Further instructions say:

While exotic and normal and abnormal crania of all descriptions are valued at the Museum for the purposes of comparison, it is chiefly desired to procure sufficiently large series of adult crania of the principal Indian tribes to furnish accurate average measurements. Medical Officers will enhance the value of their contributions by transmitting with the specimens the fullest attainable memoranda, specifying the locality whence the skulls were derived, the presumed age and sex, and, in the case of "Mound" skulls, or of those from cemeteries, describing the mode of sepulture, and any traces of weapons, implements, utensils found with the specimens, or any other circumstance that may throw light on their ethnic character.

The subject is earnestly commended to the attention of the Medical Officers of the Army. By order of the Surgeon General.[44]

A few months later, a group of Pawnee Scouts had been discharged from the army and were passing near Salina, Kansas, when the locals became disturbed by their presence and called for troops. Even though the scouts tried to show them their discharge papers, a fight ensued. The Pawnees took refuge in a cave, where attempts were made to smoke them out. They were killed trying to survive. The post surgeon from nearby Fort Harker, B. E. Fryer, ordered someone to scavenge the site for skulls but a blizzard set in. After a couple of weeks the search resumed and six Pawnee skulls were part of a shipment of twenty-six Cheyenne, Caddo, Wichita, and Osage crania sent to Washington.

All over the West, army officers and civilians alike pillaged Native graves and sacred sites to collect the bones. Long dead or recently deceased—it didn't matter.

Even being a dead Indian wasn't safe.

Chapter 5

A Boy Adrift 1868–1873

*Go then if you must, but remember, no matter how foolish your deeds,
those who love you will love you still.*
— Sophocles

The boy on the North Topeka train platform was small for the
age of ten, "clad in an unbleached muslin shirt and a pair of jean trousers
suspended by a single homemade 'gallus,' his tawny skin showing through
numerous rents in his scant garments, his legs and feet bare, his long
black hair uncovered and his small eyes a-glitter," recalled James E. Safford of the first time he met Charley.

> "I want to go to Silver Lake," I said, stepping up to him as he stood
> on the platform as motionless as the Indian I recognized him to be. I
> hardly expected him to speak, but he did without a moment's hesitation.
>   "Then why didn't you stay on the cars?" he demanded in a shrill
> childish treble.
>   "But I didn't know. I thought the road stopped here," I stammered.
>   "It goes on to Wamego now," he explained laconically.
>   "When is the next train?"
>   "Tomorrow."
>   It did not look promising. I proceeded to make a few further inqui-
> ries of the boy, who was all the time regarding me with a look of the
> most imperturbably gravity.
>   "How shall I manage it?" I asked.

"I reckon you'll have to go over, to the south side and put up at the Gordon House if you've got the nickel to pay your bridge fare," he said. "If you ain't, I reckon Cap Dowdell will give it to you. Cap keeps yon saloon."

"I'd rather get to Silver Lake," I said helplessly.

The lad shrugged and made a slight grimace. "If I wanted to get to Silver Lake mighty bad I know what I'd do—I'd foot it, you bet. It's only twelve miles. I've walked it many a time."

It was midday, very hot and the dust in the roadway along the track was black and almost foot deep. I shook my head.

"I guess I'd rather hire some one to carry me out," I said. "Do you know anybody who would like the job?"

"I'd like it mighty well," he declared, with an eager look in his glittering eyes, "if my grandfather'd only let me have the team. He wouldn't though."

"Suppose we go and ask him," I suggested, glad of any possible way out of the difficulty. The lad agreed, and we proceeded on our way to consult his grandfather.[1]

Safford was invited to supper with the Curtis family, and Grandfather Curtis asked his son-in-law, Charlie La Tourette, to take the traveler to Silver Lake. Safford asked if the "Indian lad" could accompany them on the journey, not realizing he was part of the family. "He was in no way like any other member of it that I met on that occasion," he recalled.[2]

Later on, Mr. Safford moved to Topeka and the La Tourettes were his neighbors. He saw Charley often when he visited his aunt and uncle.

"He was a hustler," Safford wrote. "There was not a suggestion of the traditional Indian aversion to labor in his makeup." He characterized Charley as possessing "unfaltering and almost perpetual industry."

"His remarkable abstinence from and even aversion for the vices that have brought ruin to his race are quite as wonderful under the circumstances," the neighbor observed. His environment was not conducive to nurturing "a temperate disposition, yet he never manifested the slightest inclination to swerve from the path he must have laid out for himself when he was very young."

"It is still and ever will be a mystery to those who remember the dissolute life of his father," recalled Safford, "the helplessness of his aged grandparents, the almost impenetrable murkiness of his environment."[3]

Mr. Safford's observations are valuable insights into Charley's young life, but the bias toward his Native ancestry is evident. Even though Safford notes that Charley's father is no role model, it is the "Indian blood" that must be overcome.

One key to Charley's success was his ability to see his circumstances in relation to those of others. There does not appear to be one self-pitying moment in his life. Even though Charley was often referred to as an orphan, in the strictest sense, he was not. His father was living, and he had family who welcomed him into their homes. Children who had been truly orphaned had been filling the orphanages and poorhouses of America's cities for decades. In 1854, the Children's Aid Society began sending children to the more rural parts of America, including Kansas, where it was believed that they would have a chance at a better life and a loving home. For some, that dream was realized; for others, the dream turned dark as they became servants or subjects of abuse. Charley would have been aware of the orphans coming from the East, and likely realized that even though his plight was sad, many children and young people were in far more dire circumstances.

In fact, the same month Charley returned to his family in North Topeka, the Orphan Train arrived bearing hopeful adoptees at the Lawrence depot. "Mr. Fry, agent of the Children's Aid Society, yesterday arrived with fifteen fine looking boys," the accounts read. "Parties were promptly on hand to obtain most of them. They have found homes with some of our best citizens, among others with Col. Learned, Col. Willemsen, and Councilman Clark."[4]

Prospective parents had been instructed to pay $15 to defray travel expenses and to be prepared to "furnish references, recommending them as suitable parties to be entrusted with the children. . . . Parties taking these children are expected to give them a good bringing up, with the ordinary advantages of education. To avoid all favoritism, choices will be determined by lot."[5]

There is no doubt Charley must have felt like an orphan at times. When he left the reservation, he lived for a while with his father and stepmother, Lucy Jay Curtis. (It is unclear when they married.) He went to school through the end of the term and then went back to live with Grandmother and Grandfather Curtis. From his accounts and the evidence of his many jobs, he was expected to provide for himself, however.

North Topeka was "most interesting" as he recalled. His grandparents' hotel, the Curtis House, was the center of activity on Railroad Street, along with the Antietam and other saloons (with gambling rooms), the post office, livery, and general store. Charley was familiar with the games of chance—poker (at which he would become quite proficient), faro, monte, chuck-a-luck—which he described as going "full blast." The frontier town attracted frontier characters:

> Once in a while Wild Bill [Hickok] would come down from the western part of the state; he always attracted a great deal of attention; he was tall and straight as an Indian, his hair was long and black and his eyes were of the piercing kind, he was a great gambler and a dead shot. When he visited North Topeka the men and boys would follow him from place to place and he seemed to like the attention he attracted.[6]

Charley recalled others like Abram Burnett, legendary in Shawnee County for his size (reportedly 450 pounds):

> [A] half breed Potawatomi Indian, but who claimed to be a full blood; he was no doubt the broadest and heaviest man who ever lived in the state, he was so large that when he rode in a lumber wagon there was no room on the seat for any other person, not even a little boy. He was educated in the schools of Indiana and Michigan. His home was on a beautiful mound a few miles southwest of Topeka. When he died, he was buried in his Indian allotment and since his death the piece of elevated ground has been and is still called Burnett's Mound. He was good natured and always full of fun.[7]

Not only did the Curtises have a hotel, but a farm as well. It seemed Charley enjoyed much the same freedom that he was afforded on the reservation. "I have many vivid and delightful memories of the years of my boyhood but none are more pleasant than those spent at the old home of My Grandparents, William and Permelia Curtis."[8]

While his Kaw family had prepared for winter by going on the annual buffalo hunt, the Curtises prepared by butchering hogs and smoking and curing the meat; making hominy; molding candles and soap; drying apples, peaches, and wild grapes; storing potatoes, cabbages, and turnips; making sauerkraut, sausages, and apple butter; gathering nuts; and putting up jams, jellies, and pickles. The cribs were full of corn, and stacks of hay and fodder were piled high.[9]

But on the plains beyond Topeka and Council Grove, the world was anything but calm, despite peace talks in September. Major General Phil Sheridan had written to Governor Crawford from Fort Hays on October 9, 1868:

> Gen. Hazen has informed me that the friendly overtures which were made to the Kiowas and Comanches at Larned on the nineteenth and twentieth of September, 1868, have failed to secure peace with them, or removal to their reservation, and I am authorized to muster in one regiment of cavalry from your State for a period of six months. I will communicate further with you on the subject on receipt of additional instruction from Gen. [W. T.] Sherman.[10]

Crawford had been expecting the message. "Everybody familiar with the character and habits of the wild tribes knew that the young Kiowas and Comanches had been with the Cheyennes, Arapahoes, and Apaches on the war-path from the day they drew their arms and ammunition from the Government in August," he wrote.[11]

The next day, having received directions from General Sherman, commanding the Military Division of the Missouri, Sheridan authorized Crawford to raise a regiment. Crawford had been itching for the opportunity and wasted no time issuing the call for troops, who began pouring into Topeka. General Sherman further instructed General Sheridan on October 15:

As to extermination, it is for the Indians themselves to determine. We don't want to exterminate or even fight them. At best it is an inglorious war, not apt to add much to our fame or personal comfort; and for our soldiers, to whom we owe our first thoughts, it is all danger and extreme labor, without a single compensating advantage.[12]

Once again, General Sherman indicates that extermination is a possible, if not desired, outcome. With the same zeal that characterized his all-out war against the armies and civilians of the American South, Sherman outlined the situation, again characterizing it in the same way he had viewed the Civil War. They made war, we will end it.

[W]e . . . accept the war begun by our enemies, and hereby resolve to make its end final. If it results in the utter annihilation of these Indians, it is but the result of what they have been warned again and again, and for which they seem fully prepared. I will say nothing and do nothing to restrain our troops from doing what they deem proper on the spot, and will allow no mere vague general charges of cruelty and inhumanity to tie their hands, but will use all the powers confided to me to the end that these Indians, the enemies of our race and of our civilization, shall not again be able to begin and carry on their barbarous warfare on any kind of pretext that they may choose to allege. I believe that this winter will afford us the opportunity, and that before the snow falls these Indians will seek some sort of peace, to be broken next year at their option; but we will not accept their peace, or cease our efforts till all the past acts are both punished and avenged. You may now go ahead in your own way, and I will back you with my whole authority, and stand between you and any efforts that may be attempted in your rear to restrain your purpose or check your troops.[13]

Once the regiment was assembled, Governor Crawford issued a Thanksgiving proclamation and resigned his office to become colonel of the 19th Kansas Volunteer Cavalry. When the regiment broke camp on November 5, Jack Curtis went with them, serving in Company H and becoming quartermaster sergeant before he was discharged the next year.

The plan was for the 19th Kansas to rendezvous with the command of Lieutenant Colonel George A. Custer. Up to this time, war had taken a break in the winter, but the US Army decided it would no longer stop to rest, but find the tribes while *they* were resting. Custer's command attacked a village along the Washita River in the Indian Territory. There were warriors, but the majority were women and children. Many were survivors of the Sand Creek Massacre, like the "Peace Chief," Black Kettle. Even after the horror of Sand Creek, he had tried to achieve peace.

Taken by surprise at the attack that November morning in the midst of a snowstorm, Black Kettle pulled his wife up behind him on his horse. They were met by a hail of gunfire as they were crossing the Washita River and fell dead into the icy waters.[14] Mochi had survived the Sand Creek Massacre but lost her husband and other family members. She escaped the Washita as well, but her little girl was wounded. Her name would be heard on the plains again. To further immobilize the Natives, seven hundred ponies were slaughtered.

The 19th Kansas did not take part, however, having been lost in a blizzard for several days. They found Custer after the battle was over, and though General Sheridan was complimentary to Colonel Crawford at the time, his later memoirs were not as kind to the 19th Kansas. The two exerted more energy laying the blame for why the regiment was late than concern for the fate of the Cheyennes, Arapahos, Kiowas, Comanches, and Kiowa-Apaches in their winter camps. The casualty numbers are not certain. Custer lost twenty-one men while the Native losses were estimated in the dozens, many of which were women and children.

Fifty-three women and children were taken prisoner and used as human shields for Custer's soldiers as they retreated, protecting them from possible retaliation from the other Native camps. They were taken to Fort Hays, Kansas.

Colonel Crawford resigned when he realized no provisions had been made to pay his regiment. Turning over command to his lieutenant colonel, he traveled immediately to Washington and met with the Secretary of War. Congress, however, had adjourned making no appropriation for the troops. He tracked down General Sherman, and since he had called the regiment into service, he paid them from his contingency fund.[15]

Black Kettle, one of the Cheyenne peace chiefs, survived the attack on the village in Sand Creek, Colorado Territory, only to be killed at the Washita in 1868.
COURTESY CAPT. MYLES KEOGH RESEARCH LIBRARY, FORT WALLACE MUSEUM

While Captain Jack was soldiering with Colonel Crawford, Charley was starting a new career. Grandfather Curtis raised livestock and bought a pair of racing horses. At eight years old, Charley rode in his first race.

"While on the reservation I had ridden all kinds of Indian ponies and had ridden in a number of pony races and was considered a good and fearless rider," Charley said. His grandfather's horses were Brown Tom ("a good-looking, fast horse") and Flatfoot ("fast but unreliable"). Flatfoot was matched against a "very fast horse that had just been brought into the locality," he recalled.

The race was a quarter of a mile on a straight track and I rode Flatfoot. It was a regular frontier crowd that gathered to see the race; betting was not very lively because of the rumors of the speed of the strange horse. The starter and judges were soon selected; we riders were lifted to our mounts—we rode bareback, and the horses were soon ready for the word Go![16]

Charley lost.

But Grandfather Curtis sold the horse and the next year bought a roan mare, Carrie, "reported to be the fastest eight-hundred-yard horse in the west," and Charley became a full-fledged jockey at the age of nine.[17] He could recall the races in great detail decades later, in the same way he could describe each election in which he had been a candidate. Politics and horse racing—his competitive spirit was keen, and these two outlets fueled that part of his personality.

Every town of any size boasted a track, which was especially busy at fair time. Charley's grandfather had confidence in him and Carrie and determined to head westward, out of Topeka and into the cowtowns often flush with money. They passed through Junction City and visited a bubbling spring; continued on to Solomon, where Charley saw a huge prairie dog town; and then passed through Fort Harker:

> We . . . camped in a clump of trees by the historic spring that breaks through the rocks which line the well-known draw, at the head of which is a great soft rock. We went up to this rock and read the names of the Buffalo hunters, pioneers and cattlemen which had been cut in the rock. There were many who were well known then but have long since been forgotten. We stayed a day or two at the spring to give our horses a chance to rest up and to give the men a chance to visit Ellsworth and select a good camping place near the town.
>
> We got well acquainted with the sutler at the fort. He was a sporting man and as he said, "loved to see the ponies run"; and he gave us lots of information in regard to the men and horses the cattlemen had with their outfits.[18]

Charley recalled the Ellsworth of those days with relish—the red-light district in such detail that he obviously had seen it himself, even though only a boy. Each of the gambling houses ran several monte layouts "because this was the game for the men from Texas." In the dance halls there were to be seen women of "every grade and condition from fresh young girls just starting out to those who had been in the game for years and followed the trail, and then there were the experienced madams who ran the places and knew the business from A to Z."[19]

A race was soon organized between Charley riding Carrie and another lad on a Texas horse that had not lost a race on the trail. "[M]y grandfather was there and had plenty of money and took all the bets he could get."[20] Charley won, apparently profiting his supporters handsomely, and he was rewarded in the process:

> [T]he madam insisted on taking me to her house and then up town and bought me a new suit of clothes, boots, hat, and all and the madam had a new jockey suit made for me. I was proud of my good luck; the suit was a good one. They gave me money and bought me candy and presents and they came to our camp every day. We could get no more races and soon left. I was anxious to stay. I had never been so petted in my life and I liked it.[21]

The grateful madam wasn't the only interesting person he encountered in Ellsworth.

Bill Tilghman was a young buffalo hunter having his horse shod when he encountered a young Indian boy at Ellsworth. They shared an apple pie and went to the racetrack together, with Charley claiming that he had quit a wagon train that day and also rode horses. When they reached the track, the planned jockey couldn't make the run and Tilghman shouted that Charley could ride. He did, and as the famous lawman recalled, "stuck like a burr to his mount."[22] Author Jim Gray assessed the incident:

> What Tilghman didn't know was that he had just participated in an age-old horse racing deception. . . . The injured jockey was merely a

ploy to get a young, seemingly inexperienced Indian boy into the race.
The bets literally soared as gamblers placed their money.[23]

Tilghman gained fame as US Marshal when he captured Bill Doolin,
of the Doolin-Dalton gang. Along with his friends Wyatt Earp and Bat
Masterson, he became a legend in his own lifetime and even starred in a
movie based on his exploits. A good many years after the Ellsworth horse
races, Tilghman visited Charley in Washington. In the Senate dining
room Charley ordered pie and was said to have commented, "But none
of it ever tastes so good as that apple pie you bought me at Ellsworth,
Bill."[24]

He encountered another Western legend at the Kansas City
Fairgrounds. Charley and others heard shots being fired as the ticket
office was relieved of its strongbox full of cash during a race. The per-
petrators were reported to have been Jesse and Frank James with Cole
Younger.[25] Accounts of the episode recounted the drama after one of the
horsemen had grabbed the cashbox:

> Quicker than we can say it, the man had mounted his horse, and the
> three broke for Twelfth street and thence eastward toward the woods at
> a speed that would have put Restless to his meddle to emulate. Whence
> they came or whither they went no one knows; but they came and went,
> and while they stayed they made a page in the criminal history of the
> country that will probably stand for many years single and singular
> for wild audacity, reckless courage, invincible nerve and UTTERLY
> INDESCRIBABLE DARING.[26]

Other than the famous robbery (which may have affected Charley's pay-
day), the season was so successful that Grandfather Curtis determined
to head south, send the horses, and Charley, to Texas to race. He missed
school (the only winter he did not go, he said) but considered the education of the trip more valuable than anything he would have learned
from books. Charley was accompanied by four men: Tip Williamson, the
manager; Doc Hinshaw, the trainer; Bill Dawson, the cook; and Mike
McCarty, the assistant trainer and owner of one of the horses. Charley
was twelve or thirteen during the trip.

They journeyed through Baxter Springs and into the Quapaw Country, then through the Cherokee Reservation and on to Fort Smith, Arkansas. They were warned to be wary of horse thieves. They were also advised that the local towns would accept venison in trade for most goods, and Charley said they managed to find something to trade at "every little town" they passed through. They crossed the Arkansas River on a ferry, went to Fort Gibson.

A toll bridge along the route was so rickety that the group feared taking their horses across. The toll keeper informed them there was a ford five miles down and when they reached it, the toll keeper had beaten them to it, just in time to collect the toll since his license extended ten miles down the river. They continued to Waco, where Charley encountered his first suspension bridge. Of all the situations he faced bravely, this one had him stymied. "I could not understand how it could hold up under the loads that were constantly going over it," he said. "I was so afraid of it that the first day I was to go over it into the main part of the city, I crossed the river at the ford, but after the first day, I used the bridge."[27]

Along the way, Hinshaw proved to be a traitor. He doped Carrie, causing her to lose a race. The next day, Hinshaw was working for the other horse's owner. It was the only race Carrie lost, though Charley said they couldn't always get up races because of her winning reputation. Upon reaching Fort Worth, it was determined to turn and head home. On the return, back at Fort Gibson, the group encountered a Cherokee Freedman who had lived in Topeka. He shared the sad news that Grandfather Curtis had passed away.

"I cannot describe how greatly Grandfather Curtis was missed," said Charley. "He was a wonderful man, a real leader among men. His death seemed to change everything."[28]

At that point, Charley was "adrift." There was an uncertainty in the loss of his grandfather, in addition to the natural grief. Charley had been employed as a jockey for him, so there was the basic concern for whether or not he would have a job. There were bills to be paid and Grandfather Curtis's estate to be settled. There may have been a question about Charley's having a home to return to. He was taking part in some races still, but was showing signs of anxiety. He was sleepwalking, according to his comrades who described his going into a stall and brushing down a horse while sleeping. They watched nervously, afraid to wake him until he was outside of the stall.

He suffered from fevers and described how an Irish woman near Salina doctored him when he was racing there. The woman took in laundry and thus knew the men who ran the stable, who recommended her to young Charley:

> She made a cot on the floor, took a lot of blankets, some I think were taken over from the stables, made me put on a night shirt and made me lie down, then she began to prepare the medicine. She rolled a lemon, boiled some coffee, made it good and strong, squeezed the juice of the lemon in a tin cup, then filled it with the hot black coffee, no cream, no sugar, and made me drink it all. It was the bitterest dose I had ever swallowed. Then she covered me with blankets. I perspired a long time. She did not let me up for hours and when I got up, I was dry and had no chill and no fever and, for that matter, I have not had a shaking chill since.[29]

No doubt, Charley was feeling the weight of the world on his young shoulders, and it may have affected his health. He was not the only person trying to find his way in stressful times. The Kaw were also adrift.

While Charley had been off on his horse-racing adventure, the Kaw had been fighting to stay in Kansas. In 1872, a delegation from Washington, DC, visited the reservation. Speeches were made, mostly propaganda, about how wonderful the next permanent home would be. The head chief, Allegawaho, rose and addressed Secretary of the Interior Columbus Delano and the other briefcase-carrying white men and the tribal leaders who had assembled. He was tall, straight, a respected leader and an effective speaker:

> Be-che-go, great father, you treat my people like a flock of turkeys. You come into our dwelling places and scare us out. We fly over and alight on another stream, but no sooner do we get well settled than again you come along and drive us farther and farther. Ere long we shall find

ourselves across the great Bah-do Tunga [mountains] landing in the Ne-sah-tunga [ocean].[30]

There were discussions and negotiations, but in the end, Allegawaho's eloquent words meant nothing. They fell like cottonwood leaves, littering the ground, trampled into dust. The Kansa were forced to pack and leave the state that was named for them. Mention of the farms and homes the Kaw had built, and the sacred dead they left behind in the hills, were of no concern. White settlers had been pouring onto their reservation for years, encroaching with near impunity. When the Kaw had set a price for their land, however, the public balked and waited for prices to drop precipitously before settling the rich countryside, thus reducing and delaying the profits to the tribe.

Wagons were hired for those too poor or too old to pack and transport their own belongings. It was a sad, anxious, but mostly uneventful trek to their new "permanent" home. On the way to the Indian Territory, tribal members stopped in El Dorado and performed a war dance. When they had finally crossed the state line, many Kansans muttered "Good riddance!"

For generations, the Kaw had been negotiating with the federal government; often, they were the "peaceful" tribe, the "civilized" tribe, as opposed to the "savage" tribes who refused to do as they were told. In the end, it didn't matter. All Indians were the same. Perhaps categorizing them as less than human helped justify lusting after their land. "Thousands of acres stretching away in either direction are given up to them, and are consequently devoid of cultivation," *Scribner's* reported. The widely reprinted article continued:

> Dirty, lazy, and in many instances dishonest, he is hardly grateful for the respect government accords his traditional methods of life. Not far from the residence of the agent, [the] government once built a number of commodious stone houses, which the Indians were solicited to occupy; but they stabled their ponies in the structure and camped in their wigwams outside.[31]

78

It was an oft-used argument: the Indians were not "using" the land, or perhaps not using it to its maximum capacity to produce. Efforts to "civilize" the Kaw, as with many other tribes, failed for so many reasons but were rooted in a total lack of understanding and respect for their culture. Every time a tribe was to be compensated for land, the funds were siphoned through the bureaucracy until the tribe received only a fraction of what they had been promised. It was like dealing with an unscrupulous landlord or the company store where every little thing is itemized, and exorbitant administrative fees are calculated to legally cheat the person who is supposed to benefit.

"The commodious stone houses" erected for the Kaw are a prime example. The complexities of the fraud are voluminous, but the crux of the story is familiar: contracts were let on the basis of relationships rather than merit, with a sizable chunk of the moneys appropriated going to the bureaucrats and contractors rather than into the homes themselves. Even the location of the houses was counter to the Kaw culture—with plans to locate them along the streams and rivers on individual tracts rather than in villages as they had traditionally lived. When the Kaw left their homes on the annual buffalo hunts, vandals or squatters took advantage, often leaving the homes bare or in disrepair for the Kaws' return. Thus, if the tribal members "camped in their wigwams" it was out of necessity or desire for comfort, not because they were not civilized enough to appreciate four stone walls and a roof.

As the Kaws were preparing to leave, a band came to Topeka to collect annuities, Charley recalled. Other sources suggest they were visiting old friends and relatives. "They were old friends from my own reservation," Charley told a reporter many years later. "Among them was Julie Pappan, my grandmother. They were glad to see me and I was glad to see them. They were very like homefolks to me."[32]

The band was camped on Soldier Creek, essentially the familiar North Topeka community each of them would have known so well. Charley's mother had left him a mare named Kate, and the horse had been running with a "semi-wild" herd of ponies near Silver Lake close by. He retrieved the pony and joined his relatives in camp.[33]

Being adrift, I threw my lot with them. They were then on their way to new reservation lands allotted them by the Government down in Oklahoma. I should go back to the Indians. . . .

We traveled for one day's journey out of Topeka and made camp. The evening meal was eaten. Our Indian pallets were made on the ground. The camp had fallen asleep.

It was then that Julie Pappan came to my bed. She awakened me. She told me of the love she felt for me, the son of her lost daughter, of the joy of having me back with her tribe. She said that she loved me above all else in this world.

But she wanted me to leave the Indians. She wanted me to go back to the white men. This was the great crisis in my life. By the action I then took I would be either white man or Indian for life. The world belonged to the white man. She, Indian woman, knew that. She, against the urge of her heart, wanted me to return to my father's people.

She got me from my bed, put me on a pony, sent me in the dead of night again over that trail which I had once traveled carrying a message for help, back to Topeka. She dominated what was probably another of the great turning points in my life, another occasion where I was balancing between the races that were in me. If I have been of service the thanks is due to Julie Pappan, Indian woman of the Kaw tribe.[34]

With his belongings in a flour sack, the thirteen-year-old returned to the white world.[35]

CHAPTER 6

The French Apple Peddler 1873–1879

Of all crimes the worst
Is to steal the glory
From the great and brave,
Even more accursed
Than to rob the grave.

—ROBERT FROST

THE KAWS WERE NOT THE ONLY TRIBE BESTED IN NEGOTIATIONS WITH the government. In the fall of 1873, leaders from the Cheyenne and Arapaho Nations went to Washington and other eastern cities to meet with the Great White Father and to bear witness to the advanced civilization (and unimaginable numbers of inhabitants). It was expected that these leaders would return to their tribes and make it clear that it was futile to resist the federal government. Agent John D. Miles escorted the group (including Cheyenne chief Stone Calf and his wife, and mixed-blood interpreter Ed Guerrier); their presence at the Eldridge Hotel in Lawrence while en route created quite the stir:

> They were the objects of much curiosity, and the office of the Eldridge House was thronged all Sunday afternoon and evening by persona anxious to get a peep at these roving red riders of the plains Those who never saw an Indian before, and had imbibed their notions of the noble savages from reading Mr. Cooper's novels, we fear suffered a worse

disenchantment than those parties who heard Bret Harte lecture, and had formed a notion of what the lecture would be like, from reading the Luck of Roaring Camp, or the Heathen Chinee. We heard a great many expressions of disgust at the beastly, squalid looking wretches. They are large, well formed, athletic looking fellows, with small heads, big coarse mouths, snaky eyes, narrow retreating foreheads, long hair, and taken all and all, as villainous a looking lot of heathens as it has ever been our fortune to look upon.

Little Robe is the principal big Indian of the lot, and he is as mild a mannered savage as ever cut a throat or took a scalp or dashed a baby's brains out.[1]

The descriptions are derogatory and degrading. In the mainstream white society, Indians—no matter what tribe—were second-class citizens at best, and at worst, animals:

Mrs. Miles informed us that White Horse was the chief or principal warrior of the s[c]abby band of Dog Soldiers. He has a fine open countenance like an alligator, and we can well believe that he is the chief son of a——of the lot. A good square look at him is enough to make a man feel for his scalp, and we should give him the road if we met him "by moon light alone" or anywhere else. Each one of the bucks wore a silver cross on his breast large enough to be mistaken for the Confederate crossroads. If any other evidence of their Christianity or civilization is needed, it is to be found in the multiplicity and variety of their ornaments. . . .

Beads, earrings big enough for mule shoes, bells, medals, feathers, worn in all sorts of outlandish, or unfashionable ways, ornamental combined tomahawks and tobacco pipes, symbolical of both peace and unpleasantness, beads where ever there was room for any, blankets and robes, embroidered to look like log cabin quilts, or old fashioned double coverlets but we never could describe fashionable costumes, and of course have to give this up for a bad job. They must be seen to be appreciated and distance in this case will lend a decided enchantment to the view.[2]

People who were best viewed at a distance, if at all. They aroused much curiosity, and little empathy.

When the delegation met with President Ulysses Grant, Stone Calf informed the president that the Cheyennes did not need the trains and wanted them to be taken away. Just as President Abraham Lincoln had been dismissive of the Kaw leader Ishtalasea a decade earlier, and Johnson had been deaf to Chief Allegawaho, Grant made it plain that progress was coming and there were few options left to the Plains Tribes.

Of course, there were always the sideshows and the circus:

> P. T. Barnum, the great showman, is negotiating for twenty Kaw Indians to go to the Vienna Exposition, and after that appear before the crowned heads of Europe. The Indians are willing to go provided Judge Huffaker [Indian agent] will accompany them, but not otherwise. Barnum has bought them a car load of fancy articles, beads, buckskin, &c, to give the Kaw the air of a respectable Indian.
>
> The Kaw should be taken in his native lousiness.[3]

The esteemed Mr. Barnum had a couple of cousins in Kansas who put him in contact with the Kaw, according to the papers. The Kansas papers further ridiculed the Kaw and the spectacle that would be made of them in Europe. "Judge Huffaker will present the Kaws to the crowned heads of Europe," proclaimed the *Western Home Journal*, "who will immediately give the Kaws permission to explore their respective palaces for cold victuals and shoot at nickels in the back yards."[4]

As one of those Indians who had "shot nickels," that had to be a painful characterization. Charley was a bright and curious young man. It is reasonable to expect that he read the newspapers, saw the condescending and degrading way all Native people—his family members as well as the "wild" tribes—were portrayed. He was recognizably an Indian; in the summer, his skin turned to copper. His hair was straight and black. He worked to support himself in highly visible jobs—racing, peddling apples at the Union Pacific train depot in North Topeka, clerking in a general store—all positions that would bring him into contact with the public. Back in school, he was teased for speaking French and Kaw and determined to forget those languages in order to fit in. Even so, he was constantly in fights. He was called the "French apple seller" or the "Indian race rider."

At last, a teacher saw Charley's plight and treated him kindly, lightly punishing him for fighting, or not at all. That teacher changed Charley's life:

> Just after school took up after the noon hour, he announced that Mr. Curtis would please take charge of the room, until he, the teacher, returned. I did as ordered and was in charge the remainder of the day. From that time on, I had no trouble. I didn't look for any and the boys seemed to leave me alone. I shall never forget that act . . . it was the best thing that happened to me while attending school.[5]

Following his grandfather's death, there was a sale of William Curtis's estate. It must have been especially hard for Charley to see the racing horses, Brown Tom and Carrie, sold away. He went with the horses as a jockey for a while, but the new owner did not understand training and thought that a trip to town was good enough as exercise. Charley quit that owner but continued to race and train. One of his clients was none other than the same Colonel Jennison his father had so admired during the war. Charley traveled to Leavenworth and agreed to work for a month to size up the situation. Though Jennison's offer was a generous one, after a couple of weeks Charley found the horses were not fast enough to be winners. He rode for other owners and went back to school.

In 1874, Charley, now fourteen years old, went to Louisville, Kansas (near Manhattan), and worked for a couple of horse owners. He was there when the grasshoppers came:

> I was out exercising Sleepy Joe and was two or three miles from the stable. All at once it seemed as though a great dark cloud had come between the sun and me, and in a few seconds, grasshoppers began to light on the ground. As soon as they lit, they began to eat everything in reach. The farmers tried to save their crops but they were unable to save much of anything. The grasshoppers ate everything that was green and tender. Taking the leaves of trees, the blades on the corn stalks,

At no time in Charles Curtis's life was he far away from a horse. His French-Kaw mother taught him to ride before he was three years old, and a horse was her legacy to him. On his Grandfather Curtis's farm, on the reservation, as a jockey, or while in office visiting the race track, he knew horses.
COURTESY DENISE COALSON, TAKEN AT AMERICAN FRONTIER PRODUCTIONS

peaches down to the pits, newspapers, old rags and in short everything they could find.

It was not long until covered wagons could be seen coming in from the western part of the State. On the sides were all kinds of printed and written phrases and comments. Some quite funny, some sad, but all reminders of the great damage that had been done by the grasshoppers. . . . They caused many of the Saturday men and women who had been among the pioneers of our state to leave their homesteads and go back to their old home states.[6]

In early September, Charley and his racing team headed south to Wichita. Not only had the grasshoppers laid the land bare, but the recent drought had also left the countryside in a dismal state. They stopped in Council Grove, where Charley had spent two years among his Kaw kinsmen. Spending a few days, they were able to schedule a race, which Charley won, so the group was encouraged to continue their trek despite the conditions:

> Finding food for the horses was difficult. The plains were strewn with the white bones of dead horses and cattle, the sun was hot, and our suffering was great. I really do not see how we stood the trip and several times we were tempted to turn back but Mr. Cooper [one of the horse owners] insisted upon going on. At one place where we were told we would find plenty of water we found a large hole in the bed of a creek that had been dry for weeks. In this hole was some water but the few cattle that were left were standing in it when we drove up and there were dead carcasses of horses and cattle, that had died of hunger and thirst, strewn all over the ground, but it was the only water we could find.[7]

The drought and plagues of locusts were likened to the trials visited on Egypt in the Old Testament. Two million acres across the Great Plains were affected, leaving no refuge for those settlers who had made homes there, and certainly none for the Plains Tribes who were being hounded and harassed, no longer a threat in Kansas. The last vestiges of the Cheyennes, Arapahos, Kiowas, and Kiowa-Apaches were being forced onto reservations in the Indian Territory. With the buffalo herds growing smaller and smaller and more difficult to find, they were facing starvation themselves. The government was counting on their weakened condition to force them onto reservations.

The great migration westward was not halted, but it had certainly reached fits and starts in the mid-1870s. The railroad boom had gone bust and contributed to the country's economic depression. Increased immigration from troubled Europe coincided with currency crises in America, massive bankruptcies, and unemployment. These were very modern issues and yet here was America still hampered by these backward people that were consuming time, resources, land, food—to what end? The American public's patience had worn thin for the Indian.

As young Charley traveled through the troubled West, he had no way of knowing that many of the issues playing out with real people—white and Native—at that moment would become policy debates when he served in Congress years later. He may not have had a great deal of formal education, but he had keen powers of observation. He learned to read people, an essential skill for a boy on the Plains or a politician in Washington. He saw firsthand what real people did to survive. He saw the risks people were willing to take to improve their lot in life, and he could relate. And through every story, every example, he was "balancing the races within him."

While Charley and company were heading south and encountering numerous settlers giving up and headed back East, John and Lydia German and their seven children were crossing Kansas headed to a new stake in Colorado. The family's story would have struck a chord with Charley, especially the father's ambition and determination to provide for his family and establish a home for them in the West. The Germans found a camping spot along the Smoky Hill River bed—the river itself was dry. John dug down a foot and a half in the sand until he found water for them to drink and provide relief for the livestock.[8]

The family had left their home in north Georgia four years prior. A Confederate veteran, John had returned to a war-ravaged country and a war-weary people. Like many Americans, North and South, he set his sights on the West. But the family did not have the means to leave until 1870 and, even then, they worked their way westward.

Finding water along their route was a challenge for them as well, and the locals, ravaged by drought and grasshoppers, were not willing to share. When they camped on the Smoky Hill Trail, their spirits must have been boosted knowing they were closer to their destination and a new home at last. When they awoke the morning of September 11, they hitched their wagon and prepared to leave, but suddenly a Cheyenne raiding party was upon them. In moments, John and Lydia and three of their children were dead and four daughters had been carried away.[9]

The news spread across Kansas and the Plains. Troops from Fort Wallace had reported the attack, and soon the headlines had spread to Eastern papers as well.

The Red River War plagued settlers in the Texas Panhandle. The US Army had been assigned to bring the renegade tribes to reservations, among them the Cheyennes and Arapahos who had been enemies of the Kaws for generations. Nelson Miles (a colonel in the postwar army, a general during the Civil War, and an ambitious officer who would rise to the rank of General of the Army) led the far-flung troops assigned with this task. When word was received that a raiding party had attacked a family and kidnapped four girls, Miles was determined to see them rescued, as was Major Frank Baldwin serving under him.

The two younger German sisters were rescued in the Battle of McClellan Creek, in the Texas Panhandle, during the fall of 1874. The older girls were surrendered at the Darlington Agency, Indian Territory, with Stone Calf and his band in March 1875. Some of the Cheyennes, including Medicine Water and his wife, Mochi (who were identified as leading the attack on the German family), were taken to Fort Leavenworth, where they were essentially put on display for the curious public. They later were transported to prison at Fort Marion, Florida.[10]

The mighty Cheyenne who had struck fear in the hearts of the Kaw in the end fared no better than they. Following the discovery of gold in the Black Hills and the ensuing conflicts on the northern plains, the Northern Cheyenne were ordered to leave the Black Hills and join their Southern kinsmen in the Indian Territory. The two branches of the tribe had lived separately for many years, long enough to become very different groups. The Northern Cheyennes had become more like their neighbor, the Sioux. In 1878, almost a third of the tribe left the reservation to return to their homeland in what became a deadly journey for them and settlers they encountered along the way.

James N. Leiker and Ramon Powers, authors of *The Northern Cheyenne Exodus*, discuss the attitudes that prevailed in America at the time, as well as the situation with the Cheyennes themselves:

> All that can reliably be said is that at this crucial juncture the Northern Cheyennes were divided and the U.S. government exploited their division. Indeed, Euro-American society seemed equally divided. By the mid-nineteenth century, the United States had become a continental power, loosely unified by a central government but with enormous, ethnic, religious, and political diversity. Since the Second Great

Awakening, a growing body of reformers exerted influence over their nation's dealings with non-Europeans. Before 1870, the superintendents of Indian Affairs were army officers. Now, though, Congress had relieved officers of this duty, and soon various church denominations assumed the role; Episcopalians, Presbyterians, and Quakers oversaw about two-thirds of all agencies.[11]

The reformers believed that if only the Natives were converted to Christian farmers, they would fit into society. "Take the Indian out of the Indian" was the common theme. For those like the band of Cheyennes resisting all efforts at assimilation, there was almost no sympathy for their plight from the Kansas population. In fact, one of the most sympathetic voices was that of former captive Catherine German. She and her sister Sophia kept Stone Calf from prison by insisting that he had been kind to them since they came under his protection, and he had not been a party to the attack. It was a rare quality to distinguish Native Americans as individuals rather than holding the tribe or the race accountable for the actions of a few.

As Charley traveled, the events of the Red River War were playing out in the press. He was obviously an Indian; everywhere he went he would have been recognized as such, often inviting fear or insult. What must have been his reaction knowing that the Cheyennes, too, were being forced to accept reservation life? If many of those same Cheyennes had triumphed just six years earlier at Council Grove, his family and friends would have been among the casualties.

He did not comment. He got by and hoped for better days.

News of "Indian atrocities" flooded the media. Occasionally, the atrocities perpetrated on the tribes themselves made the news, but (with the exception of the Sand Creek Massacre, which was not wholly condemned) most were reported with impunity and without fear of judgment.

In December 1874, the Austin papers reported on troop activities. When nine Comanches encountered an encampment of soldiers about 160 miles west of Austin, a skirmish ensued. Five Comanches were killed and one was captured. In reference to the returning soldiers, the *Austin*

Weekly Statesman reported, "The boys brought some fresh scalps with them, and they report that Scott Cooley, who was fired at and run into camp, not only cut a wounded Indian's throat, but stripped a large piece of skin from his back, saying that he would make a quirt out of it." The official report only gave the numbers killed and captured and stated, "No men were killed or wounded on our side."[12] No mention of the outrages on the bodies of the Comanches was made in the report to the Adjutant General.

The 1875 Census lists Charley as living with his father and step-mother, Lucy Jay Curtis, and another sibling, "T. P.," who was listed as seven years old at the time, making her year of birth 1868. His half sister's given name was Theresa Permelia but she would ever be called "Doll" or "Dolly," even in official documents. Other census records give birth dates of 1873, 1875, 1876, and 1877. Her grave marker indicates the birth year of 1872, but her obituaries indicate she was born in 1867. No matter her age, it appears that she and Charley did live in the same household as children, for a while at least. By December 1876, Lucy Jay Curtis had filed for divorce, and Charley went back to Grandmother Curtis's home. Lucy and Dolly moved fifty miles or so east to Olathe, Kansas, and lived with Lucy's brother.

Charley continued working at whatever jobs he could find. During the winter of 1873–1874, while attending school, he helped a local store-keeper who was illiterate; Charley, a mere teenager, was balancing the books on the weekends as well as minding the store on Saturdays. He was peddling apples on the Union Pacific train platform in North Topeka every day at noon until the railroad officials forced him to stop. Since the Curtis family had given the land for the depot to the railroad, it would seem the company's memory was rather short.[13]

That same winter a buffalo hunter rode into town with a wagonload of meat, possibly the last one that came into town, and asked Charley to help him sell it. His commission was a "big piece of a hind quarter," which fed the family for days.[14]

Charley would return to racing periodically and acknowledged, "All I knew was horses," but he was getting heavier and "outgrowing" the sport, since size was not a desirable trait for a jockey. He was invited to race

MRS. WILLIAM CURTIS
Dolly Gann's grandmother, who ruled
the Curtis clan in Kansas.

Permelia Hubbard Curtis, devout Methodist and Republican, urged her grandson,
Charles Curtis, to leave horse racing and get an education.

at the 1876 Centennial Exposition in Philadelphia, but this was when Grandmother Curtis once again intervened.

"My Grandmother Curtis, there in Topeka, talked to me always of the value of education. Upon my return . . . it was she who urged me to go to school. I should make the money I had saved go as far as I could, and while it lasted I should go to school. This advice I took," Charley related in a later interview, "and, with what I was able to earn, I was able to maintain myself for two years. This schooling was the first apparent progress I had made toward bettering my condition, toward building a future with possibilities in it."[15]

Despite his sporadic schooling until that point, Charley had earned the money to buy books and clothes and had sufficient education to attend Topeka High School, on the south side of the river.

One of his teachers later recalled that Charley "knew what he was in school for." When other boys and girls of the freshman class were "wont to pass notes, whisper and otherwise disturb the classroom quietude back in 1878," Charley had no time for such "trifling." She also recalled that Annie Baird, who later became Charley's wife, was there at the same time, and recalled their being in programs together. Annie's name often appeared in the papers singing or performing recitations at school or club events.[16]

Charley was especially involved in debating society, where "we settled all the public questions of the day to our own satisfaction, if not to that of the men who were making the laws for the National Government and the states."[17]

His teacher recalled that Charley was a freshman in 1878, making him eighteen years old at the time, and given the infrequency with which he had attended school, that might be accurate. He said the first school he attended was "in the old log school house, with its wooden benches and its old fireplace." The school was about two miles from his grandparents' farm. "Why I was allowed to go is not known to me," Charley wondered. "I was too young to study." He also made reference to school being held in the log cabin in which he was born, and another school in the second story of a house near the Union Pacific Depot, both in North Topeka. J. H. Foucht, a North Topeka hardware dealer, taught school for a short time in North Topeka and claimed to have taught Charley to read and write upon his return from the reservation. Charley did not dispel his claims, and it is very possible that he did not read and write until he was at least eight or nine years old.[18]

Since Charley was six years old when he went to the reservation, he was no more than five or six when he attended that first log school. He surmised his grandparents had sent him to school to keep him out of trouble, but school may have simply been used as a babysitter, as his grandparents had their hands full with running the farm and stage stop.[19] In fact, biographer Don Seitz indicates that the reason Charley was sent to live with his maternal grandparents was the hardship facing Grandmother and Grandfather Curtis.[20]

Charley was determined to get an education and credited his grandmothers with instilling that desire. "My two grandmothers," he said, "I have always held, were responsible for any success that I may have attained."[21]

CHAPTER 7

The Indian Rider 1880–1888

God works wonders now and then; Behold a lawyer, an honest man.
—BEN FRANKLIN

Nothing spoils a good story like the arrival of an eyewitness.
—MARK TWAIN

LUCIA CASE WAS A SMART WOMAN. THE WIFE OF ONE OF TOPEKA'S LEAD-ing attorneys and early settlers, she was independent and open-minded. In fact, she would eventually become an attorney herself and was asked to be a candidate for attorney general. Mrs. Case attended the commencement exercises for Topeka High School, and one student stood out among the presenters. There were the usual bands and inspiring speeches; the salutatory address by Miss Annie Baird "elicited earnest commendation" and her duet with another student "was beautifully and loudly applauded." But "The Duties of the Chief Magistrate," written by noted jurist Oliver Wendell Holmes, was "an earnest, patriotic, magnanimous selection, and spoken with clearness and force" by a handsome, black-haired young man. Mrs. Case had to speak to him.

Although nineteen years old, Charley was only a junior in high school; his schooling to this point had been sporadic, interrupted by racing and earning money. But he had promise. Mrs. Case caught up with Charley after the ceremonies and asked about his plans for the future. He had none, though he may have already been thinking that any plans might include the talented Miss Baird. Their names had often been linked in high school presentations and church events.

Mrs. Case said that her husband could use some help around the office, and that Charley was just the type of bright young man that would benefit from such an arrangement. Charley consulted with Grandmother Curtis and, with her encouragement, visited Mr. Aderial "Hib" Case the next day.

Pioneering lawyer Case had been in town as long as the Curtises and had served as the attorney for William Curtis and for Captain Jack. He felt "warmly" toward the family, according to Charley. At first Case discouraged his young companion from pursuing law, glibly remarking that there were too many poor lawyers in Topeka. To which Charley confidently responded by asking if there was room at the top:

> This seemed to please him and he told me I could come in the next morning. I was to keep the office clean, keep fresh water in the tank and keep the desks, tables, chairs and books dusted and, in the winter, I was to build the fires and I was to be in the office every morning at eight o'clock. I agreed to the terms. I began by reading Blackstone, Kent and other standard law books, and I continued to drive the hack at night and frequently took one of the law books with me when I read while waiting for the passengers.[1]

It was another way of paying for his education—cleaning the office for access to law books as well as Case's mentoring.

One evening, Case presented a promissory note signed by Captain Jack and payable to Case. Charley's shoulders slumped but he said that he would repay the debt. Case threw the paper into the fire and Charley put his face on his arms and cried. "He had the warmest heart of any man that I ever knew," Case recalled.[2]

Charley's father was a never-ceasing source of embarrassing moments. While the Curtis family was firmly Republican (the party of Lincoln, of abolitionism, of reform), Captain Jack was a founding member of the Hancock Club. The nationwide organization was founded to support the candidacy of Winfield Scott Hancock for president in the race against

Republican James Garfield. In fact, Captain Jack was on the committee to select speakers for the club meetings, and it was he who suggested musical entertainment also be provided. While Charley was becoming more entrenched in the Republican machine, Captain Jack had done the unthinkable and become a Democrat. He even collected money to finance Democratic candidates.

Both Hancock and Garfield were veterans, but Hancock had earned the sobriquet "Hancock the Superb" for his actions during the Civil War. In the Plains Indian Wars, however, his actions were less than stellar. "Hancock's War" in 1867 had inflamed the situation rather than resolve it, though he garnered praise in Congress. For Captain Jack to go against his stalwart Republican family there must have been a strong personal motivation. But if we dissect the Plains Indian Wars, the war waged by Hancock and his contemporaries was conducted mostly against traditional enemies of the Kaws. Captain Jack maintained a relationship with his Kaw in-laws until his death on the Kaw Reservation in 1893. Perhaps his loyalty to them somehow led him to support the man who had attacked their enemy.

Meanwhile, Charley's duties in the Case Law Office were growing; he was entrusted with collections and received half the fees he collected. His lot in life was improving. He was often seen at night, waiting for fares under a streetlamp, reading fundamentals of law. Case eventually sent him to police court and then cases before justices of the peace.

In just a few months, Charley was able to give up the hack-driving and devote all his time to the practice. He increasingly filled in for Case. One such example was before the justice of the peace in the little town of Muscotah, several miles north of Topeka. Charley raised a constitutional issue (rarely are such arguments raised in minor cases). The other attorneys teased him, no doubt taking him for an upstart showing off his newfound knowledge. The presiding judge ruled in Charley's favor, however, and the decision was upheld on appeal.

By the time he passed the bar, Charley had two years of experience, and knowing, *truly knowing*, the law and using it to his or his client's advantage was his specialty. His preparation was thorough, and this would be a hallmark of his professional and political life. Many times, he was better prepared than his opponents both in researching the facts of the case and the law as it related to the situation.

He was twenty-one years old, and he was headed to New Mexico to make a career in Las Vegas. His sister Libby and her husband had moved there, and several people in the business community had promised to be his clients. But before he left, Case made him a proposition, and his trip to New Mexico turned into a vacation rather than a relocation. Case offered him one-third of the practice. Charley quickly accepted and when he returned, the sign "Case and Curtis" welcomed him. The *Topeka Weekly Times* reported: "Our old friend and fellow townsman, Charles Curtis, today entered into a partnership with A. H. Case for the practice of law. . . . This is a successful and well deserved termination of a long and thorough course of study and a strict attention to business. The firm has our best wishes for its success."[3]

While Charley was a working attorney, Captain Jack was working as a lawman—sometimes a jailor, sometimes a deputy. In 1882, the Grand Army of the Republic (Union Civil War veterans) had a reunion in Topeka coinciding with the state fair. Units marched through town in formation, waving flags accompanied by drums and fanfare. Captain Jack was one of those deputized to provide security for his former comrades in arms.

Hundreds of veterans attended including Boston Corbett, famous for having slain John Wilkes Booth. He had moved to Cloud County, Kansas, and filed a homestead claim. The veteran was quite poor, and a collection was taken up for his benefit. Corbett was also recognized when the former prisoner-of-war veterans met; he had been a prisoner at Andersonville, the most notorious of the war's POW camps.

When not providing security for events or otherwise enforcing the law, Captain Jack frequented Topeka's saloons. Whether he was employed as a "spotter" (informant) or he just took advantage of his firsthand information, he would serve as a prosecution witness against those saloons.

One such example was the Wyman liquor case, in which Captain Jack was called as the primary prosecution witness against fellow North Topeka resident William Wyman. The trial resulted in a hung jury after ten days of deliberation, but a letter to the editor of the local paper expressed dismay at the verdict and said, "The testimony of Curtis was clear and explicit that he had bought both beer and whisky of the defendant a great many times. No man who heard him testify could doubt that he was telling the truth."[4]

The only attempt to discredit Captain Jack's testimony came from another saloonkeeper by the last name of Taylor who said that Jack had come into his establishment complaining of ill treatment from Wyman and indicated that was Jack's motivation in testifying against the defendant.[5] When the defense attorney questioned Captain Jack on the matter, he was appalled to be accused of lying about liquor, but qualified the statement by offering the circumstances under which he would lie:

> Capt. O. A. Curtis, popularly known as "Jack" Curtis, was congratulated yesterday upon the manly and straight-forward manner in which he testified in the Wyman liquor case. When he turned his flashing eyes upon the cross-questioner and said, "I would only perjure myself for my old mother and little daughter; I would not swear to a lie and perjure my soul for any man who ever sold liquor on the face of God's eternal earth," the scene created quite a sensation in court. He had testified to purchasing whisky of Wyman from four to six times a day—every day he was in town and had the money.[6]

There was one holdout on the jury, the proprietor of a local mercantile. Another liquor case around the same time ended the same way—with one juror holding out, resulting in a hung jury. A letter to the newspaper declared:

> The saloons of Topeka are run openly, without any attempt at concealment, other than the usual screen before the door. Every one that passes them knows, if he observes at all, what business is carried on within, and yet it is notorious that in the trials that have taken place under the prohibitory law it requires more direct and incontrovertible evidence to secure the conviction of one of these saloon-keepers of selling intoxicating liquors than it would to convict a man of the best repute in our community of horse stealing or highway robbery.[7]

Captain Jack's eagerness to prosecute the whiskey peddlers coincided with his newfound sobriety. The convert is the most zealous advocate, and that made the notorious Captain Jack, frequenter of saloons, an asset for the temperance forces. He became a regular speaker at the temperance gatherings in the city park, some of which attracted as many as seven hundred people. In his characteristically straightforward manner he noted members of the audience "with whom he had drank and got drunk and advised them to quit drinking, telling them that the main thing necessary was to keep away from the saloons, for they will not come to you."

He had advice for the women in the crowd on how to manage their husbands, sons, and brothers who drank, advice for the city government, and then he turned his attention to the police: "He had drank with some of them, and they had bought liquor for him." Then he proceeded to discuss the saloonkeepers and the juries deciding these cases. No one escaped his critique. "He wanted it understood that he was the enemy of all saloon-keepers, and would fight whisky as hard as he fought the 'Rebs' during our late war." Even though he was a Democrat, he supported Prohibition and wanted to see it prevail all over the state.[8]

While Captain Jack was aiding in the prosecution of saloon operators, Charley was defending them. Case and Curtis enjoyed a solid reputation for strongly representing their clients, and it appears they did not discriminate against the saloonkeepers, minorities, the disenfranchised, or just plain odd. And as colorful as Captain Jack's courtroom appearances were, some of Charley's clients were equally interesting. Among them was a medium.

Mrs. Rachel Johnson was an attractive, well-dressed, prosperous-looking African American woman who wanted a divorce. Not every law firm would have welcomed her business, but Case and Curtis did not hesitate. She walked into the office, up to Mr. Case, and described the attorney she wanted: he was young, with black hair and black eyes.

"I saw him while in a trance," she told Case, who quickly sent her to Charley's office.

"That's the man," she exclaimed when she saw Charley.

In due time, said Charley, her divorce was granted, and Charley had made quite the impression on her. Many clients came to his door by her recommendation. She had a brisk business, and was well known for her gifts. Charley recalled examples of her powers: Two women visited her because one of them had lost some jewelry. In her trance, Mrs. Johnson said the jewelry was in the second lady's purse, to which the guilty woman responded that she had been playing a trick on her friend. Whether that friendship survived the test was not related. Another gentleman had lost a valuable blooded calf and believed it stolen. Again, Mrs. Johnson went into a trance and said no, the calf had escaped through a loose wire and joined a nearby herd. That is exactly where the farmer found the lost beast. These and many other similar stories added to Mrs. Johnson's esteem.[9]

There were other instances when Charley defended minorities— other Black defendants, Native Americans, and Romani.

Two Romani had been charged with stealing a raccoon. The facts of the case were simple: the travelers were camped near the place where the coon had been taken, and they were in possession of a coon. "They had been there for weeks; the men trading horses, the women telling fortunes, dancing and singing to entertain visitors," recalled Charley.

The case attracted a large crowd. After the state presented its case, Charley moved to dismiss on the grounds that a raccoon is a wild animal and cannot be stolen. The justice agreed and the charges were dropped. Charley became a hero in the tavelers' camp. "I was wonderfully treated," he wrote. "Every woman, young and old, insisted on telling my fortune. They entertained me with their songs, music and dances. For years after that trial the [Romani] who came to Topeka always looked me up and I was employed in a number of cases after that where the [Romani] were defendants."[10]

Charley insisted that he had no plans to enter politics but had been an active member of the Young Republicans for some time; it was an energetic organization across the state, and Charley was a popular lad with his professional reputation growing. Despite his youth, one paper described him as "taking rank with the leading attorneys of the state."[11] Soon members of his party were pressuring him to run for county attorney. His law partner advised him to abstain but finally acknowledged that even though it would not pay as well as the practice, the experience would be invaluable. As with every major decision, Charley consulted Grandmother Curtis before agreeing, and on June 25, 1884, he announced his candidacy.

The issue was Prohibition. It was the law, but obviously not the practice as illustrated by the Wyman case and so many others. At a rally where Charley was asked to explain his position, he told the audience "that thousands of dollars had been expended; that spotters had been employed and used and yet the law had not been enforced; that there were then nearly one hundred open saloons in Topeka." Charley said that personally, he did not agree with the law, but if elected, he would enforce it.[12]

When Charley drove away with his friends, they pulled out liquor bottles and proceeded to pass them around. Charley did not imbibe, which they found funny and spread the word in the courthouse. Rather than diminishing Charley in the eyes of others, their gossip caused his stock to rise. Still, his election was far from a given. G. W. Casey commented:

> [H]ad the choice for County Attorney been left to me I should not have chosen Charley Curtis, but he having been fairly chosen by the Republican county convention, and he being, as I understand, a "teetotaler," and as well qualified in point of legal attainments at least as some of our former County Attorneys, I hold it to the duty of every true Republican in the county to support him. . . . This is Charley's first effort in politics. He has by his own energy and efforts risen from a jockey boy to an honorable position in an honorable profession, and I think he and all other young men of like ambition and noble aspirations should be encouraged and endorsed.[13]

On election day, there was a show at the Grand Opera House and election results would be announced from the stage. Charley had invited Miss Annie Baird to accompany him; in fact, the two were engaged to be married later in the month. As precincts were announced, he began to doubt the wisdom of inviting her, but when he won, he was glad she was there to share the moment.[14]

The two were married on Thanksgiving Day, and Charley assumed the duties of county attorney on January 12, 1885. A year later, they welcomed their first child, Permelia Jeannette, for Grandmother Curtis, but they called the little girl "Perm."

As the new county attorney, Charley wasted no time in prosecuting the saloons and various establishments selling spirits, which came as a surprise to many people, including some among his supporters. People talked Prohibition, but *actually enforcing* it, that was a different matter. It was expected that Charley would look the other way as his predecessors had done, especially since Case and Curtis had not only represented saloon proprietors but also represented the liquor lobby at a retainer of $500 per month.[15]

But he meant what he said about enforcing the laws. He went after the big offenders first, rather than taking the low-hanging fruit and only making a show of prosecution. "I shall never forget that first trial," Charley wrote.[16]

The defendant was Frank Durein, one of the "richest and most prominent violators of the law." The defense dream team included Charley's law partner, Aderial "Hib" Case, and other high-profile lawyers. A committee of radical Prohibitionists were assigned to watch the proceedings, keep tabs on Charley's progress, and report back to the Prohibitionist community. They were disappointed when the new county attorney exercised none of his peremptory challenges and allowed seven men known to oppose the law to sit on the jury. Obviously, Charley was no more interested in enforcing Prohibition than his predecessors, and the committee members spread like quail to scatter that news. They offered help from more-learned members of the bar, but Charley declined.

After two days of testimony it took fifteen minutes for the jury to return a guilty verdict against Durein—guilty of all seven counts in the indictment. One of the jurors told Charley they took so long because they were trying to find other counts to add. With that verdict, the next saloonkeeper facing trial entered a guilty plea. Charley was trying them as fast as he could. "In a couple of weeks there were eighteen men in the county jail and that many more waiting sentencing. The jail would not hold any more," he recalled.[17]

Reelected to the position in 1886, Charley continued prosecuting the whiskey peddlers, no matter how wealthy and no matter who represented them. Occasionally, father and son were on the same side. Information offered to the county attorney indicated that saloons were in operation near the Atchison, Topeka and Santa Fe Depot. Warrants were issued and placed in the hands of deputies A. Kuykendall and Captain Jack, who raided the establishments in question and arrested George Ferguson and J. Kuykendall:

> Ferguson was keeping a joint in the rear of H. C. Wilson's restaurant, and at the time of his arrest by Captain Curtis, was surrounded by about fifty fellows, all drinking and carrying on a great rate. Captain Curtis made a flank movement by running in at the back door, and the first intimation any one had of his presence, he had nabbed Ferguson. He was given time to change his slippers for boots, and was then taken to the county jail. . . . It was amusing to see the way in which the crowd of drinkers scampered when Captain Curtis made his appearance. Each man made a break for a door and in half a minute not one was to be seen.

The reporter affirmed, "County Attorney Curtis, who seems to be ever on the alert to bring malefactors to justice, yesterday gave another very forcible illustration that prohibition does prohibit."[18]

Whiskey was not responsible for one of the more bizarre and high-profile cases to come across Charley's desk, however.

Boston Corbett was a household name. The greatest manhunt in American history ended with Corbett disobeying orders and fatally wounding John Wilkes Booth, the assassin of President Abraham Lincoln. Born Thomas Corbett in England, he emigrated with his family to New York. He worked as a hatter, and people now realize that the mercury used in the profession produced symptoms of mental illness, hence the "Mad Hatter." Corbett married but lost his wife and baby in childbirth. He became despondent, drank heavily, but experienced a religious conversion while in Boston that so affected him, he changed his name. He was so zealous in his commitment to following a Christian path that when confronted by prostitutes, he castrated himself. He missed no opportunity to proselytize, often preaching on the street corners.

Corbett served in the Union Army during the Civil War, but often chastised his comrades for their language. He was sent to the guardhouse for rebuking Colonel Daniel Butterfield for taking the Lord's name in vain. His actions were so disruptive that he was court-martialed and sentenced to be executed, but the sentence was commuted and he was dismissed from the service. However, he reenlisted and months later was taken prisoner and held at Andersonville, Georgia.

Released through a prisoner exchange, Corbett eventually rejoined the 16th New York Cavalry, and in April 1865 they were assigned to capture Booth. Orders from Secretary of War Edwin Stanton were explicit—take Booth alive! Attempts to flush Booth from the barn where he was hiding were futile, even as the building burned and filled with smoke. Peering through a crack between the boards, Corbett heard God's voice telling him to shoot. He fired, and the bullet passed through Booth's neck, mortally wounding him.

Stanton was livid and determined to court-martial Corbett yet again, but cooler heads prevailed. Corbett had become a national hero overnight. Instead, the army quietly discharged him. Eventually, he made his way to the Soldier State—Kansas—so called because so many veterans were taking their homestead claims in the state. He made his home in Cloud County, in the rolling prairie of north-central Kansas, where he lived in a meager dugout and made little improvement to the land. Taking pity on the plight of this veteran, a local legislator secured a job for Corbett at the statehouse in Topeka:

> Boston Corbett, the man who shot John Wilkes Booth, the assassin of President Abraham Lincoln, was yesterday elected third assistant doorkeeper of the house of representatives, and that, too, by a unanimous vote; he was the only officer who received the unanimous vote of the house—republicans and democrats alike. . . . He is scarcely able to obtain enough to eat or clothing to keep him warm. Mr. Knapp, the representative from Cloud County, will very generously pay Corbett's way to Topeka.[19]

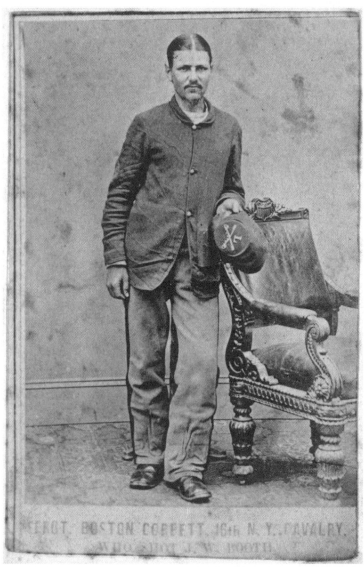

Boston Corbett gained nationwide fame by killing John Wilkes Booth, the assassin of President Abraham Lincoln. He later homesteaded in Kansas and worked at the capitol in Topeka, where his threatening behavior resulted in arrest and trial. Young Shawnee County Attorney Charles Curtis prosecuted Corbett and had him judged insane.

As the same paper reported weeks later, when the good legislators voted they had no idea that "Corbett has for years been erratic and at times almost crazy, particularly on the subject of religion. The few who knew him entertained fears that he would cause some trouble. . . . (One former house member even predicted that Corbett would kill someone before the session was over.) . . . Everything went well, however, until yesterday."[20]

The accounts vary, but at the very least Corbett brandished his pistol and threatened to shoot other doorkeepers, the sergeant at arms, a journalist, and at least one legislator, if not more. Some accounts say shots were fired, and some tour guides will point out nicks in the marble at the statehouse as evidence. Corbett was arrested and even though the headlines read "Crazy Corbett," the trial did not descend into the media circus it could have been. Topeka, with many veterans who were no doubt suffering themselves, seemed very sympathetic to the plight of this deranged man. From newspaper coverage of the proceedings, court personnel appeared respectful of Corbett even when his responses were nonsensical. Topeka's *Weekly Commonwealth* recorded the exchange:

> Charles Curtis, the county attorney, asked the witness a question, to which Corbett objected on the grounds that the probate judge should not put words in the witness's mouth. Mr. Curtis said that he was not the probate judge, to which the prisoner replied: "I hope you never may be, for a man who puts words into a witness's mouth is not fit to be probate judge."[21]

Not surprisingly, Corbett was adjudged insane and was committed to the state asylum in Topeka. A year later, he escaped. While the patients were enjoying their "constitutional" outside, Corbett spied a pony tied nearby and was mounted and gone before the guards had time to respond. "While interest always attaches to the escape of a lunatic, on mischief bent, and fear is entertained of the consequences of his being at large, unusual interest attaches to the escape of this insane patient because Boston Corbett is a historical character . . . as every school boy and girl of the country knows," said the *Daily Commonwealth*.[22]

Corbett headed south; stopped in Neodesha, Kansas, where he left the stolen pony with veterans he knew with the request of their returning it; and then disappeared. Reports would surface from time to time—he was seen in Enid, Oklahoma, and Old Mexico—but those were never confirmed.

Charley would have been one of those schoolboys who read of Lincoln, Booth, and Corbett—events that shaped the course of the nation. If he had particular feelings about the role he played in Corbett's commitment, that record has not been found. But what could have been used for grandstanding and publicity—the trial of one of the most recognized names in America—was not.

Corbett's time in Topeka, however, was remembered with sympathy for his predicament:

> Poor Boston Corbett. He had run under McDowell, fortified under McClellan, charged under Hooker, fought under Grant, hunted Wilkes Booth to death, headed a salvation army in the east and braved the terrors of the western frontier, but when compelled to listen to the ravings of the late Kansas legislature, his reason took a tumble and he is now hopelessly crazed.[23]

While Charley labored at law in Shawnee County, he maintained contact with his relatives in the Indian Territory and, as a voracious consumer of the news, he knew about the Dawes Act, passed on February 8, 1887. Whether or not he had an inkling how important that would prove to him is not known.

The federal government, rather than moving tribes from one spot of land to another as a tribe, determined to break up the tribal system with individual ownership of land, encouraging agriculture and Christianity, and simply encouraging Natives to be more "white." Senator Henry Dawes (R-Massachusetts) was the author of the bill. He visited the Indian Territory to research the situation, but his efforts did not make a favorable impression on most of the people he studied. This new plan would make the individuals in the tribes independent and no longer in need of annuities and the various welfare programs that had come to characterize the relationship with the government. As in the past, what the various tribes themselves wanted was not a consideration.

A missionary serving in Michigan gave a succinct, firsthand account of the problem with implementing the Dawes plan:

> From my own observation, I can state that after the cessation of the government annuities, and when the Indians were thus compelled to derive their living from farming, hunting and fishing, too many of them ran short and contracted debts. When, therefore, they received their title-deeds to lands apportioned to them as homesteads, they were unable to withstand the temptation to mortgage a portion of such lands for ready money.
>
> The better the land was allotted to them, the more numerous were the white men at hand, eager to advance them money or store credits, secured of course, by mortgages on their land. Thus, in numerous cases, many poor Indians were compelled to mortgage one piece after another; and this, oft-times, for a mere trifle. Every advantage was taken of their want of experience.
>
> They were discouraged. They found themselves unable both to pay the taxes and exorbitant rates of interest. A common remark among fair-minded whites, observing this state of things, was, "What a pity to leave the helpless Indians protection? The government should employ some capable and faithful lawyer to defend them in their land title."[24]

Only a few weeks earlier, the writer of this account, passing an Indian home on a tract of 40 acres, worked by a rather Christianized and sober Indian, was informed that he had already disposed of 120 acres, and was still scarcely able to maintain his family. "It is too soon to compare the Indian with the trained white farmer," the missionary wrote. He wrote too of the evils of alcohol and how "a rather intelligent Indian" had said "the Indians should reside more together, and retired from the whites, where intoxicating drinks should be withheld from them." The missionary added that "by the Severalty bill the tribal Indians will become a prey of the greed of avaricious and designing white men, and will surely lose their land."[25]

Another feature of the Dawes Act that drew angry reactions from tribal members was the caveat about Native women marrying white men losing their allotments. However well intentioned the condition was, that particular clause backfired. It was intrusive and paternalistic to presume to tell a woman who she could and could not marry. Some questioned why the government, who had long encouraged these relationships as a "civilizing" tool, had decided such alignments were undesirable. Many women interpreted the law as insulting, that if a woman chose to marry a white man he was only interested in her property—that a white man could not be interested in an Indian woman because she was beautiful, smart, desirable—any of the qualities he would have seen in a white woman. The provision further stated that if a Native woman married a white man, she would become a US citizen and lose her tribal member-ship. The Dawes Act was like quicksand, with Natives drowning slowly and painfully, and there was no help to pull them out.[26]

As the fate of "squaw men" and their wives and families was debated, what must Charley have been thinking? By the definitions in the Dawes Act, Charley's father and maternal grandfather were "squaw men"; their wealth (at least in land) had been secured through their marriages to Native women. He would have had a personal insight that few politicians possessed at the time, but would it have made him more or less sympa-thetic? While he did not criticize his father, he surely saw his flaws. Had his mother's death been hastened by his father's behavior, as his aunt suggested? And as for his Grandfather Pappan, he is rarely mentioned—certainly never with the same affection shown for his other grandparents. But even if such arrangements were not always good or healthy for those involved, who had the right to dictate to anyone else who they should marry? More importantly, how would that insight serve Charley, and his Kaw relatives, in the challenging days to come?

CHAPTER 8

Hello, Dolly! 1888–1892

Permanence, perseverance and persistence in spite of all obstacles, discouragements, and impossibilities: It is this, that in all things distinguishes the strong soul from the weak.

—THOMAS CARLYLE

LUCY JAY CURTIS REMARRIED FOLLOWING HER DIVORCE FROM CAPTAIN Jack Curtis. When she passed away, at only forty-two years of age, she and Dolly were living on her brother's farm in Olathe, Kansas, south of Kansas City. Her new husband does not appear to have been there at the time. As she lay dying, one of her friends comforted Dolly, a teenager. She wrapped her arms around Dolly and said that her mother would be leaving soon. Dolly recalled the sad day. "I went home and looked at Mother, so white, lying on her pillow, and knew it was true," Dolly wrote in her memoirs. "Not long afterward she slipped away. My brother Charles came for me, and I went to live with him and his wife, who from that day was a real sister to me."[1]

Dolly was fifteen (best guess) years old when her mother passed. Despite the pain and losses of her childhood, she shared her brother's optimism. She rarely indulged in sadness or self-pity and possessed the same straightforward attitude toward life. In her autobiography, she makes no mention of her parents' divorce, or of a stepfather. She wrote of living on her Uncle Jay's farm (her mother's brother) but does not explain why. Both her mother and an aunt lived with Dolly's uncle.

Dolly spoke fondly of her mother and Grandmother Curtis but said that Grandmother Curtis was the "outstanding influence" in her life, and that of her kinsmen:

> She ruled the family. So strong in mind and body, yet so gentle, she brooked no opposition. Not that any of us wished to oppose her; if we strayed momentarily, by accident or inadvertence, from the fold of her orthodoxy, she needed only to remind us of our allegiance, which lasted to her death at the age of ninety-six years. . . . And we loved her as much as we admired her Spartan character.[2]

Dolly was much like her namesake, firm in her Republican politics, absolutely devoted to her family, no-nonsense, and opinionated. When she joined her brother's household, they became her true family. Her devotion to Charley and Annie was unconditional and unwavering. Also like Charley, she did not criticize their father, publicly at least, even though there was probably ample reason. He was often absent, probably frequenting saloons, or arresting others who did. But it was Captain Jack who gave Dolly her pet name. Though named Theresa Permelia, she was such a tiny baby, just four pounds, that Captain Jack would take his sombrero-style hat and lay it over her, covering her completely, as if she were a "doll."

The name stuck.

Dolly did not look like her half brother and sister. They had inherited the olive complexion of their mother and had smaller features, typical of the French. Dolly was blonde, freckled, broad, tall—as tall as her brother. Even though Libby was older, Dolly always referred to her as "Little Sister" because she was so tiny by comparison. Charley was always "Brother," not Charles, or Charley. Dolly described herself as a tomboy and was told she was "plain" and "unattractive" as a child. Her mother or grandmother had decided that blue complemented her complexion and thus it was the only color she ever wore. She was envious of her cousins who wore pinks and reds, and grateful when she moved in with her brother and was allowed more freedom in choosing her clothing.[3]

Charley was finishing his second term as county attorney when Dolly joined the household. He went back into private practice and continued to be very active in Republican politics. He found himself in the running to be the party's nominee for Congress but did not secure the votes for the place on the ticket. Nonetheless, he campaigned tirelessly for other candidates, he met people, he learned the ropes. He witnessed the intrigues and the infighting.

In October 1890, a son was born to the Curtises—Harry King Curtis, no doubt named for Annie's younger brother who had died tragically a generation earlier. Ten-year-old Harry Baird and thirteen-year-old Tommy Jones were killed when the sandy soil of the dugout they and other boys had carved into the bank of the Kansas River caved in on them. The community had been devastated by the tragedy and newspapers carried every detail of the accident, rescue attempts, and the sad funeral services. The friends had been buried side by side in Topeka Cemetery.

With another mouth to feed and the election behind him that fall, Charley turned his attention to catching up on his caseload. Soon, he was part of another high-profile case, this time in the western reaches of Kansas.

The western third of Kansas was relatively young, as governance goes. Forts Dodge and Wallace had been the outposts of civilization, and those communities saw railroads and settlement before the countryside around them filled up. Those early communities were eager to secure status as the county seat, as that translated to government jobs and supporting businesses. Kansas, as well as other western states, were scenes of "county seat wars" as factions sometimes took up arms to decide the issue. While the turmoil of the Bleeding Kansas, the Civil War, and the Plains Indian Wars defined the first thirty years of the state's history, the county seat wars defined the 1870s and 1880s.

"Without a doubt," wrote historian Robert Collins, "the struggle over the seat of Stevens County was the bloodiest of all the battles in Kansas over a county seat." Comparing the conflict to a "Kentucky feud" or a "Sicilian vendetta," Collins said, "This struggle shows quite well what happens when the contestants have no restraints and are willing to wage war to the death."[4]

Many county borders had changed with population fluctuations, and in 1886 the Kansas legislature reestablished Stevens County in south-western Kansas with Hugoton as the interim county seat. This set off the county seat war with nearby Woodsdale. The town of Woodsdale had been established by attorney Sam N. Wood, who had been in the thick of every Kansas conflict since Territorial times, up to and including the disposal of the Kaw lands at Council Grove. The residents of Hugoton considered Wood "an interloper" and resented his involvement in county affairs.

Never one to let resentment stand in his way, Wood dug in his heels. Both communities knew they needed a railroad line to survive and went about trying to lure one to their location. The seeds of violence were planted during a public forum for a bond referendum to support the railroad. Guns were drawn and no shots fired, but a couple of banged heads and bruised egos resulted in the issuing of warrants, and the back-and-forth began.

The ugliest of the conflict occurred in July when one of the factions went on a "picnic" south of the state line and into an area called "No Man's Land" because it seemed no government entity had authority to enforce the law there. The other side rushed to catch their enemies and serve warrants (ignoring the fact they had no authority either outside of Stevens County), and as the groups were going back and forth, the Woodsdale men decided to make camp in a hayfield. The Hugoton faction surprised them there and shot them. Thinking all were dead, they returned to town and said there had been a gunfight. However, one of the Woodsdale men survived and said they had all been captured and executed.

The state militia was called out to keep the peace. The Hugoton men responsible were tried by a federal court in Paris, Texas, with Sam Wood prosecuting. They were sentenced to death. However, the US Supreme Court overturned the convictions on the grounds that the Texas court had not had jurisdiction.

In the meantime, anger was directed at Wood and bogus warrants were issued for his arrest for made-up crimes. Finally, Wood was to stand trial in Stevens County on bribery charges. The trial was held in the Methodist church. Wood was outside on the steps when James Brennan, a notorious man who had become one of the strongarms of the Hugoton lot, shot Wood in the back. Wood tried to run but Brennan shot him again. Wood was carried into the church, where he died soon after. There were rumors that the presiding judge had been involved in the assassination.

Kansas Attorney General John N. Ives had his doubts that the prosecution in Stevens County would be vigorous enough and determined that he and Charley would aid Stevens County Attorney William O'Connor in prosecuting. Because of "certain charges as to his connection with the case," the district judge was replaced by one from Wichita who could be impartial. News reports of the case read like a B-Western script:

SAM WOOD KILLED!
Shot Four Times by a Witness Whom He Tangled up in a
Cross Examination in the No Man's Land Murder Case.

The state of Kansas is astonished and shocked today by the news of the death of Sam Wood, who was shot four times in the heart while standing on the court house steps at Hugoton, yesterday morning. The particulars are, that the man who did the shooting was James Brennan, a witness in the celebrated "No man's land murder case," in which Sheriff Cross was killed, and in the cross examination, Sam, who was one of the attorneys, mixed and tangled the fellow all up in his evidence, this making the witness mad.

Yesterday when Brennan, who is said to be a desperado generally, heard that Sam was at Woodsdale, he declared his intention of killing the well-known attorney and political agitator, and started out in search of him. Mr. Wood was standing on the court house steps when Brennan stepped up in front of him saying "You are the man I am looking for," pulling his revolver at close range and fired four times with so deadly an aim that it is said every bullet went through his victim's heart, who fell dead. James Brennan, who did the shooting, is and has been chief of the desperadoes of Hugoton.[5]

During the summer and into the fall, the news spread across the state, with newspapers choosing sides on Wood's reputation and the tragedy, or the good fortune, of his death. As the state of Kansas was trying to redeem its reputation as the center of the Wild West, occurrences like these were unwelcome reminders of a lawless past. Among Wood's staunchest supporters was former governor Charles Robinson, arguably the "father" of Kansas and among the most ardent Free-Staters:

> Speaking today of the murdered Colonel Sam N. Wood, ex-Governor Robinson said: "In the death of colonel S. N. Wood, Kansas has lost is ablest and one of its best citizens. It is doubtful whether the tide of slavery would have been turned back from Kansas without his assistance. His services were invaluable and indispensable. He understood the conflict in every particular, was thoroughly in earnest a man of firm conviction and with sufficient courage for all emergencies. He was physically and intellectually a giant, and a heart full of love and good will for his race. He was always found on the side of the oppressed and in the thickest of the fight.[6]

If Sam Wood's traits were exceptional, his independent nature was not in the frontier towns of the era. Power struggles were often violent and the arrival of "outsiders" to interfere with local business was not welcome, as twenty-nine-year-old Charley soon found. Even the trip itself underscored the remoteness of this area, almost as far from the seat of government in Topeka one could travel and still be in the confines of Kansas. Stage travel in the eastern part of the state had not been supplanted completely by the train, but those routes passed farms and signs of habitation. Between Liberal and Hugoton, there was wide open space. Charley described the train ride to Liberal and then the stage ride on to Hugoton and passing a lake with thousands of wild ducks upon it. The passengers regretted they were going to try a case rather than hunting.[7]

Charley noted that the trip was also lined with abandoned homesteads; in fact, the mortgage banker traveled with them, noting the sad tale of foreclosed properties where even the fixtures from the windmills had been stripped away. All that remained were the tumbleweeds.

His first morning in Hugoton, Charley was confronted by a judge and a deputy US Marshal who was his bodyguard; both were carrying Winchester rifles on their shoulders:

> I followed the men who fell in behind the Judge to the building where the court was being held. The Judge walked up to the bench, laid his Winchester over it. Mr. Short [the bodyguard] walked up to the side of the Judge and stood by the bench with the butt of his Winchester resting on the floor.
>
> The court was opened. . . . I had not been in the room long before I discovered that nearly every man in it, except myself, was armed. Big revolvers showed below their coats or bulged at their hips.[8]

Attorney General Ives announced that Charley was to be lead prosecutor in the case, and jury selection began. The division in the community was evident as men wanted to be on the jury to avenge Mr. Wood or acquit Mr. Brennan. The attorney general headed back to Topeka, but before he did, Charley asked him to put in writing that he, Charley, was to prosecute the case. It was a fortuitous request, for no sooner than the official left town than the county attorney protested Charley's presence and asked for a private conference. Others advised him not to go, but Charley would not be cowed. The attorney was agitated, and asked if Charley intended to bring out all the facts surrounding the killing of Wood:

> I told him I did. I had hardly completed my statement until he was on his feet and talking loudly about not having been given fair treatment and then turned to the stove and pointed to a big round hole in the stove pipe and then to a like hole in the board partition and said, "Do you see that bullet hole in that stovepipe and the one in that partition?" I told him that I did. He said, "Well, this faithful old gun of mine went off accidentally the other day and made those holes and it might go off accidentally again and kill a man."
>
> I said with all the men out in the street I was not afraid of his gun going off accidentally or otherwise; that I intended to try the case in

my own way and if he had any further communication he might submit the same in open court; that I happened to have been born in Kansas and that I was not afraid of guns nor of men who carried them and I bid him good day and walked out of his office.[9]

It proved impossible to seat a jury since none of the men called could be impartial. The case was continued, whereupon it was still impossible to seat a jury and thus Brennan was never tried; the murder of Sam Wood was officially unsolved. It was rumored that Brennan became insane, which seemed to bring some satisfaction to Charley.

Nonetheless, to have been selected by the state's attorney general to accompany him and be a part of this trial had to have been both a compliment and a good paycheck. Charley may have doubted whether either was worth it after the experience, but it was evidence of his growing reputation as an accomplished lawyer.

"Of the twenty-eight murders I tried, or assisted in the trial of," he wrote, "the prosecution of James Brennan for the killing of Sam Wood attracted the most attention in the newspapers."[10]

Pundits began mentioning his name as a candidate for Congress.

Charley was confident he could secure the nomination, but his only hesitation was the popularity of Union veteran Captain J. B. Johnson. It was not only that the veterans would support him, but Charley also held Johnson in high regard. He met with him to discuss their options. When Johnson decided not to run and instead threw his support behind Charley, the congressional seat was nearly a foregone conclusion.

The veterans were always a consideration. According to William Allen White, it was the members of the G.A.R., "whose cause he championed and defended on the stump," who began referring to him as "Our Charley" because of Captain Jack's service. "He 'Our-Charleyed' his way in Kansas politics and in the Republican organization of the nation for more than thirty years," White asserted.[11]

When crowds gathered at Lukens' Theatre in North Topeka to celebrate Charley's nomination, the decor was decidedly patriotic. Flags hung from the chandeliers, bunting covered the bottom of the stage, and portraits of President Grant and Generals John Logan and Phillip

Sheridan were in front of and flanking the speaker's podium. Marshall's Military Band performed patriotic tunes. Speakers echoed the fact that Charley was the son of a veteran and remarked that Captain Jack was among the bravest of Kansas soldiers.[12]

There were many tributes throughout the night, including that of Elder Barker, who was introduced as a representative of "the colored people" who would support Charley in November. He said: "There always is a black sheep in every flock. I am the one in this one."[13]

But the most heartfelt tribute came from Charley himself. His voice trembled as he spoke, according to the reporter:

> He said, "I see in the audience friends, who in the grasshopper year, when we had hard [times] getting along, sold me apples at a reduced price and advanced me money on my work to get us something to eat, and I owe so much to my dear old grandmother, who sits before me—" Here the speaker's voice broke and he ended abruptly by saying: "Friends, I can't talk any longer." There was great applause and the reception concluded with a general hand-shaking, while Klingaman's orchestra furnished some music.[14]

Only weeks before, Annie had given birth to another girl, Leona Virginia. Leona and Dolly would be especially close through the years, though Dolly adored each of the children. She never had babies of her own, so the role of doting aunt suited her well.

While Grandmother Curtis was present to witness this milestone in Charley's life, Captain Jack was not. "He is a great fisherman," the reports read, "and for three weeks has been camped on the river below Lawrence, with his boat, net and lines, he was at home last Sunday, and left word to have the papers sent to him when 'Charley would be nominated.'"[15]

After getting his office affairs in order, Charley hit the campaign trail, visiting every school district and ordering newspapers favorable to his campaign to be delivered to his constituents, even sending the *Western Veteran* to a mailing list of former soldiers.[16]

Many of those veterans had participated in not only the Civil War but the Plains Indian Wars, a topic once again filling the newspapers.

The Honorable Charles Curtis as a young congressman in 1891.

Accounts of events from twenty-five years earlier became headlines with recollections from the Medicine Lodge Peace Treaty, the Battle at Beecher's Island, the Battle at Fort Wallace, the Kidder Massacre, and so many other events of those pivotal years. Most of the Native Americans in the news were thus cast in a negative light—reminders of attacks on travelers and settlers.

Charley knew that his Indian identity was a disadvantage in the political arena. In a later interview, he remarked, "I was an Indian and had been a Jockey. Also, as a school boy, I had driven a hack." In other words, he did not have the illustrious background one might expect of an elected official. Even though being an Indian may have made for colorful copy, it would always be a quality that should be overcome or compensated for somehow.

Charley did not dwell on those issues; rather, he honed his skills as a politician. He developed a habit for which he would become famous and proved invaluable for a politician: he remembered people. "I made note of facts and names and taught myself to remember names and instances," he explained, "so I could call men by name when I met them and tell them what had happened the last time we met. It was hard at first but soon became easy to recall names and places."[17]

William Allen White wrote of his friend's method for remembering and how Charley referred to it:

[H]e pulled out a little book . . . and like a pious worshiper out of a prayer book he began mumbling their names to impress them on his memory. It was a curious rite, I thought, and funny, and I giggled. But it was dead serious to Curtis. He had a little book like that for every township in Kansas, and carried the county's Republican poll list when he went into a county.[18]

Despite how hard Charley was canvasing, the National Congressional Committee said the Kansas Fourth District race was hopeless and that they would not financially support his candidacy, so he personally financed his campaign. Charley won by 2,800 votes, a healthy margin. News spread quickly that Kansas had elected an Indian to Congress:

Kansas is always doing something unexpected in political fields, and at the recent election it again did a notable act in choosing a quarter-blood-Indian to represent the Fourth District, including the capital of the State. Charles Curtis, Congressman-elect, is the son of a quarter-blood Kaw Indian and Captain O. A. Curtis, of the Kansas Volunteers, Fifteenth Regiment. His grandmother still lives on the reservation in the Indian Territory and is very proud of her offspring's prominence.[19]

The article went on to describe Julie Pappan's standing in the audience and listening to one of Charley's speeches. Since she passed away in 1890, Grandmother Pappan was not there to see him elected to Congress, though there could have been other relatives happy to see Charley and hear his "big talk."[20]

The happiest man in Topeka over this victory (aside from family), according to Charley, was Judge John Guthrie. A native of Indiana and a Civil War veteran, Guthrie had served in the Kansas legislature and enjoyed a successful legal career before becoming a judge. He was "the one man who at all times and under all circumstances was praising me to the people of Kansas," wrote Charley, and had encouraged him to enter public life since his serving as county attorney.[21]

When the position of postmaster for Topeka was open a couple of years later, Charley rewarded his old friend with the appointment. Guthrie's health was failing, and the duties of the postal bureaucrat were not as demanding as those of a judge or attorney. There was a "roar that could be heard in Washington" when Charley put forth Guthrie's name over the younger men vying for the job. Even Guthrie told him not to sacrifice votes for his sake, but the congressman was firm. "You were my friend when I needed one," he told Guthrie. "I have not forgotten. I don't care how many votes it costs. You take the office."[22]

Being a US congressman did have its rewards.

CHAPTER 9

An Indian in the House 1892–1905

A life spent making mistakes is not only more honorable, but more useful than a life spent doing nothing.
—GEORGE BERNARD SHAW

FOR DOLLY CURTIS, WASHINGTON, DC, WAS A LONESOME TOWN. IT WAS the first time in her life she was not surrounded by family, and her brother was immersed in his work, learning the ropes and proving his worth to the House leadership. But Dolly had no friends, and the inclement weather only added to her woe. The normally optimistic Dolly wrote:

The rains of 1893! I shall never forget the dismal weeks of that late summer and fall. A downpour every day, not a ray of sunshine. Never have I since seen such weather in Washington, nor so much of it. I wept. Finally I reached the point of asking Charles to send me back to Kansas. I hoped he would let me stay there forever. Perhaps my homesickness hastened his decision to have me for a secretary. Although he had a small office in the Capitol, his real office was a room in our home, the Manning residence, at 200 East Capital Street, which he had rented. He had a secretary, a very competent man, who resigned for some reason or other; so it came about that I got my chance to work and forget how lonely I was.

From then until now I have been busy.[1]

In those early days, Annie and the children joined Charley during the long sessions of Congress; for the short ones, they remained in Kansas. Eventually, the children were enrolled in Washington schools. When Annie was in town, Dolly received visitors with her each Tuesday—the "at-home" day for the wives of congressmen where refreshments were served to endless guests.

Dolly also began keeping "systematic records for campaign use—books filled with the names of Kansas voters, the citizens of every county and town. All the names we could get. A short biography of each voter, with his achievements, sometimes with a description of his personality, all the facts we could gather about him."[2]

Charley was noted for working long hours, for always being prepared, just as he had in his law practice. Duties for his home and interests in Topeka were left to various family members or friends. Whether it was to keep him employed and off the river or Charley truly believed he was the best person for the job, Captain Jack was tasked with property management for some of Charley's rental properties. The congressman counted many attorneys among his old friends in Shawnee County that he could call on when legal matters arose, and it fell to his sister Libby to keep the Curtis home in order and ready for their return.[3]

Washington became their primary home, and even though they maintained strong ties to Topeka, life in Washington would dominate the rest of their lives.

Charley's first speech as a congressman was about money—silver, gold, and their ratio to paper money. (He always said he represented tenets of the Republican Party whether he personally agreed with them or not.) William Allen White, Emporia journalist, commented on another occasion Charley addressed the topic and characterized the remarks as "a very carefully poised straddle on the currency question (which, I was satisfied then—and still think—that he knew little about, and cared nothing for). For his politics were always purely personal. Issues never bothered him."[4]

When challenged by the other representatives on the merits of gold and silver and where he stood, Charley's ability to spar was evident. His confident and quick responses, his ability to turn barbs back on his attackers, his unflappability—these qualities garnered cheers from the gallery. He concluded, "I am for currency to support the business and common people of this country." Just as White had said, Charley's stand on the matter was difficult to discern.[5]

As critical as White was of Charley's political acumen, he was nonetheless seduced by Charley's charm. His description fairly drips with admiration. "He was a handsome fellow, five feet ten, straight as his Kaw Indian grandfather must have been, with an olive skin that looked like old ivory, a silky, flowing, handlebar mustache, dark shoe-button eyes, beady," wrote White, "and in those days, always gay, a mop of crow's wing hair, a gentle ingratiating voice, and what a smile!"[6]

Charley made a name as a man of the people, and even though he was capable as a public speaker, he was not exceptionally eloquent. His strong suit consisted of his straightforward manner, his fearlessness, his ability to read people, and his charm. As his stature grew, ironically, he led from the back of the room and not the floor. He became the master of backroom politics. When he spoke, it was to his constituents, not before his fellow legislators.

He built his reputation on personal relationships, being everyone's friend. Kansas State Representative E. W. Hoch "paid a high compliment to Congressman Charles Curtis, who he said was a living proof that the Republican party did not elevate plutocrats to high places, as had been charged by the populists. He said Curtis was a man from the people."[7] If one should ever doubt Charley's down-to-earth background, news of his father's exploits was there to remind them.

While Charley and Dolly navigated the Potomac, Captain Jack was once again navigating the Kaw River. There is no direct mention of it, but one is led to believe that Jack had abandoned his temperance philosophies. Rarely did the Topeka papers fail to mention one of his adventures, including the time he caught a fifty-pound catfish and the fact that he knew every fish in the river.[8] His various boats were referred to as "floating shooting galleries" as they docked here and there along the river.[9] In 1894, however, he had commissioned the building of a deluxe flatboat and had elaborate plans for earning money along the way. There was the air of the circus's arriving whenever Captain Jack put in, and people flocked to see him:

BOUND FOR NEW ORLEANS
Capt. Curtis Casts His Moorings at Day Break.

The little packet "Hail Columbia," commanded by Capt. "Jack" Curtis, that was moored near the dam of the Kaw river for several days past, was cast loose this morning at day break and started on its way down the river towards New Orleans, its destination.

The little craft attracted much attention while it put up in this city and there were many visitors who went on board. The flat boat is 48 feet long with an inside clearing of 10 feet long and 9 feet high. The interior is divided into three compartments; cabin, dining room and carpenter shop, and everything is kept in perfect neatness by Capt. Curtis and his two assistants. The carpenter room has a complete outfit for making traps which will be sold along the route to farmers.

Capt. Curtis also has a splendidly equipped medicine chest, and will make medicine for veterinary use to help pay his necessary expenses. The party will stop at Desoto tonight and go onto Kansas City, where they will remain about three weeks. They expect to reach New Orleans early next fall. Capt. Curtis is about 63 years old, and this is his fourth trip by flatboat to the lower Mississippi. He was urged by his son, Congressman Charles Curtis, to give up this journey, but as he was raised to run boats on the Wabash river, he is not contented to remain on land. He is a great fisherman and takes the trip for pleasure.[10]

A month later, Captain Jack returned to Topeka, having sold his boat in Kansas City. He remarked that it was the worst trip he had ever taken down the river.[11] He was never one to sit still, though, and there were other adventures to be had, other work to be done, including managing property for Charley. A dispute arose between a woman leasing a home and property from Charley and a gentleman who drove his wagon across her yard. As luck would have it, Captain Jack was not only the property manager but a witness to the event, so his testimony was key to the case. Quite unlike his son who preferred to stay in the background, Jack was the center of attention. He made quite the appearance in the courtroom:

> Charley Curtis' father has the agency for the place and he was a witness in the case. Mr. Curtis himself said that he was about four parts Dutch

and it took him a long time to say anything so he slid down comfortably in his chair till he simply hung to the chair arms by his armpits and put his feet in a friendly way on Judge Ferry's desk that the judge might have a free uninterrupted view of his generous and expansive sole. There is no putting on style about Old "Jack" Curtis who came here before there was any Topeka.

McNary [the defense attorney] undertook to cross examine Mr. Curtis for Taylor but gave it up.[12]

Every time Captain Jack made news, reports reminded the public that he was the father of Congressman Curtis. Such was the case when the Cherokee Strip opened for white settlement. The lands that had been reserved to the Cherokee Nation attracted crowds to the first-come, first-claim land rush. Captain Jack was among those lining up waiting for the race to begin. Other headlines said he was headed to the Indian Territory to visit his Kaw relatives. He was with them in 1897 when Charley was in Arkansas City (just a few miles into Kansas from the Kaw Reservation in the Territory). Captain Jack and General Fred Hardy, treasurer of the Kaw Tribe, met Charley at the train depot. He was on an official visit to the Kaw and Osage, "the exact nature of which is not a matter for publication at the present time," but he was to remain for two weeks. Captain Jack told the reporter he was proud of Charley, and General Hardy added, "Yes and the whole tribe of Kaws are proud of him."[13]

A year later, Captain Jack was dead. He died suddenly while living on a Kaw allotment near Newkirk, Indian Territory, land his grandchildren had inherited through his wife, Helen Pappan.

Charley immediately reached out to his friend and attorney, A. A. Hurd, to arrange for Captain Jack's body to be brought to Topeka for burial. As the news was shared in the Kansas capital, a reporter went at once to interview Grandmother Curtis, then ninety-one years old. It was feared the shock would be too much for her, but Permelia Curtis was made of tougher stuff and "bore the shock without flinching." She spoke calmly about her eldest child's death and his visit months earlier:

"I always tried to do everything 1 could for Orrin [sic]," said she. "It is too bad that I could not be with him. He always knew that when he wanted his mother to do anything she would do it if she could. The last time he was at home he said, Mother, I wish I had a pair of double mittens like you used to make. Do you think you would be able to knit them for me? I told him I would be glad to knit them but I had no money to buy the yarn and he went and bought the yarn and I made the mittens for him before he left. That is the last thing I ever did for him."[14]

The lengthy obituary went on to chronicle Captain Jack's record as a veteran of the Civil War and Indian Wars, as well as his personal and professional failures—his failed marriages and the fact that "[a]t one time he owned the greater part of North Topeka, but through bad management and improvident habits, he lost everything." He was a "born rover," and had been planning a wagon trip through Arkansas later in the year.[15]

Charley and Dolly came from Washington as quickly as possible, and Captain Jack's funeral was held in the home of a US congressman. But another, far greater, tragedy was soon to engulf the Indian Territory, and Charley's name was all over it.

The Act for the Protection of the People of Indian Territory was signed into law by President William McKinley on June 28, 1898. Introduced by Charley as House Bill 8581, it went through so many revisions by the time it was passed that it had little resemblance, according to Charley, to his original bill, but it bore his name nonetheless: the Curtis Act. The *Weekly Chieftain* reported from Vinita, Oklahoma, on the repercussions of the bill:

Congressman Curtis, of Kansas, has introduced a bill in the house which is intended to be a substitute for the Dawes commission bill, as reported in a Washington dispatch. It will provide that all criminal cases in the territory must be tried in the United States courts. It also provides for an equitable system of leasing lands, for a period of from one to twenty years.

Another provision is that no Indian shall hold over 160 acres of land, all the rest to be held in common, for the benefit of the tribe. As far as civil cases are concerned either party is to have the right to take the case into the United States courts, if he desires, but where both parties prefer to have the decision of a tribal court it is permitted. It will be seen that the bill is hardly less radical in the reforms which it proposes than the Dawes commission bill. The fact that it is to be proposed by Congressman Curtis, who has all along been the Indian's chief champion on the committee, indicates that Indian legislation by the present congress is now a certainty. In losing Congressman Curtis as a supporter the Indians have lost their last hope of holding off action.[16]

The *Chieftain* went on to outline a brief to be filed by the Cherokee Nation in opposition to the bill. One of the most egregious elements of the bill was related to abolition of tribal courts:

There could not be a more direct and flagrant violation of the solemn promises and plighted faith of the United States as contained in the treaties of 1835 and 1866. It would not only result in taking the jurisdiction from the tribal courts, but it destroys their governments as well. Without a judiciary to interpret and enforce law a legislature would be a farce and an executive officer a painful reminder of false promises and broken pledges.[17]

As to the plan for allotments, the Cherokee brief asked:

How can you divest one of the use of lands patented to the tribe, legally acquired, when the laws of the respective nations, under which he acquired it, were authorized by the treaties with the United States? Congress has no more right to force a division of the use of the lands of the Cherokees than it has to compel heirs to an estate to individualize their interest, or shareholders of a corporation to divide their stock.[18]

As to Charley's role in the bill, the reporter observed:

The Indians are completely disconcerted by the conversion of Congressman Curtis to the Dawes side of the case. He was undoubtedly disposed to favor the Indians to the limit of his conscience, but the facts which have been brought out both before the Indian Affairs committee and the judiciary committee as to the corruption of the Indian courts were too much for him, and he is now convinced that the institution of reforms is imperatively necessary.[19]

There is no elaboration on the alleged corruption in the Indian courts that may have motivated Charley in his course of action. A later issue of the same paper carried a far more bitter assessment of the law. The article was written by Cherokee attorney and author DeWitt Clinton Duncan. Educated at Dartmouth, he signed his work with his Cherokee name, *Too-qua-stee*. The headline declared, "THE CURTIS LAW IS A CALAMITY. A Pandora's Box Opened in Indian Country. The Communal Interests of the Past Displaced." His words wholeheartedly condemned the measure:

> But what now, has this miserable Curtis law done with all this noble people? It has disbanded them as a nation; abolished their social organization, and reduced them to the condition, (in a legal sense,) of a mere band of strolling savages, nay a herd of prone cattle, and has placed over them a special executive agent, (well, a herdsman,) with authority to prescribe, direct and compel, what they shall and shall not have, do, or enjoy. They are allowed no voice in making the laws by which they are governed; no voice in the selection of the men that rule over them; no voice in the choice of the magistrate who is to try and sentence them; no voice as to who shall be the hangman that is to give them their passport into eternity; no more voice than so many rats, in anything of a political nature. It is not easy for one who has no personal knowledge of the facts, to get anything like an adequate idea of the humiliating condition to which these Cherokee people have been reduced by this unjust law.[20]

"The bill I drew, introduced and passed in the summer of 1898 was intended to protect the interest of the people of the Indian Territory," asserted Charley.[21] However sincere that intention might have been, it was not well received, and while he intended that Native Americans be recognized officially as citizens of the United States, at what cost would that be achieved? The greater question, never asked, is why the

Indigenous peoples of America were not automatically recognized as citizens in the Constitution.

Too-qua-stee's article continued:

> Prior to the enactment of the Curtis law, the people of this country were socially organized; they were living under what was known as the Cherokee government. But the spirit of that legislation was decidedly destructive; its aim was not to build up, protect and preserve; but rather to pull down, undo and annihilate. It swept, in effect, over this territory like a devastating tornado. There was no kind of obstacle, however formidable, that caused it to falter, or hesitate, for a moment. It kicked aside the Decalogue and all the fundamental principles of God's moral universe, as worthless obsoletions; laws and constitutions were but vapor; solemn contracts and treaties were smoke; plighted faith, moonshine-national honor, staked as a guarantee, it trampled underfoot as the merest trash.[22]

While America had issues at home to resolve, there was always a conflict abroad to divert attention. This time, it was war with Spain.

Cuba and the Philippines were chafing under the rule of Spain, an empire in decline, and clamoring for their independence. When Cuba's rebellion began in 1895, President Grover Cleveland declared the United States would remain neutral, but public sentiment did not always align with public policy.

Kansan Fred Funston heard Civil War veteran General Dan Sickles speak in New York City. The general had lost a leg in the Battle of Gettysburg and was a most convincing speaker. Funston was determined to join the Cuban resistance. His bravery and ability earned him notice but did not keep him from contracting malaria. He was granted leave and returned to the United States. The five-foot-four-inch officer weighed only ninety-five pounds.

In 1898, the USS *Maine* was attacked and sunk in Havana Harbor, giving the United States an excuse to join the war. "Remember the Maine, to Hell with Spain!" was the rallying cry. Upon Funston's recovery he was commissioned in the regular army as colonel of the 20th Kansas. News of the regiment's heroism filled the newspaper reports, and Funston and others among the 20th Kansas were hailed as heroes for actions in the Philippines. Meanwhile, Colonel Theodore Roosevelt achieved fame in Cuba charging up San Juan Hill.

Roosevelt rode the wave of fame into the New York governor's mansion and was aiming for the White House when he visited Kansas in 1899. A crowd of three thousand met him at the Santa Fe Railroad depot in Topeka, where Charley clambered over the iron rails of the platform to introduce him to the crowd. The press reported on the spirited speeches and the enthusiastic crowd:

> The crowd yelled: "Hurrah for Charlie," "Hurry up, Curtis," and other similar expressions.
>
> "Hello, Curtis; how are you:" exclaimed Roosevelt, changing his hat from his right to his left hand and extending his sword arm to aid Curtis in climbing over the rails. The crowd began cheering when Curtis landed on the platform and gave Roosevelt's hand a hearty shake. Curtis raised his right hand and motioned silence to the crowd with his left hand, in which he held his hat. "This is Colonel Roosevelt, one of the greatest men in this country and a hero in the minds of the American people. I take great" then the cheers drowned his voice and the distinguished Visitor leaned against the rail and opened his mouth to speak. The crowd cheered and Roosevelt admonished them to be silent with a wave of his hand.
>
> He said: "When I heard the trumpets I thought the 20th Kansas had reached home and you were all celebrating as you have a right to do on that occasion. I have been through here before but I would gladly come again to help you honor the 20th and Funston. We all honor Funston, not alone because of what he has done, but because the cause he represents stands for the highest and best thought in this country. We honor him, too, because he is ugly, honest and has horse sense." When he used the word "ugly" the colonel gave a sly wink and crooked his index finger towards his own person.[23]

At the Republican Convention of 1900, Roosevelt was chosen as the vice-presidential candidate, not the top spot as he had hoped. President William McKinley was riding a wave of popularity himself with the victory in the Spanish-American War and the acquisition of valuable territories Puerto Rico and the Philippines. The election was a rematch between the president and his former opponent, Democrat William Jennings Bryan. Bryan's anti-imperialist ideology gained little traction. America liked having more land. McKinley won with nearly double the electoral votes.

In December, Charley accompanied the Kaw chief Washunga to Washington. Several members of the tribe filled out the delegation, and they met with officials about allotments and payments. The *Arkansas City Traveler* reported on the event:

> President McKinley's visitors today included Wash Shun Gah, chief of the Kansas tribe of Indians.
>
> He was in full war paint, from his thoroughly smeared face to his gay colored moccasins and fiery red shawl, but he was not in a bellicose humor. He was, in fact, the best natured and most talkative Indian who has been to see the "great white father" for a long time. He was so full of talk that he wanted to make a speech to the president in English. He was not allowed this pleasure, but he shook hands with Mr. McKinley in the most free and easy way, extending his right hand in a gay and cordial manner.
>
> Wash Shun Gah has made two speeches since he came to Washington. One was to Secretary Hitchcock of the interior department and the other to Commissioner Jones. Secretary Gage went to the white house while Wash Shun Gah was there and was introduced to the chief. The interpreter explained that Secretary Gage was the man who had all the Indian money. Wash's face brighted [*sic*]. He patted Secretary Gage on the shoulder and said: "Me no go home till git mon." Wash was accompanied to the white house by Representative Curtis.[24]

The *Arkansas City Traveler* ridiculed the fact that Washunga had been treated as well as a foreign dignitary during his state visit. "The people have seen this old Indian about the streets so often they have forgotten he is a chief."[25]

About six months into President McKinley's second term in office, he spoke at the Pan American Exposition in Buffalo, New York. It would

Chief Washunga of the Kaw Nation and Indian Agent on the Kaw Reservation in Oklahoma. Congressman Curtis escorted Washunga to meet two presidents, William McKinley and Theodore Roosevelt.

be his last speech. The president eschewed protection details: he enjoyed meeting people and mixing with the crowds. At an appearance in the exposition's Temple of Music, a young man who had lost his job in the Panic of 1893 shot the president in the abdomen. Sadly, McKinley's secretary had been concerned about the Temple of Music event and had taken it off the calendar twice, only to have the president put it back.

Vice President Roosevelt had been vacationing in Vermont when notified of the president's condition. His first six months of serving as vice president had been boring; he only presided over the Senate for a few days before it adjourned, so he went fishing. He hastened to see the president, but thought McKinley was improving. Roosevelt returned to his vacation, only to be notified of the president's death. Hurrying back to Buffalo, Roosevelt was sworn in by a federal judge in a local home with only a handful of people in attendance on September 14, 1901.

Once assuming office, he assured the country, and Republican leaders, that he would continue McKinley's policies.

In 1902, Chief Washunga, with a delegation of his tribesmen, again went to Washington to meet with the president. "The chief was adorned with paint and feathers to an extent that is seldom seen. He wears the native dress throughout," wrote a reporter.[26] Another reporter sent this dispatch to the *St. Louis Republic*:

> A delegation of Kansas, or Kaw, Indians called on the President today to see about making a treaty for the division of their tribal lands among the individual members. Their chief, Washunga, headed the delegation, which was accompanied by Agent O. A. Mitcher of Oklahoma. Representative Curtis of Kansas will introduce a bill in the House on Monday to authorize the Indians to make this disposition of their lands. The treaty that Chief Washunga has with him provides that the tribal land shall be distributed among the individuals during the next ten years, at which time the tribe will disintegrate and merge into citizenship.
>
> The tribe owns about 100,000 acres of fine land in Northern Oklahoma, which would be divided among 217 persons. It is worth about $5 an acre. Fifty years ago the Kaws numbered 4,000. Representative Curtis is himself of Indian forefathers. Chief Washunga was dressed in full Indian garb, from feathers to moccasins.

Old Washunga told the newspaper correspondent in the President's ante-room that he was 207 years old. After seeing the President, Chief Washunga was asked how he liked him and said: "Heap fine boy. Mighty young for big Chief.[27]

The first steps to dismantle the tribe had been taken.

Early in President Roosevelt's term, the nation's attention once more turned to the Philippine-American War as the First Philippine Republic mounted armed resistance to American rule. Fred Funston was instrumental in the capture of Emilio Aguinaldo, the Filipino president. As soon as the news had been received of Funston's feat, Congressman Curtis called upon President Roosevelt, urging Funston's appointment to a brigadier generalship in the US Army.[28]

After Congress adjourned in the spring of 1903, Charley was home in North Topeka looking forward to Decoration Day (later designated Memorial Day). He had been asked to deliver speeches in many towns throughout the First District in honor of the nation's veterans. Then an epic flood intervened.

Charley rescued his Grandmother Curtis when informed the rising water from the Kansas River had reached her living and dining rooms. The home was built in 1867, but the water had never been known to rise that high. Grandmother agreed to leave only if Charley promised to bring her home as soon as the water receded. He carried the ninety-six-year-old woman from her house to the buggy. She was not afraid, Charley said. She had seen floods on the Wabash. Nonetheless, he saw that she was safely in place with his sister Libby and returned home to watch the water. The family sat on the front porch and waved and visited as the neighbors waded by. When the water reached the top step of his porch, he phoned the weather service and was told it would only rise another foot.[29]

"We felt perfectly safe," recalled Charley, "because it was still five feet to the first floor." But they were not safe:

We heard an awful sound and on looking in the direction which the noise came we saw the water pouring into a hole at the side of the basement wall under what was about the center of the dining room. I thought the foundation had given in and at once phoned for a carriage to take the family over to the south side. We locked the doors of the house and left things just as they were. When we got in the carriage the water was running through the doors on either side.[30]

Once his immediate family was safe with friends, he returned to help evacuate other citizens of North Topeka. Having thought his grandmother was safe, he realized the rising waters now threatened his sister's home. He sent a boat for Libby and Grandmother Curtis, and when it arrived, the rescuers rowed up to the porch and lifted his grandmother and sister over the porch railings and into the boat. The Kansas River had risen eleven feet the night before.

All that day and night we were rescuing people from their homes and some from trees and tops of buildings. To add to our worries, the lime in one of the lumber yards set the lumber on fire; this drifted against some of the houses and set them on fire and there were all kind of reports as to the fire and the damage it was doing. My father-in-law and his wife were not rescued until the second day.[31]

The destruction was unimaginable. When Charley inspected his own house, he found the mantle clock had stopped at 11:20, the water having reached more than six feet from the floor. Adding the height of the foundation, the water was more than eleven feet high around his house.[32]

The aftermath was so discouraging that people were willing to give their properties away. "To stop a real estate panic, I bought all the places that were offered and stopped the selling," Charley said. "After a day or two, people would come to me and want to buy their house back and I sold them back at just what had paid for them with the understanding that they wanted to move into them and would repair their homes and live in the houses."[33]

Charley developed a case of blood poisoning from spending so much time in the floodwaters, and the usually unstoppable public servant was sidelined for a few days.[34]

The economic impact of that natural disaster on North Topeka was felt for years to come.

A few months earlier, Charley had been in Chicago when a friend dragged him into the parlor of a "palmist." Charley protested but was also curious and allowed the woman to examine his hand. She studied the lines and contours and concluded that Charley was a lawyer and had the potential to be a successful politician. But she also saw land and thought that he should be successful in real estate as well.

Charley was impressed by the woman's insight: as a lawyer and politician, he was indeed successful; as for real estate, he had been investing widely there as well. But soon after the consultation, the flood came and "almost destroyed a few little houses which Mr. Curtis had built in North Topeka out of his savings." The reporter added that Charley had been working all summer making repairs and "paying out money to save them from utter loss." The report concluded, "Now he wonders why the palmist, who knew so much about real estate, didn't warn him."[35]

Charley was reelected to Congress in 1904. In 1905, he was selected by President Roosevelt to be part of a delegation to East Asia. "Roosevelt wanted this mission to be part fact-finding, part goodwill, and part saber rattling," wrote Alice Roosevelt Longworth's biographer, Stacy A. Cordery.[36]

The president took advantage of his daughter's popularity and hoped her diplomacy would be an advantage to Secretary of War William Howard Taft leading the entourage. There were seventy-five people in the official party, including Alice's future husband, Congressman Nicholas Longworth.

The *Topeka Daily Herald* reported in late June, "Congressman and Mrs. Chas. Curtis, Miss Dolly Curtis, Miss Permelia Curtis, Leona and Harry Curtis will leave Monday for California and the Pacific coast. Mr. Curtis will go on to the Philippines and the family go to Portland and other western points."[37]

The Americans were enthusiastically received, in great part due to Alice's charm and celebrity status. It had served her country, and her father, well. The delegation visited Manila, Tokyo, and Hong Kong, among other cities. President Roosevelt was attempting to negotiate the end of the Russo-Japanese War, and a strong American presence in the region was to his advantage. The delegation returned to San Francisco in September, and Dolly was on hand to greet her brother after his months at sea.[38]

There was much work to be done before the family headed to Washington in November for the next session of Congress.

CHAPTER 10

A Marble Battleground 1906–1915

If, of all words of tongue and pen,
The saddest are, "it might have been,"
More sad are these we daily see:
"It is, but hadn't ought to be!"

—BRET HARTE

NO SOCIAL EVENT IN ANY PART OF THE NATION ECLIPSED THE INTEREST in the wedding of "Princess Alice," President Theodore Roosevelt's daughter, to Congressman Nicholas Longworth of Ohio. The press clamored for details, especially of Alice's wedding dress and trousseau. The lists of wedding gifts were an embarrassment of riches and home-made handcrafts, with everyone from the Empress Dowager of China to rural potato farmers sending presents and good wishes. The invitation list was a who's who of American society and politics. Only three of the congressional delegation from Kansas were invited, including Charley and Annie.[1]

Prohibition was still an emotional issue for many people, and the Women's Christian Temperance Society and others began campaigns to see that wine would not be served at Alice's wedding functions. An enterprising gentleman from Leavenworth wrote to Governor Edward Hoch and said Kansas was missing its opportunity for national press as "home of the cranks" and urged Governor Hoch to send a resolution demanding that the president see that all wine and beer were kept off the

Nicholas Longworth, Alice Roosevelt Longworth, and President Theodore Roosevelt. The wedding of Alice Roosevelt to Nicholas Longworth was the social event of the decade; Congressman and Mrs. Curtis were among the guests attending the nuptials. Alice and Dolly Curtis Gann would be embroiled in a social feud throughout Charles Curtis's vice presidency, even though the families were allies.
COURTESY LIBRARY OF CONGRESS

White House grounds. Hoch did not send such a demand and it likely would not have mattered; as President Roosevelt famously said, he could run the country or control Alice; he could not do both. It is doubtful that a resolution from Kansas would have swayed Alice, but it might have amused her to see them try.[2]

Later that year, the senior senator from Kansas and Charley's close associate, James Burton, resigned his seat, having been convicted of bribery. The discussion of who would assume his office began before the verdict in his trial was rendered, and Charley's name was prominent. For a few days, the seat was vacant. Since the legislature was not in session, it fell to the chief executive to choose a replacement, and Governor Hoch appointed fellow Republican Alfred Benson to fill the position. He only served six months in the office because once the legislature *was* in session, they took up the duty of electing a senator.

In 1907, the Kansas legislature elected Charley to fill the remaining months of Burton's term as well as the next full term. Charley's relationship with President Roosevelt was well known, and State Senator Edwin Tucker referred to it in his nomination speech:

I rise to nominate for this office a man who has already served Kansas for fourteen years in the lower house of Congress. His record is free from taint and above criticism. He has always protected public interests and has ever been on the side of the veterans. He is good enough for Theodore Roosevelt and the man who is good enough for Roosevelt is good enough for Kansas. I name Charles Curtis.[3]

The president was among the first to congratulate the new senator:

White House, Washington, D.C., Jan. 12th.
My Dear Senator Curtis:—Pray accept my hearty congratulations. I look forward to seeing you upon your return to Washington.
SINCERELY YOURS, THEODORE ROOSEVELT.[4]

Dolly, so personally and professionally invested in her brother's career, was permitted to sit on the floor in the Kansas Statehouse while the voting occurred. "I had a list of the members and checked them off as they voted," she recalled. "Far down the alphabet, in the W's, a man named Woodyard cast the deciding vote. Then, as usual, they all came over. What a night that was for me!"[5]

Charley received over five hundred telegrams in Topeka congratulating him on the nomination but had time to open only a few, including those from the president, Secretary Taft, and a dozen other congressmen and senators.[6]

The celebration was not universal. An old editorial resurfaced denouncing Charley along with James Burton and former state treasurer Tom Kelly. Kelly had publicly stood by Burton during his high-profile trial. The article had been published in the *Troy Chief*, October 27, 1904, and it was still relevant, the paper asserted:

"BURTON-KELLY-CURTIS." The combination which has been running the politics of the state, Burton, Curtis and Kelly, have long-been known to be a crooked trio. Burton's record is well known.
Before he [Burton] was elected United States senator it was an open secret that he was a grafter and a dead beat and is now a convicted felon. Kelly robbed his own county and when caught paid back the

money, and not only escaped punishment for the crime, but was elected state treasurer. He is now in the toils again. Curtis has been in congress ten years at a salary of $5,000 a year. He is now worth $500,000. He has no other known income. His connection with the Indian land grabs are [*sic*] well known. It is thought that it will only be a matter of a short time until he will be in a worse predicament than either of his boon companions, Kelly and Burton.

These three men are a heavy load for the party to carry. It can't carry them much further and survive the strain, it is a good old wagon or it would have broken down with an outfit like that riding upon it.

"Curtis, Kelly and Burton, don't forget the name of this firm," the writer continued. "The election one week from next Tuesday will put the firm of Kelly, Burton and Curtis, political grafters and confidence men, out of business."[7]

Charley decried the accusations, asserting that he had owned real estate (mostly in North Topeka) for years and that claims of his wealth were exaggerated. Alas, grafter or not, Charley was elected and was sworn in on Kansas Day (the anniversary of Kansas statehood), January 29, 1907. He had marked his forty-seventh birthday just four days earlier. He wore the same suit he had worn at the other end of the Capitol, a black double-breasted sack coat and modest striped trousers. His lapel, along with those of several colleagues, displayed a red carnation in honor of the birthday of the late President McKinley.

Kansas Senator Chester Long formally presented the credentials of his colleague to Vice President Charles Fairbanks, who administered the oath of office. Dolly watched from the gallery along with several visitors from Kansas. General W. E. Hardy, Charley's relative and Secretary of the Kaw Nation, was also on hand to support his old friend.

Later in the day, Charley was named chairman of the Committee on Indian Depredations, which had rooms on the Capitol's terrace. It also provided for the staff positions of clerk and messenger. Dolly became clerk with a salary of $1,800, and Senator Burton's former secretary became messenger with a salary of $1,440.[8]

Annie remained in Topeka for the winter. Harry and Leona ("exceptionally attractive and brilliant young people," according to the newspaper) were enrolled in Topeka High School and rather than moving them in the middle of the school year, it was decided that Annie would remain with them in Kansas. The eldest, Perm, was away at Wellesley. Harry, a junior in high school at the time, bore "a striking resemblance to his father" and is "identified with the high school fraternity sets." The reporter guessed that Harry was thinking "more about Delta dances and pledges than life at Washington." Although Harry was considered bright, and a "great wit," there were signs that he was not as serious about school, or life in general, as was his father. Leona was in her first year of high school and was described as much like her older sister in appearance and personality, possessing the same dark hair and eyes, olive skin, and "happy manner."[9]

The family planned to wait until September to travel to Washington and would remain until the following July. The Topeka press was fairly bursting to share a clip from the *St. Louis Globe Democrat* in praise of Annie:

> Mrs. Charles Curtis, the wife of the new senator from Kansas, will be at home in Washington, where her husband has served several terms in Congress. She is like most Kansas women, a club woman, and takes a great interest in all the liberal and broad-minded measures that these women advocate.
>
> She is, besides, a very domestic lady, and does not only make friends, but has the happy faculty of being able to keep them. Upon the whole Mrs. Curtis will be quite an addition to the senatorial set in Washington.[10]

It seemed that Annie was above criticism, for no one offered any. Certainly not Charley or Dolly, not her children, not her neighbors, not any of Charley's political foes. Her demeanor was genteel, and she kept Charley grounded in a world where people often lost their compass. The *Pawhuska Capital* said, "Mrs. Curtis is of domestic trend not much given to social fads—a plain practical motherly woman."[11]

Another milestone event in 1907 was the Curtises' move from North Topeka. No doubt influenced by the devastating flood four years earlier, Charley and Annie bought a home south of the river. The imposing

Annie "Anna" Baird Curtis was married to Charles Curtis from 1884 until her death in 1924. An invalid in the last years of her life, she was still his strongest supporter and believed he should be president.

"eclectic Italianate" at 1101 Topeka Boulevard had been built in 1878 for a former mayor. Subsequent owners had hired renowned architect Seymour Davis to make changes, which included the addition of two turrets and "jeweled" windows, windows that perfectly framed the Kansas Statehouse a block away. This spacious home would be the center of the family's events for decades to come—funerals, weddings, receptions, and campaigns—and would be Charley's official address for the rest of his career.

For a time, Charley was the only Indian in the Senate, and then Oklahoma became a state on November 16, 1907, bringing another of Native ancestry to Washington. Robert Owen, one of the state's first two senators, had been born into an affluent Virginia family and attended Washington and Lee College, but the fortunes were lost, and his father passed away. His mother had Cherokee ancestry and they eventually moved to the Indian Territory, where Owen became a lawyer, teacher, and Cherokee activist. He had only been in the Senate a few weeks when he and Charley disagreed—vehemently:

Redskin Senators, Owen and Curtis, in Tilt.
AUTHORITY TALK IS CAUSE

Question of Whether Secretary of Interior Is Governing Power Incites Word Battle Replete with Tragic Utterances.

Washington, Feb. 28. Those at the capitol, who are familiar with the regard in which the Kaw holds the Cherokee, and vice versa, Friday expressed opinions upon the tilt Thursday between Senator Robert L. Owen of Oklahoma and Senator Charles Curtis of Kansas. The trouble started when Senator Owen, a Cherokee, insisted in tragic tones that his band is not under the Jurisdiction of the secretary of the interior. The event was rendered all the more interesting by the fact that Senator Owen was sharply engaged in controversy by Senator Charles Curtis (Kan.), himself a Kaw Indian. It was the first time that two men with Indian blood in their veins had ever locked horns as senators in the senate chamber.[12]

The argument began over the "Indian bill" and Senator Owen's attempt to amend the bill "as to recognize the citizenship of the five civilized tribes."

Charley interrupted the Oklahoma lawmaker and said, "Your property is under the control of the secretary of the interior, and you know it." The retort was just as quick when Senator Owen said, "I do not!"[13]

"The two senators of Indian blood now were facing each other 20 feet apart," the press reported. "Both appeared to have lost sight of parliamentary rules and were carrying on a personal colloquy."[14]

A colleague intervened before the men lost all dignity and came to blows. He tactfully pointed out that both senators were correct, and that Senator Owen's resentment over the idea that he was under the control of the Secretary of Interior was perfectly understandable. His remarks eased the tensions and the confrontation passed. But the issues were far from resolved.[15]

For many observers, the face-off was comical—two Indians whose tempers flared just as they had in the past, further proof that there was a limit to just how "civilized" Indians could be. In truth, however, there was a chasm separating Charley from his Cherokee colleague.

Even though both were mixed bloods, Owen, a Democrat, was an aristocratic Southerner whose father had been an officer in the Confederate Army. Charley's dad, Captain Jack, had an entrepreneurial streak but he was about as far from gentlemanly upbringing and behavior as someone in the same country could be. He had been an officer in the Civil War too, but in the Union Army. At the turn of the twentieth century, the legacy of the war still loomed over the country and old prejudices died hard. Tribal loyalties in the Civil War had been divided, creating deep animosity on the Kansas-Oklahoma border, and between some of the tribes themselves.

The Kaw Tribe received a devastating blow when Chief Washunga died of heart failure in February 1908. He was found beside the gate to his home, having gotten out of his wagon to open it and been overcome. The cold may have contributed to his death, and he was found frozen the next morning. His death was symbolic of the tribe's situation, seemingly unable to pass through the gate to the safety and security of home.[16]

Once again, Charley found himself going head-to-head with a senator to the south. This time, it was Senator Thomas Gore, also a Democrat. Gore, who had gone blind as a youth, accused lobbyist and oil millionaire

Jacob Hamon of attempting to bribe him to vote for contracts to sell Chickasaw and Cherokee lands, contracts worth tens of millions that Hamon would reap a hefty percentage of for himself. There was an investigation and Hamon denied everything. Charley was called to testify, but before leaving for Muskogee he spoke to the Topeka press:

> Senator Curtis, before he left Topeka, said: "I shall tell the committee that President Taft sent for Vice-President [John] Sherman and myself in order to discuss this Indian matter. . . . The conferences with President Taft should alone set at rest any further consideration of the vague charges made by Senator Gore in this matter. We have proof beyond the shadow of' a doubt as to our standing in this case."[17]

Ironically, Vice President Sherman had been a US senator making Indian policy when Charley was a boy living on the reservation. The two became friends and often worked together, most often behind the scenes. No matter what issues confronted Congress or the president, the primary preoccupation of elected officials was getting reelected.

The presidential election of 1912 was a bitter race, with both incumbent President Taft and former president Theodore Roosevelt, as a Progressive, entering the race against Democrat Woodrow Wilson. The Socialist Party, as ever, ran Eugene Debs.

"[P]ersonally I thought more of Colonel Roosevelt than I did of President Taft," Charley said, "but I felt for the good of the party that Taft should be renominated. I knew if the Colonel entered the race there would be a hard fight."[18]

Charley was also concerned about his own campaign for reelection and feared that having both of these men in the race would erode his own base of support. Governor Stubbs had announced that he was challenging Charley for his seat. Being consumed with business in Washington, Charley's campaign at home in Kansas had faltered. "Curtis Clubs" had disbanded because of the Roosevelt-Taft fight. Charley lost the fight for renomination and Stubbs became the candidate. He was defeated by Democrat William Thompson in the general election as both Taft and Roosevelt, and Debs, lost to Wilson.

After the election, Charley returned to his Senate duties as energetically as though he had won, finishing his term on March 3, 1913. The next day, after adjournment, he was lunching with a handful of senators in a room reserved for the members of one of the most exclusive clubs in the world—the US Senate. Charley recalled the day vividly:

> While we were eating Senator Bristow of Kansas entered and as he passed our table, after we had all spoken to him, he turned toward me and said, "Curtis, what are you doing here? I thought this room was for Senators only." I retorted as quickly as possible, "It is, and two years from today I will be entering here as a Senator and you will be retiring as an ex-Senator." Mr. Bristow passed on without making a reply. Some of the Senators turned to me and said that was an awful shot. I said, "You watch."[19]

The next two years were devoted to accomplishing exactly that. But politics was not the only thing occupying the Curtises while at home in Kansas. There was a wedding to plan.

In January 1914, the eldest of the children, Perm, was married to Lieutenant Charles P. "Toddy" George. The young officer served in the 6th Field Artillery at Fort Riley, about sixty-five miles west of Topeka. The lieutenant had grown up in the army; he was born at Fort Concho, Texas, while his father was stationed there. The *Topeka State Journal* declared:

> The wedding will be the most important social event of the gayest holiday season Topeka has known for many years, and besides the interest that attaches to a wedding in a prominent family, the ceremony tonight will be a military affair, which is a rare event in Topeka circles. About 260 or 300 guests will witness the service which will be read in the library of the Curtis home.[20]

The wedding was in the evening, by candlelight, and red being the color of the artillery, there were red poinsettias and roses throughout the home. Members of the groom's regiment were in their dress uniforms. Dolly joined Charley and Annie as they greeted guests, and younger daughter Leona was one of her sister's attendants. There was no mention of Harry's attendance, and as he was studying law at the University of Michigan in Ann Arbor, there may have been a conflict.

However, when Harry wed that summer in Ann Arbor, his mother was the only family member who made the trip:

> The wedding of Miss Elizabeth Walker, a well known society girl of Ann Arbor. Mich., and Mr. Harry Curtis, the son of former Senator Curtis and Mrs. Curtis, of Topeka, will take place this evening at Ann Arbor. The news of the wedding will be a surprise to the friends of Mr. Curtis, as no formal announcement of the engagement had been made. Mrs. Curtis left for Michigan last month to attend the graduation exercises of Mr. Curtis, who received a degree in the law school in Ann Arbor in June, and she will be present at the wedding ceremony this evening.[21]

It appeared that Annie was also the only family member to attend Harry's graduation in June if she had indeed traveled to Michigan for that event. Dolly would later write that she had been sorry not to attend but did not explain why she could not be there.

After his 1912 defeat, Charley reopened his law office and handled cases in Oklahoma and Washington, DC, as well as in Topeka. He took some of his income and invested in some oil wells throughout the state. But mostly, Charley spent his time figuring out how to get back into the Senate. He had kept up with the senators he had lunched with the day Senator Bristow embarrassed him, and from time to time he would remind them that he would be back. Dolly was focused on the same goal, and this time, she took command:

> I had charge of his campaign headquarters while he was out in the state. I did the work at the house, and every evening many of our friends came in to help. They included the young friends of Charles's three children and my friends from all over town—every one of them enthusiastic over Charles's campaign. We sent out over one hundred and fifty thousand letters in that campaign. . . .
>
> A small kitten, the children's pet, made hours of work for us. I had envelopes addressed to different groups of voters, carefully placed in

boxes and labelled to await the proper letter. The kitten upset the boxes, the slips marking them fell out in every direction, and for days thereafter we had heart palpitations from fear that the letters intended for old soldiers had gone to members of the W. C. T. U., or that communications intended for prominent doctors and lawyers had found their way to the peaceful occupants of the Old Ladies' Home.[22]

Those were good times, and Dolly described the family and volunteers gathering for suppers at midnight after the work was finished. She also recalled the family's cook going after the ice man with a carving knife when he said that he was voting against Charley.[23]

While family and friends were putting in long hours at home, the "official" campaign office appeared quiet. Said Charley,

> I had the names of 110,000 active Kansas Republicans living in cities and villages and on farms. I wrote them letters. Then I had a campaign committee of my own. I spoke, however, under the direction of the regular state committee and only went where I was sent. My public headquarters in Topeka that is to say, my office was a harmless looking establishment. In it sat my secretary and one clerk. Seemingly, I was taking things easily. Up at my house, however, there were nine typists and stenographers working under the direction of my sister, who knows as much about politics as any man in the state.[24]

Dolly not only was involved in her brother's campaign, but worked for other Republican candidates as well. Dan Anthony (son of D. R. Anthony, who had been so prominent in Kansas politics from Territorial days, and also nephew of famed suffragist Susan B. Anthony) was running for Congress in Charley's old district. Dolly was a veteran campaigner, up for every challenge. Politicians were everywhere. Their longtime friend and next-door neighbor, Arthur Capper, was running for governor. (He had lost in the 1912 election, Charley suspected, because he had come out for the Progressive candidates and angered the Republican base.) One day, Capper's campaign manager called Dolly and insisted she at once head to a nearby town for a speaking engagement.

"He made it quite clear I was the last resort," Dolly said.

They had wanted Brother, who was out campaigning, and they had invited Arthur, who was also traveling over the state. In fact, they had tried everyone, but all were busy. A substitute speaker who had been assigned to the meeting was ill, and so I would have to go. I did not feel particularly happy over the assignment, but hurriedly started to fill it. When I arrived I did not see anyone I knew. An elderly, kind-looking old gentleman was presiding. He introduced me in a very flowery manner. Then, looking carefully at a printed program, he announced: "The lady's name isn't here."[25]

While Charley's career saw more successes than failures, the fickle nature of politics was evident to him at the 1914 Kansas Day Dinner in Topeka. "The treatment I received . . . shows how a man in public life is treated after he has been retired from office," he said. "For twenty odd years, yes, from the organization of the Kansas Day Club up to and including January 29, 1913, I had always been given a place at the head of the table." But in 1914, Charley noted, there was no place for an ex-senator at the head table. "I was down with the others who had not received much recognition as would entitle them to sit at the head table, but I was happy with them and they gave me the glad hand all around."[26]

The election was unique in that it was the first one held after the passage of the Seventeenth Amendment. The amendment, whose authors ironically included *the* Senator Bristow, required US senators to be elected by popular vote rather than by state legislature. No one was quite sure how much difference that would make in strategizing, but Charley's team had been up to the task.

In the Republican primary, Charley beat the incumbent Senator Bristow to become the party's candidate in the fall election, where he faced Democrat George Neeley and his longtime friend, Progressive Victor Murdock.

In 1915, Charley was again at the head table at the Kansas Day Dinner. And on March 4, 1915, he ate lunch in the reserved dining room as Senator Curtis of Kansas and Mr. Bristow was the ex-senator.

CHAPTER II

Weddings, War, and Want 1915–1928

*It is good to love many things, for therein lies the true strength, and
whosoever loves much performs much, and can accomplish much, and
what is done in love is well done.*

—VINCENT VAN GOGH

DOLLY CURTIS MADE A LOVELY BRIDE, WHEN A WEDDING DAY FINALLY
came.

In 1906, Charley and Annie announced the engagement of *their*
sister to Phillip Metzger, who was a Pennsylvanian but had moved to
Oklahoma to be a banker. He was a delegate to the Oklahoma Constitutional Convention, but also had a home in Washington, DC, where he
and Dolly met. It was a very high-profile match. When the engagement
was confirmed, the *Wichita Beacon* acknowledged that "while frequent
reports of Miss Curtis' engagement, now to one admirer, now to another,
have been made and have proved to be merely gossip," this one had been
confirmed. The paper continued, "Miss Curtis is the most widely known
and popular young woman in Kansas."[1]

When the nuptials were announced, there was no date for a wedding,
just months in the future. But the wedding never happened. Dolly made
no mention of it in her memoirs, and in 1910, Mr. Metzger married
someone else.[2]

In time, Dolly, too, moved on.

She had been introduced to Edward Everett Gann, "Billy," a few years earlier through mutual friends. He was an attorney and had worked for the Santa Fe Railroad in Topeka but had returned to Washington, where he served as a special assistant to the Attorney General. At first, he would come calling and Dolly would invite another single lady to join them, thinking she would "fix him up" with an eligible woman. Finally, Billy told Dolly it was *her* he was interested in and would she please stop inviting other women to join them. It took her by surprise; Dolly took great care with her appearance, but having been told she was "plain" as a child, she did not see herself as particularly attractive. Others commented on her looks, not always in a flattering way. She was tall and imposing, not the most feminine of qualities. She was smart and outspoken, independent in her thinking and opinions—all qualities of questionable value in a mate.

But with Billy, it was different. He was quiet and introspective, the perfect complement to Dolly's personality in many ways. He understood her devotion to her brother and his career, and rather than feeling threatened, he became part of the team. When they announced their engagement in 1915, Topeka was electric with the news of Dolly's nuptials. There were luncheons with old friends in Dolly's honor and gifts and messages from all over the world delivered to the Curtis home. More than a thousand invitations were sent out and many of them were accepted, to Dolly's delight. The news was shared in the nation's capital, where the occasion was reported in the society pages of the *Evening Star*:

> The bride, who was escorted by Senator Curtis, wore the handsomest and doubtless the most costly wedding gown that any Topeka bride has been fortunate enough to possess. It was of heavy bridal satin, combined with rose point lace, and was richly embroidered in gold on the skirt and the bodice. The embroidery was done in India, and it carried with it the touch of the rich and lavish eastern hand. The gown was made in Paris and was a gift to the bride from Mrs. Elizabeth Bourne, who is now living in London.[3]

Mrs. Bourne was divorced from Charley's Senate colleague, Jonathan Bourne of Washington. She also gifted Dolly with a diamond and emerald necklace for the occasion. The *Evening Star* erroneously identified Dolly as being one-quarter Kaw. Keeping up with who was who and their ancestry in the Curtis household was challenging for the press. Dolly never claimed to be Native; she did proudly trace her lineage on her mother's side to John Jay, America's first Chief Justice of the Supreme Court.

Surrounded by lawyers working with her brother, it was probably not a surprise that she should marry one. Billy was accomplished, a gentleman from a prominent Kentucky family, and, gasp, a *Democrat*. Though of different parties, he and Dolly were of like minds:

> My husband's politics, perhaps because it is not of a violent or over-assertive sort, makes no difference to me, nor mine to him. As he is informed on more subjects than any man I know, I could forgive him even if he were a more vociferous partisan on his side of the political fence. Anyway, I am glad to have a Democrat in the family. As I am a red-hot, die-hard Republican, it is well for me to have at home a constant reminder that there are many worth-while Democrats in the country.[4]

She wondered what Grandmother Curtis would have thought of her marrying an "office-holding Democrat!" and doubted that Grandmother would have forgiven her even if she had personally liked Billy. She knew that the staunch abolitionist would have been horrified to think that Billy's family had once been slave owners.

"The fact that he was a Presbyterian might also have militated against him," Dolly pondered, "for according to her ideas only the doctrines of John Wesley insured entrance into the gates of heaven."[5]

As for the other most important man in her life, Dolly said that her brother and Billy were "inseparable pals."[6]

The couple honeymooned briefly in Chicago, but Dolly was anxious to get to Washington and begin married life in a new home, and to help Annie get settled in a new home on Belmont. In frail health for years, Annie was becoming weaker. She relied more and more on Dolly to help carry the burden of being a senator's wife.

When attorney Edward Everett "Billy" Gann married Dolly Curtis, he became a part of the Curtis team, despite the fact that he was a Democrat. He was one of Charley's most trusted confidants and handled some of his legal affairs. Following the death of Annie Curtis, Charley lived with his sister and brother-in-law. From left, Charles Curtis, Dolly Curtis Gann, Edward E. Gann, unidentified.
COURTESY LIBRARY OF CONGRESS

Charley's "comeback" in the Senate was big news. Journalist James B. Morrow, whose insightful interviews were shared in many newspapers across the nation, visited Charley to learn the secret of his return to Washington and gain insight into his personality. Morrow expressed some disappointment that Charley did not disclose more, but the carefully crafted narrative of his life was a cornerstone of his success. He varied little with each telling. But Charley did reveal more than usual when asked about his stand on Prohibition and feelings about alcohol:

"I had no high-flown moral principles at that time." he said to me, "but I saw what liquor had done and was doing for all sorts of men, how it broke them down physically, took away their pride and made them hang around the racing stables just for a drink. The sight of them disgusted me. They were loafers and beggars, tho they had once been self-respecting fathers, husbands, brothers and sons.

"Moreover, they were unclean and I never could stand that."[7]

That comment may be as revealing as anything Charley ever said to a reporter. "Disgust" is a strong word, and noting that he "could never stand" their being "unclean" is quite damning. Alcohol abuse had a profound impact on Charley's family. Captain Jack's use of spirits was widely known, and even though Charley made no specific mention of his father in his comments, it is not difficult to read between the lines. Moreover, his repulsion at men being "unclean" brings to mind Captain Jack's fishing expeditions and no doubt his coming home reeking of whiskey and fish. Prohibition was a law he could sink his teeth into enforcing and a policy that he could champion.

Another presidential election loomed in 1916, and it was another hard-fought and bitter campaign. Incumbent Woodrow Wilson was challenged by Supreme Court Justice Charles Evans Hughes. War was raging in Europe, and Wilson's mantra, "He kept us out of war!" obviously appealed to Americans who wanted to avoid becoming entangled with Europe's issues. Perhaps it was the fear of war that pushed the voters to Wilson; the Electoral College belies the popular votes where the margins were slim, sometimes razor thin. But it was enough, and Wilson was reelected.

One month into Wilson's second term, America was at war.

On April 2, 1917, President Wilson called Congress into "extraordinary session." The boy who had watched defeated Confederate soldiers march home to Georgia following the Civil War was now asking his country to enter the largest war since that conflict:

With a profound sense of the solemn and even tragical character of the step I am taking and of the grave responsibilities which it involves but in unhesitating obedience to what I deem my constitutional duty I advise that the Congress declare the recent course of the imperial German government to be in fact nothing less than war against the government and people of the United States that it formally accept the status of belligerency which has thus been thrust upon it and that it take immediate steps not only to put the country in a more thorough state of defense but also to exert all its power and employ all its resources to bring the government of the German empire to terms and end the war.[8]

The resolution passed the Senate 82–6, with eight members not voting; the House vote was 373–50, with eight not voting. The loudest opponent in the Senate was Robert M. La Follette, a Progressive Republican from Wisconsin. A couple of nights later, he and a colleague were hanged in effigy four blocks from the White House:

> An effigy intended to protray [sic] both Senators Stone and La Follette at 10 o'clock last night was hanged in Fourteenth street near H street within four blocks of the White House. For perhaps an hour the figure swung from an electric light pole and a large crowd gathered. It was made of white cloth, five feet high, with eyes nose and mouth crudely marked with black paint and stuffed with newspapers. On one side the name "Stone" appeared and on the other "La Follette." Down the back was a broad streak of yellow and dangling from the feet was a streamer bearing the inscription "Traitors."
>
> La Follette and Stone were two of the twelve senators who prevented the armed neutrality bill from becoming a law and were two of the six who Wednesday night voted against a war declaration.[9]

On April 6, the "Great Peace President" was transformed into the "War President." The news spread almost instantaneously across the world:

> With the ink still wet upon the page, Lieut. Cmdr. Byron McCandless, from a window of the White House, signaled by semaphore to the Navy Department the one word "war," and at the sight of it the lightning flashed the message to our every ship waiting upon the seas . . . and in every army post, inland and border, every officer unsheathed his sword.[10]

One of those officers was Charley's son-in-law, Major Charles P. George Jr. The senator had to be keenly aware that every vote related to the war effort was personal, and thus having a direct impact on his family, and his household. A few months later, Perm would move in with her parents while Toddy was deployed in France.

Another relative in the fight was Moses Bellmard, one of Charley's Kaw cousins. Bellmard had gained fame in some circles as he rodeoed all over the western states before enlisting in the army in 1916. He was commissioned as a first lieutenant in the 142nd US Infantry. Bellmard would distinguish himself by suggesting that Indians be stationed at each message relay station using their language to avoid decoding by the Germans. That system carried over into World War II's famed Code Talkers.[11]

Funding the war, drafting soldiers, ferreting out the disloyal—these were among the issues facing the lawmakers as they arrived at the Capitol each day. The days were long and the city was quickly transformed:

> From every state the war workers, civilians and men in uniform, flocked to the capital Financier and clerk, employer and labourer, general and lieutenant and enlisted man—all of them arrived in such numbers that there were not enough hotels, rooming houses, and barracks to hold them, nor enough business buildings to give them office space. As the throng moved about the city, crowding the streets and restaurants to overflowing, traffic in the once quiet town became a jam of packed street cars and cabs, and in the downtown section jostling pedestrians elbowed their way along sidewalks as populous as New York's Broadway or Chicago's Loop.[12]

In looking back at that dark time, Dolly wrote, "the country entered an epoch of which the end is not yet."[13]

If people were crowding into Washington, they were also crowding into Kansas. There were sixteen cantonments established throughout the country to train troops. The largest was Camp Funston, named for Brigadier General Fred Funston, who had died suddenly in February. Camp Funston was on the Fort Riley Military Reserve near Junction City. It was also the most expensive, with at least 2,800 buildings and maybe as many as 4,000 to serve 40,000 soldiers with a cost of nearly $10 million.

It was more than an army camp; it was a city unto itself with theaters and barber shops, soda fountains and gas stations—everything a town needs. Major General Leonard Wood was the camp's commander.

The war effort translated to money and jobs in Kansas. Even the barbers were asking Charley to find them a job at Camp Funston, and since dozens of them were needed, he did. In true Charley Curtis fashion, his efforts were aimed at practical matters. He introduced a bill prohibiting discrimination by businesses toward soldiers and sailors, and a bill that would establish a loan program for soldiers and their dependent families to buy farms, and he was working for women's suffrage. These were practical and optimistic, for he was looking beyond the impact of the war. What would become of these soldiers when the work of war was done? Indeed, that question would become a dark cloud over the next decade.

Even in the midst of global events, the mundane demands of office continued. Charley was always mindful of answering letters, proving himself helpful whenever possible. In response to William E. Connolly, secretary of the Kansas State Historical Society, Charley agreed to have certain government publications sent to him. He added, "Hoping that the publications will be duly received, and that you will write me whenever I can be of service to yourself or friends."[14] Unlike so many other public servants, however, Charley followed through. He was famous for getting pensions for veterans, and one account said he was responsible for as many as six thousand pensions being granted through his efforts.

Annie was busy with her spousal duties, receiving guests most Thursdays (but always with Dolly and sometimes Leona and other ladies to assist). But when Annie's and Charley's names were recorded together in the newspapers, it was as patrons of the women's suffrage movement. After the war, Charley would introduce the Equal Rights Amendment in the Senate and Susan B. Anthony's nephew, Dan Anthony of Leavenworth, would introduce it in the House. Oddly, Dolly did not champion the cause. She believed that women exercised political power in other ways and the vote itself was unnecessary. For all her forward-thinking this seems so out of character, or it could have been strategic thinking on the part of the Curtises to cover all their political bases.

The person who had the greatest impact on Washingtonians and people across the nation, perhaps even the globe, however, was Herbert Hoover. "His name became known to every woman in the country," wrote Dolly. "We learned to 'Hooverize,' vying with one another in observing the 'meatless days,' cutting down the waste in our kitchens, and studying the almost daily bulletins on economy."[15]

Hoover had been appointed to head the specially created wartime agency, the US Food Administration. When the war began in Europe, food supplies and starvation were a major concern, and Hoover, a millionaire with global experience and perspective, created the Commission for Relief in Belgium. Kansas farmers were among the greatest contributors to the efforts to supply flour to the suffering country. Those same farmers had benefited from high grain prices, driven up because of the war. By November 1914, Kansas had contributed fifty thousand barrels of flour to the effort. When the ship *Hannah* left New York Harbor for Belgium in January 1915, the Kansas flag flew from her mast. Hoover might have been the hero, but Kansas was supporting him.[16]

As if a Great War were not enough, in 1918 the Spanish influenza swept the world, from an epicenter at Camp Funston. The death toll was staggering. A Topeka resident who was a child at the time remembered the trains coming into Topeka from Camp Funston with coffins "stacked like cordwood."[17]

Then, in early November 1918, news arrived that the war was over and "the capital took on the appearance of a riot scene, with shouting celebrators pouring from every building as if on a preconcerted signal. The streets were filled with battalions of marchers shrieking their joy to the accompaniment of whistles and bells. Hours passed before the report was corrected," wrote Dolly. The news was premature; the war was not over until a few days later.[18]

"On the signing of the Armistice, November 11th, came another celebration, mild by comparison with the earlier outburst, for the whole population had exhausted its emotions," she said. "We were all incredulous of the truth, fearful of another disappointment, even when the news was verified beyond question."[19]

When the presidential election of 1920 rolled around, a Republican victory was almost a certainty no matter who the candidate was, Dolly speculated. The country was weary and wanting change. Senator Warren Harding fit the bill. He was one of Charley's best friends and Dolly liked him as well, and his handsome features didn't hurt either. "From a woman's viewpoint, I must say that he looked as if he ought to be President," she gushed, "though perhaps it is too critical of my sex's political acumen to include a candidate's good looks among his assets." But men liked him too, Dolly noticed, men from both parties. "He was a most gregarious person, wanted his friends around him continually," she wrote. "Amiability was his unfailing characteristic."[20]

At the Republican Convention in Chicago, Charley was among Harding's intimates who helped negotiate his nomination. There were outcries of his candidacy's arising out of "smoke-filled backrooms," but don't they all? Charley said there was nothing that was out of the ordinary in the process. In those smoky backrooms, Harding emerged as the compromise candidate over other luminaries including Major General Wood.

Ironically, Harding's campaign ads screamed, "Do You Want Your Boys to Go to War?" Paid for by the Republican National Committee, the ads claimed that if the League of Nations Pact, so famously championed by the Democratic candidate, President Wilson, was to be enforced in its present form, there would be an ever-present danger of war. In fact, the campaign was an all-out attack on Wilson's policies. "The republican party has pledged itself to conclude a peace treaty such as will stabilize the business and industrial affairs, solve transportation difficulties, relieve the labor situation on the farms and reduce abnormal fluctuation of prices on farm products," the ad proclaimed. "The republican party proposes to so revise the tariff as to preserve a home market for American agriculture and industry."[21]

That pretty well summed up the Republican Party's platform. Harding's running mate was Massachusetts Governor Calvin Coolidge. The Democrats countered with their own Ohioan, Governor James Cox. His running mate was the Assistant Secretary of the Navy, Franklin D. Roosevelt, who resigned his post to campaign. While the Republicans railed

The essential Charles Curtis—the personal touch characterized his political style. As Assistant Senate Floor Leader, he is deep in conversation with the House Floor Leader, Congressman Frank Mondell, R-Wyoming, in 1922.

against the League of Nations and touted a return to "normalcy," the Democrats advocated for the organization as the only way to maintain peace and move the country forward. In the end, Harding won handily with 404 electoral votes to Cox's 127 and more than 60 percent of the popular vote.

The country was facing a staggering national debt and millions of men were unemployed when Harding took office. Congress and Secretary of the Treasury Andrew Mellon focused on reducing taxes and attacking the national debt. Thus began an unprecedented era of prosperity. The twenties had roared in.

With 20–20 hindsight Dolly looked back and said, "In those days no one—not even a Democrat—arose in the land with sufficient wisdom to read the future. No small voice—not even a Democratic prophet's wail—was raised to point out the lack of vision which in later years the opposition's afterthought attributed to our leaders of that golden era. We prospered, and the multitude applauded."[22]

Like most households, the Curtises experienced losses and blessings. In May 1919, Annie and Charley welcomed their first grandchild. Toddy had returned home from the war and was stationed at Fort Myer, and Perm gave birth to a little girl, Ann, in a Washington hospital. In June, Annie's mother passed away in Topeka. She traveled to Kansas for the funeral, but it is unclear if other family attended.

In July, Leona married at her parents' home in Washington. It was a smaller affair than Perm's or Dolly's ceremonies, with only a hundred guests. The groom, Webster Knight II, came from a prominent New England industrial family, and the couple would make their home in Providence. A little more than a year later, the Knights welcomed a son, named for his grandfather, Charles Curtis Knight.[23]

The Knights were one of the largest manufacturers of cotton goods in the world and marketed under the name "Fruit of the Loom." They were also known as great breeders of horses. Love of horses ran through the Curtis family as strongly as brown eyes or olive skin.

As Annie's health failed, she was not able to travel to Kansas when her father passed away less than a year after her mother. She and Charley enjoyed movies, and he would carry her small frame to the car and place her in the theater seat each week as long as she was able. Increasingly, Dolly filled in for her sister-in-law as well as seeing to her care.

The family kept growing. On April 12, 1921, Charles Curtis George was born to Perm and Toddy. In the summer of 1923, the fourth, and last, of the Curtis grandchildren arrived, Constance "Connie" Knight.

The senators from Kansas made news when Charley's next-door neighbor and longtime friend, Governor Arthur Capper, was elected to that office in 1918. They were photographed on the street in front of their houses and were said to have been the only senators in the nation to be neighbors. Capper was the son-in-law of former governor/general Samuel Crawford. He had been a reporter in Topeka when he first met Charley, who was only five years older but much more senior in some ways. From his days as a reporter, Capper went on to build a media empire second only to that of William Randolph Hearst. He was skinny, almost sickly in appearance. His wife, Florence, more than compensated for his dour looks. She was vivacious and beautiful. They had no children, but Capper devoted much of his career to helping children in some way.

The two senators were friends, but not confidants. Though of the same party and era, they were two different faces of Kansas.

The forgotten face of Kansas was that of the Kaw. Though the US government said the tribe no longer existed, the tribe refused to die. According to Crystal Douglas, former director of the Kanza Museum, in 1922 the tribal elders went to Lucy Tayiah Eads, the adopted daughter of the late Chief Washunga, and asked her to help regain their identity.[24] Her election as chief was widely reported, but even the more complimentary stories were loaded with judgmental language. The *Wichita Eagle* proclaimed in 1923, "Kaw 'Squaw' Is Tribal Leader."[25] She was described as "cultured and educated," but these were characterized as surprising qualities. J. C. Clendinning, the Indian Agent in charge of the Kaw Indian Agency, described Chief Lucy as the "finest type of a proud aristocratic tribe of Indians" and that she was an "unusually pretty and charming woman."[26]

Chief Lucy *was* a remarkable woman. Chief Washunga had adopted her and her brother when their parents died, and she attended Haskell Indian Nations Institute in Kansas. She became a nurse and moved to

In 1922, Kaw elders approached Lucy Tayiah Eads, Washunga's adopted daughter, and asked her to be their chief and help regain tribal recognition and money due the tribe. Educated and determined, Chief Lucy was an effective leader.
COURTESY PAULINE EADS SHARP, GRANDDAUGHTER OF LUCY TAYIAH EADS

New York City, where "she has enjoyed being an Indian has got a lot of fun out of it."

[P]eople in New York, New Jersey and other eastern communities could not understand that she could be both a trained nurse and an

Indian; always they expected to see moccasins, a headdress of feathers, and a gaily colored blanket, and they would not have been surprised to see a tomahawk, a string of wampum beads and a bow and arrows. And they were always surprised when they met instead an unusually cultured young woman, an expert in her profession, in tailored suit, who ate with her fork and understood how to feel perfectly at home on any social occasion.[27]

The Associated Press interviewed Chief Lucy and noted that she was married to a white man and they sent their children to white schools. Her family lived on the allotment inherited from Chief Washunga, eight hundred acres where they raised livestock of all kinds and were "thrifty." They had not sold or lost their lands as had other Indians who were less capable of managing their affairs. It was also reported that Chief Lucy's husband, John, was a cousin of the architect James Buchanan Eads, who had built the Eads Bridge over the Mississippi River at St. Louis.[28]

In every instance, reporters emphasized Chief Lucy's connection to the more civilized and progressive white world. Her husband remarked, "She is an excellent wife, a fine mother, the best nurse living and understands the needs of her people." He listed all the admirable traits a woman should have.[29]

None of these speak to how smart Chief Lucy was. The press wrote about how she was an exception to most of the Kaws who "have sold and dissipated their holdings and are now reduced to poverty." The papers emphasized the poverty of the Kaws in comparison to the success of the Osages. "Although their lands join those of the rich Osage, and oil derricks can be seen rising in the distance," a reporter noted, "the Kaws have reaped no mineral benefit as yet. A number of tests have gone down, but oil in paying quantities has not been found."[30]

The new leader was well aware of the disparity between the two tribes. She announced that "the principal task of her administration will be pressing a claim of her tribe against the government for $15,000,000, which the Kaws allege is due them as payment for lands they owned in Kansas before their migration to the Oklahoma territory." The Osage

Tribe offered to advance the money to enable the Kaws to press their claims in Washington.[31]

The "unusually pretty and charming" Chief Lucy meant business, and Charley Curtis would hear from her.

President Harding had been visiting Alaska, America's last frontier. He made good use of the cross-country train trek. He stopped along the route to make speeches and greet the party faithful. In Kansas, Arthur and Florence Capper joined the excursion for a while. The entourage ventured all the way to the Arctic Circle. On the return trip, Harding became ill near Seattle. Forced to interrupt the trip, the president's staff summoned doctors to his San Francisco hotel. Harding appeared to rally, and his wife was sitting by his bedside reading to him. He was listening intently and said, "That's good. Go on. Read some more." Then he shuddered and collapsed. The president was dead.[32]

Charley was at a dinner party but getting hourly updates from the White House on his friend. Dolly and Billy were out for a drive when a man shouted the sad news from the sidewalk.[33]

The nation's capital prepared to receive her son. In Vermont, Vice President Coolidge was roused from his bed to the news that the president was dead. His father administered the oath of office in that little house where he had been raised, and he left the farm that morning as President Coolidge.[34]

In San Francisco, the sad and hurried duties and decisions of moving President Harding's body had begun. He would only be moved once—from the hotel to the train. There was a small, very private ceremony as that occurred. The same train that had brought the joyous party west would now take them east. The train was to leave the city at seven o'clock Friday evening and arrive in Washington on Tuesday morning. The car bearing the president would have two soldiers and two sailors as guards and would be lighted throughout the trip. There would be no stops except as necessary for operation. The route was announced: the train would pass through Reno, Ogden, Cheyenne, Omaha, and Chicago. The press referred to it as "the saddest transcontinental journey in the history of the nation."[35]

Dolly recalled it vividly:

As the funeral train crossed the country, it was received in cities and villages by mourning throngs. Never in recent history has there been such a manifestation of public sympathy or sorrow. Millions paid their respects to the dead president and his widow as she kept her vigil while the train travelled mile by mile, hour by hour, from the Pacific Coast to Washington. At the state funeral in the rotunda of the Capitol, Brother was on the committee named by the Senate.[36]

In his capacity as head of the Rules Committee, many details of the funeral fell to Charley for approval. It was a solemn duty; the Hardings and Curtises were close. Dolly said that hardly a day had passed without Mrs. Harding's sending flowers from the White House conservatory to Annie or coming by to visit in person, despite her demanding duties as First Lady. Dolly went to Mrs. Harding's side immediately upon their arrival in Washington:

> [S]he received me with the old cordiality, but I could see she was crushed. Her entire conversation was of President Harding—his work, his aims and ambitions. She spoke of his campaign for the Presidency in great detail. Then her mind turned to the incidents of his last illness. She seemed to live over again the scene. . . . Mrs. Harding appeared utterly lonely. She felt that her life was finished, and so it turned out. She died a few months later.[37]

When Coolidge became president, Charley was one of the first people he contacted. There was a close personal relationship between the families as well as the frequent contact required by their official duties. The Coolidges stayed at the Willard Hotel as long as Mrs. Harding needed to remain in the White House. Dolly and Florence Capper, who was a close friend of Grace Coolidge, went to the hotel to see them as soon as they arrived. When President Coolidge entered the room, the two ladies stood, as is proper etiquette. He told them they didn't have to do that until he was in the White House. Dolly recalled that they had picnic parties in the park that summer—the Coolidges with their sons, John and Calvin; Senator and Florence Capper; and a handful of other party stalwarts joined Dolly and Billy. The company was comfortable.[38]

The Coolidges and Cappers appeared to have strong marriages, as did Dolly and Billy, but marital devotion is sometimes difficult to find. Harry Curtis's first marriage to the Ann Arbor society girl had ended. In November 1923, he married Beatrice Cameron, a divorcee with a small son. The ceremony was held in Washington. It was hard not to look at Harry and see traces of his grandfather, Captain Jack.

The wheels of Washington rolled on. Laws were debated, some were made. On June 2, 1924, President Coolidge signed the Indian Citizenship Act:

> Be it enacted by the Senate and House of Representatives of the United States of America in Congress assembled, that all non citizen Indians born within the territorial limits of the United States be, and they are hereby, declared to be citizens of the United States: Provided that the granting of such citizenship shall not in any manner impair or otherwise affect the right of any Indian to tribal or other property.[39]

One would think this would simplify matters and that if all Natives were citizens, they would automatically be eligible to vote. But that was not the case and it would take decades to have those rights.

Politics is an all-consuming beast and there was always another election. Soon it was time for the Republican Convention in 1924, which was held in Cleveland. Annie informed Dolly that she must go because, she said, "I think Charles should be President."[40]

Annie had become an invalid, unable to walk or use her hands, requiring continual care. Dolly visited every day, bringing flowers or a small gift, and said that Annie "smiled through the seasons with a patience at which all of us marvelled. . . . Charles's attentions were unceasing. Anna seemed to attract enough devotion to atone for her helplessness."[41]

As for lobbying for Charley's bid for the presidency, Dolly was prudent and told Annie that President Coolidge deserved to be nominated. With a sigh Annie responded, "Well, then, Charles should be Vice President."[42]

Charley considered Dolly and Billy his personal representatives to the convention and instructed his colleagues that they could speak for him. As discussions of candidates became more intense, Dolly called her brother and said if he would come to Cleveland in person, she believed he would secure the nomination. But he replied that Annie had suddenly become ill and he could not leave her. Dolly offered to come and stay with Annie so that he might be free to attend the convention.

"Dolly," he replied, "I would not leave Anna now to be President of the United States, and certainly not for the Vice Presidency."[43]

The convention was in mid-June and after much wrangling Charles Dawes became the vice-presidential nominee, but Annie had slipped into unconsciousness and never knew the outcome. She died on June 20, 1924.

Annie's body was taken home to Topeka for burial. Charley purchased plots in Topeka Cemetery, where her parents and siblings rested. The flag on the Kansas Statehouse flew at half-mast in her honor. It would have never occurred to her to be recognized so.

Theirs was not the only household visited by grief that summer. The president's son, Calvin Jr., was playing tennis barefoot and a blister on his foot developed into blood poisoning. Young Calvin passed away at Walter Reed Army Hospital on July 7, 1924. The services were held in the East Room of the White House.

"I have never seen such calm self-control, nor yet such unmistakable marks of pain as I saw on the faces of the President, Mrs. Coolidge, and John," wrote Dolly.[44]

The time for grieving was limited. There was an election in the fall.

Times were good and President Coolidge received much of the credit, garnering the majority of the votes that November. He defeated Democrat John W. Davis and Progressive Robert M. La Follette (the same La Follette who was hanged in effigy as America entered the Great War). The vice president was the former brigadier general Charles Dawes, of the American Expeditionary Forces. He had served as the Comptroller of the Currency and was the first director of the Bureau of the Budget. He had an impressive résumé but it remained to be seen how he would perform as the head of the Senate.

CHAPTER 12

Second Place 1928

The American people will vote dry as long as they are able to stagger to the polls.

—WILL ROGERS

NOT SINCE ANDREW JOHNSON TOOK A SWIG OF WHISKEY BEFORE entering the Senate Chamber to be sworn in as Abraham Lincoln's vice president in 1865 had such an embarrassing display taken place during an inaugural. And just like Lincoln, all "Silent Cal" could do was sit and watch.

Vice President Charles Dawes, newly elected and now assuming his role as presiding officer of the Senate, took the opportunity to chastise the august body and rapped the gavel for emphasis. He was particularly critical of the filibuster, calling it undemocratic and calling out senators by name. There was none of the dignity of an inaugural speech; it was more a rant. President Coolidge, with a front-row seat, turned crimson.

Upon completing his tirade about how the senators waste time in debate, it was the vice president's duty to swear in the senators for the new session of Congress. It is customarily done four at a time, but Dawes grew weary:

Speaking raspingly, using arms and legs to point his periods, his color heightened by the stress, General Dawes castigated the body over which he is to preside for four years for its dilatory practices. His acrobatic delivery did not pass unnoticed under the sardonic eyes that met his from the chamber. Then at the end of his inaugural the Chicagoan delivered a crushing blow to the Senatorial dignity. After two batches of statesmen had been presented to him General Dawes grew impatient. "Call them all up at once," he whispered to the clerk. The remaining twenty-four were summoned to the rostrum amid much confusion.[1]

The confusion continued when Dawes failed to return to the chamber to officially dismiss the body after the president was sworn. They waited an "uncomfortable" long time before one of their number performed the action. Democratic senators were quick to express outrage, like Virginia's Claude Swanson who said it was "farcical" and Georgia's W. F. George who said the address was "brutal and clownish." Republicans were noticeably agitated but remained quiet.

If Charley, as chairman of the Rules Committee, had an opinion on Dawes's vociferous attack on the rules, he kept it to himself. But it is hard to imagine that he did not take the attack personally. Furthermore, it was an embarrassment to the president, Charley's close friend and political ally. In fact, Charley was chosen to ride with President Coolidge and the First Lady in the inaugural procession, quite the honor.

Charley had served as Republican Whip from 1915 through 1924, and with Coolidge's full term in office, he was now Majority Leader. Thus, he had been a vital cog in the Senate's leadership for a decade. If there was a problem, some of the responsibility lay with him. With Dawes presiding over the Senate, if the two men had a difference of opinion, it would soon be obvious.

Charley had developed a quiet style of leadership, despite his outgoing personality. A reporter for the *Baltimore Sun* described it well, if not in biased terms: "Curtis can tell you beforehand how every man in the room is going to vote. Like the Indian at the listening post, he seldom talks. It is said that in one whole session of Congress he consumed no more than thirty minutes in debate. His great forte is his ability to listen."[2]

Following Annie's death, Charley had moved into Dolly and Billy's home on Macomb Street. The three of them became a team, with Dolly

When Calvin Coolidge was inaugurated for his first full term, Senator Charles Curtis was afforded the honor of accompanying him and the First Lady in the parade. From left, President Calvin Coolidge, First Lady Grace Coolidge, and Senator Charles Curtis.
COURTESY LIBRARY OF CONGRESS

at the helm. She was in her element caring for the two most important people in her life, but the focus was always Charley and furthering his career. Billy had his work, but everything hinged on Charley's schedule.

President Coolidge often hosted what became known as "griddle-cakes-and-sausage breakfasts" and invited men to join him, only men. These early morning discussions and male-bonding activities were a source of speculation. What did they discuss during these private affairs? For Dolly, "the routine of my household was shattered when Brother had an invitation, and the Presidential car called for him each time."[3] Her comments leave no doubt that it was *her* household, even if it was *his* schedule.

Billy and Charley had much in common, despite their differing political views. As a Kentuckian, Billy was inherently a follower of horse races. "They . . . would watch the horses together every day if they had the time and opportunity," Dolly observed.[4] And Dolly had found her soulmate after waiting so long to marry. She commented on the close relationship she enjoyed with her husband:

> My husband and I have never had to hunt for congeniality; we just have it, without effort. Our opinions may be at times, as far apart as the poles, or the diversion which one of us seeks may be sometimes a trial to the other. . . . We enjoy so many of the same things, however, that an occasional divergence of taste does not matter. When he takes an afternoon off with Brother or some other man, I am glad of it. Men should go out and play with other men. It is not good for them to stay tied down to their womenfolk all the time.[5]

However, Billy's law practice could be demanding and affairs of government kept Charley busy, so there was not a lot of leisure time for either man. All three members of the household stayed busy.

At the beginning of the new session of Congress in 1916, *Time* reported on the new officials entering the chamber and commented that regardless of party, "these Senators will soon learn to admire the Republican leader in the dark suit in the back row—Sen. Charles Curtis." The reporter acknowledged that Senator Reed Smoot, "the tall, lean Mormon," speaks "with a dry holy passion for financial soundness" and Senator Curtis "rarely speaks," but together "they steer, or attempt to steer the Senate. Last week they brought peace into the Republican ranks, placated the insurgents with good committeeships."[6]

Charley assumed the role of mentor to the new men and made an effort to teach them the ropes and the rules. This served him well as they later turned to him for advice, no matter which party they belonged to.

In 1928, the Republican Convention was held in Kansas City. Leona and Harry attended and the boys—Charley, Billy, and Harry—took rooms at the Hotel Muehlebach while Dolly and Leona were hosted by Mrs. Jacob Loose. The mansion was large enough to accommodate not only the Curtis supporters but other entourages as well.

"We were fight-to-the-finish foes as far as the convention was concerned," wrote Dolly, "but all good friends under Mrs. Loose's hospitable roof."[7]

Charley had announced his candidacy for the presidency in October. He waited until he was sure Coolidge would not run and would not accept if nominated. Dolly determined endorsements were needed and went to prominent Kansans, including Senator Capper, and asked for them.[8]

Secretary of Commerce Herbert Hoover was the frontrunner, and his supporters attended in great numbers and arrived early to establish his dominance. Charley lambasted him, loudly and frequently. Dolly thought (as did Charley) that while Hoover had an impressive résumé, he did not understand politics. It was said he had no understanding of the legislative process. According to Dolly, "the old-line Republicans . . . were loath to give him the preference over one who had worked faithfully for the party through nearly forty years."[9]

Charley wanted to be president. He and every other man who wanted it knew they had to topple Hoover for them to have any chance at the top spot, and they joined forces to take him down. Hoover "had the jump for the nomination" they agreed, and "no time is to be lost in snubbing the Hoover boom." In response, those managing Hoover's campaign "drove serenely ahead, insisting nothing can be done now to stop their man."[10]

But that didn't stop Charley from trying and making a fool of himself in the process in the eyes of some observers. When other "allies" in the cause dropped out, Charley refused and stayed in the fight against Hoover even when the nomination appeared eminent. "I shall not withdraw," Charley said, "no matter what others may do. And if I am asked about it again I shall cease being polite about it."[11]

Perhaps buoying his stand was the determination of the farmers not to elect Hoover. "Anybody but Hoover!" was their rallying cry as a crowd of three hundred men paraded through the streets and into political headquarters, shouting also, "Thirty million farmers won't vote for Hoover." They descended on the hotel lobbies and shouted their messages to Hoover operatives. They stopped at Charley's headquarters as well and demanded a speech, but he was "in conference devising means of stopping Hoover." His representative made a rousing speech in his stead.[12]

The farm women were equally firm, if not as loud. Following their husbands to the election hall, they wore buttons proclaiming, "You can nominate Hoover, but you can't elect him." Joining their husbands' chorus, they cried, "Nominate Hoover and we will vote for Smith."

"The farm women are desperately in earnest," said one of their leaders.[13]

Maintaining friendships in the midst of such politicking was difficult, if not nearly impossible. Dolly described such a circumstance during the convention when Colonel Theodore "Teddy" Roosevelt Jr. attended a dinner given for Charley by the Traveling Men's National Association. Though a strong Hoover supporter, he was asked to speak following Senator Capper. He obliged, but then made a quick exit to attend an event for Hoover. Hoover's gatekeepers refused to admit him, having heard he had "flopped" to Charley. Finally proving his loyalty, he was allowed to join the Hoover folks.[14]

When Hoover was nominated and the second spot was offered to Charley, he stopped trashing the Secretary of Commerce and got on board. Charley's longtime friend and poker-playing buddy, Senator William Borah of Idaho (who had been working for Hoover and advocating for Vice President Dawes to be renominated), placed Charley's name before the convention. The *Chicago Tribune* said his speech was the best of the entire event:

> I am about to place before you for your consideration as vice president a man who is the most universally known and the most universally beloved of all the public servants now in the congress of either branch of the United States.
>
> He is a child and product of the middle west, but his sympathies and conceptions are as wide as the nation and as broad and deep as humanity itself. . . . For 40 years he has stood in the fierce light of the public gaze and at this time no man would dare to challenge either his integrity, his ability, his patriotism or his loyalty to the Republican party.[15]

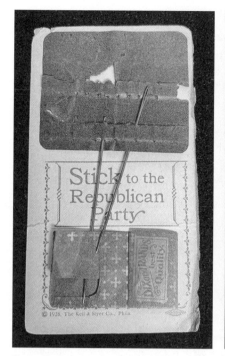

Campaign promotional materials took every shape and form including this pack of needles with the images of Hoover and Curtis, proclaiming, "Stick to the Republican Party."
COURTESY DEBRA GOODRICH

Charley's daughter, Leona, a delegate from Rhode Island, had the honor of seconding his nomination.

The *Baltimore Sun* called the nomination a "consolation prize to the farm bloc." In truth, they would have preferred Vice President Dawes but "he was ruled out as a disloyalist to the President."[16] That would be a reference to President Coolidge who may not have been loud, but was not always silent. When asked his opinion, it was a thumbs-down to Dawes.

Even as the convention was finishing its business, including formalizing Charley's nomination, convention-goers were pouring out of the hall and heading for home. They were simply worn out by the whole process. So was Charley. When he and Harry arrived in Topeka there were thousands on the south lawn of the Kansas Statehouse to greet him.

When asked for a speech, he thanked them briefly and said his main desire was to "go to bed" since he hadn't had a night's sleep in five days. "[T]hough I spent those wakeful nights working for the Presidential nomination," Charley admitted to his neighbors, "I was proud to accept the second place on the ticket when, it was offered to me unsought."[17]

Then he began spouting the party line as only a diehard Republican could do after such a struggle. "I am glad tonight to be on the ticket with that able and experienced man, Herbert Hoover," he declared.[18]

When Dolly and Leona arrived a short time later (Billy had stayed behind to close down headquarters and, as usual, do all the little jobs behind the scenes), the statehouse was jammed. There were estimates of fifty thousand people crowding into downtown Topeka. A policeman stopped the car and informed them, "You can't get in here, we are entertaining the future Vice President of the United States." Then he recognized them, and they "fought" their way through the crowd.[19]

They were in Topeka for forty-eight hours with a steady stream of callers, photographers, newspapermen, and messenger boys. From President Coolidge, who was fishing in Wisconsin: "The report has just reached me. . . . The long service which has made you the leader of the Senate has given you a knowledge of affairs and of parliamentary law such as is possessed by few. To the gratitude I have always felt for your help to me, I now add my best wishes for your success in your new office."[20]

Will Rogers commented on the results with his usual wit and insight, bemoaning the fact that Charley was in second spot: "Well, she is all over. Hoover and Curtis. What have I been telling you for days about Curtis? I knew he was a cinch for that. The Republican party owed him something. But I didn't think they would be so low down as to pay him that way."[21]

On another occasion, Will referred to Charley's place on the ticket as "the first time we have ever got a break—the only American that has ever run for that high office. . . . Come on Injun, if you are elected let's run the white people out of this country."[22]

Meanwhile, the *Baltimore Sun* censured Hoover's success. "Notwithstanding his stupendous convention vote, the Hoover nomination was grudgingly made," the paper asserted. "No Presidential candidate in

The two most famous "Indians" in America, Charles Curtis and Will Rogers, and an unidentified gentleman on the steps of the Capitol. As a political commentator, Rogers—a Cherokee and a Democrat—often commented on the Native background of his friend from another tribe and party.
COURTESY LIBRARY OF CONGRESS

modern times perhaps was named under stranger circumstances. To the last the bitter and irreconcilable opposition turned its barbs upon him, questioning his Republicanism and assailing the platform dictated by his friends."[23]

Dolly thought the election was a foregone conclusion, but Charley campaigned hard. He was a poker player, after all, and he played the hand the Republicans had dealt him. The Hoover-Curtis ticket won handily with 444 electoral votes to the 87 cast for New York's "wet" Roman Catholic governor, Al Smith.

John Adams, the first person to hold the office of Vice President of the United States, called it "the most insignificant office that ever the invention of man contrived or his imagination conceived." Charley knew that. He also knew that being a breath from the presidency was not a bad place to be, and he had certainly been in Washington long enough to know that situations changed in a moment. Most of his duties would be ceremonial, the "official diner-out." For Dolly, it was the pinnacle of her aspirations, even if her brother occupied the number-two spot.

On the morning of the inauguration, Dolly was in the procession with Mrs. Dawes. The outgoing and incoming First Ladies rode together, and Dolly said the day belonged to Grace Coolidge, for the applause and shouts were loudest for her as the cars passed the spectators. Upon reaching the Capitol, Charley's inaugural address was much different than that of his predecessor four years earlier. Dawes was gracious in introducing his colleague and Charley spoke about the role of the vice president, but with a different tone than his predecessor:

> Senators: The United States is to-day one of the most distinguished legislative bodies in the world—one of the greatest actual and potential powers for the promotion and advancement of civilization. . . . I may, therefore, be pardoned in declaring here the feeling of pride which I experience that through my election as Vice President of the United States such a signal honor has come to me. I hope that I may prove worthy.[24]

In Lawrence, Kansas, at Haskell Institute, one thousand students "representing every tribe in the United States" gathered in the chapel, where they listened to the inaugural address of the vice president. One of the most prominent buildings on campus was named for Charley.[25]

Following the administering of the oath to the president, the newly installed officials joined the procession down Pennsylvania Avenue to the White House. It was pouring rain, but the president and vice president put the tops down on the cars so that that the crowds could see them. The water puddled on the floorboards and soaked Dolly and Charley. Dolly noted the kindness of First Lady Lou Hoover, "one of the most considerate persons in the world." While they were dining, Mrs. Hoover had Dolly's coat sent out to be dried so that she would be presentable on the viewing stand in front of the White House where officials would watch the inaugural parade.[26]

Among the bands and military units, the "one lone Indian, riding bareback, clad only in a breech-cloth" made the greatest impression on Dolly. "He looked like a bronze statue."[27]

But he was not the only Native American represented. Following a dozen Oklahoma cowboys who "yipped and cut up to the delight of the throngs watching" came the United States Indian band of Tulsa and 250 "Indians in native garb" who added "further color to the moving spectrum."[28] Other Oklahomans attending the inaugural events included Kaw Chief Lucy Eads.[29]

That night, Charley and Dolly attended a charity ball and shook hands with eight thousand people. The Indian Band provided the entertainment. The band, representing sixteen tribes, then launched a world tour. The $3,000 fireworks display, including pyrotechnic images of Hoover and Curtis, was delayed for a couple of days because of the weather. The vice presidential party retired in the wee hours of the morning, leaving Dolly wondering if this would be an indication of the next four years.[30]

Little did she know at that moment, but social events would play a greater role than she could have imagined. With all the issues facing the nation in 1929, who would have thought that the biggest news of Charley's career, and nearly that of the administration, would be where Dolly would sit at the table?

Dolly would call it a "tempest in a teapot."[31]

Since the Curtises had arrived in Washington in 1893, Dolly had known nine presidents and ten first ladies. She had been a keen observer and a participant in every imaginable situation. She knew what was expected of the vice president and his hostess and considered it her duty to perform in that capacity for him, just as she had done while he was a senator, especially during Annie's sickness and since her death. It came as a surprise when Charley received a letter from the State Department that at state dinners Dolly should be seated behind the ambassadors' wives, which was at the bottom of the list. Charley immediately fired off a letter to Secretary of State Frank Kellogg stating that a member of his household would not go to the back of the line.

In the meantime, however, Kellogg retired and Henry Stimson took his place. He did not want to start his tenure reversing a predecessor's ruling, nor did he want to anger the vice president. So in true Washington fashion, he passed the buck. The Diplomatic Corps would decide. They met at the British Embassy and agreed, according to Dolly, that the "Vice President's sister was entitled to the ranking place and would welcome 'with great pleasure' my presence in the capacity of his hostess."[32]

But the story had grown legs. Alice Roosevelt Longworth, wife of the Speaker of the House, thought she should have preferential seating. Dolly heard that it was actually her husband, Nick Longworth, who claimed to outrank the vice president.

"Evidently Speaker Longworth had overlooked the fact that the Vice President, elected by the people, is under the Constitution the successor of the President," Dolly wrote. "In any event, we paid no attention to the protest—if indeed, one was ever formally made."[33]

As soon as the name of Alice Roosevelt was linked to the controversy, it would not die, even in the midst of the greatest economic disaster in American history.

The stock market began plunging on October 24, 1929, and reached a new low on Tuesday, October 29. That Black Tuesday marked the beginning of the Great Depression. Low interest rates, overproduction, and excessive credit were simply unsustainable. Banks and factories began closing. Unemployment would rise to 25 percent of the nation's workforce. Farms and homes were foreclosed on, and a significant number of the population faced the real possibility of starvation. How ironic that the man who had been responsible for feeding Europe during its darkest hours was now blamed for plunging America into this hopeless situation.

President Hoover was not the only person blamed; Democrats and disgruntled Republicans pointed to Coolidge, Harding—the entire Republican leadership. But it would be Hoover's name linked to the homeless communities of shacks known as "Hoovervilles," the cardboard used on the soles of shoes called "Hoover leather," and "Hoover blankets," newspapers the homeless used for cover. Increasingly, Hoover appeared

At the White House for an event in 1931, Edward E. "Billy" Gann, third from left, with Dolly Curtis Gann in the foreground next to Vice President Charles Curtis.
COURTESY LIBRARY OF CONGRESS

cold and aloof, as he did not believe in federal aid to help the unemployed—those things should be left to the states and private charities. Not until his term was nearly over did he assent to some federal programs to stem the growing depression.

As vice president, Charley for once had no real power. It was the highest office he had ever held, yet he probably had more real authority as a freshman congressman. He was not without influence, however, and there were still some who sought his counsel. But he increasingly was seen as a figurehead, perhaps even without purpose. President Hoover did not invite him to attend most of the cabinet meetings. In fact, Senate historian Mark Hatfield described the relationship between the two men as a "marriage of convenience."[34]

Hatfield cited George and Ira Gershwin's Broadway musical *Of Thee I Sing*, a spoof on Washington politics that included the character of Vice

President Alexander Throttlebottom. Throttlebottom could only access the White House by getting a ticket on the public tours and spent his time sitting on a park bench feeding the squirrels and birds. Audiences laughed heartily at the obvious caricature of Vice President Curtis.[35]

The endless dinners and social events garnered more attention than ever, partly because of the Longworth-Gann Social War, but also because these brilliant affairs were more and more in stark contrast to the way the rest of the country lived. But that wasn't only Charley's cross to bear. The president was one of the wealthiest men in the nation, far beyond any financial success Charley ever achieved. Likewise, Treasury Secretary Andrew Mellon was among the nation's superrich. Charley had managed well, but it would have been impossible for him not to occasionally feel out of place in those circles.

It is doubtful, for example, that any of these prominent men were handling the trifling details of their tenants themselves. Charley did. But Charley's tenants were not anonymous—they were people he knew and took time to know. Not many letters from landlords would be originating from the vice president's office, as this one concerning one of Charley's properties in Oklahoma to his tenant, W. A. Row of Kaw City:

THE VICE PRESIDENT'S CHAMBER
WASHINGTON
August 8, 1931.
My dear Row,

I have your letter and was sorry to hear of the death of your wife and assure you of my deepest sympathy. I know what a great loss you have sustained.

I note what you say about desiring lower rent. If you will write me what you think you can afford to pay I will let you know and send you a letter which you can show to the agent. I know you have had a hard time of it and want to do what is right by you until times get better.[36]

Early in the administration, rumors began around his taking rooms at the Mayflower Hotel. (It was not unusual for officials to rent suites or apartments for convenience and space, especially as they were receiving many guests and hosting meetings.) A story circulated through Washington that the hotel was giving Charley rooms for advertising purposes because there was no way he could afford the annual $22,500 price tag on his $15,000-a-year salary. *Time* covered the brouhaha:

> His nerves already raw from the public interest taken in his social battle on behalf of Mrs. Gann (TIME, April 15), the Vice President last week exploded on the matter of his Mayflower rent. Said he with hot feeling, "I know the story! . . . I want to denounce it as a miserable lie. I wish I could see the scoundrel who started it. . . . I wish people would mind their own affairs and leave mine alone. . . . Of course I do not pay regular rates for a great big hotel apartment. What I do pay is nobody's damned business! I can afford to pay what they charge me."[37]

For the record, the diligent *Time* reporter went to Mayflower management and learned that they had offered Charley a deal—$10,000 a year for the space and that it was worth that in advertising for them.[38] Also, for all the reporters that claimed Charley never cursed, well, the *Time* reporter scooped them on that one too. He would not back down from a fight, and he could scrap with the best of them.

While Charley was not a member of Hoover's inner circle, he made the most of the public persona afforded the office of vice president. In 1932, he was asked to deliver the commencement address at the University of Vermont, the alma mater of former First Lady Grace Coolidge. He was awarded an Honorary Doctor of Laws degree. The topic of his speech was self-reliance, which "is not a natural quality at all," he informed the audience:

> We all have within us a great foe to self-reliance, and that is a fear of the unknown. It is a common habit to fret and worry, to create obstacles for ourselves, to magnify the difficulties and dangers which we foresee in the path before us, to create difficulties and dangers which may not exist.
>
> All study is pointless if we'd not develop this one quality.[39]

In 1932, Washington was in turmoil. The "Bonus Army" had been camped in the city for weeks—veterans of the Great War demanding bonuses that had been promised them. However, many suspected that Communists were behind the protest, and had either instigated the events or infiltrated them. During debates over the bonuses, veterans had crowded into the galleries and throughout the Capitol and the surrounding grounds. Charley became concerned as the situation became more tense. He called for US Marines to be sent to the Capitol and to remain out of sight, but then called them off. The House passed the Bonus Bill, but the Senate overwhelmingly voted it down. The veterans did not leave.

Charley was sent to California to open the Olympic Games, no doubt a welcome escape from the volatile situation in Washington. President Hoover ordered the veterans to be cleared away by police. When the veterans resisted, police shot into the protestors and two men died from their wounds. The president authorized military action. General Douglas MacArthur, Chief of Staff of the Army, sent in a contingent of infantry, cavalry, and tanks to remove the people. Then the shantytown was burned.

At the same time as the riots in Washington, Charley arrived by train in Las Vegas, Nevada, on the route to Los Angeles. He was scheduled to make a few remarks, but the local officials feared violence because of the events in the nation's capital. Machine guns were mounted at vantage points around the train station. Police were armed with tear gas grenades.

Charley began, praising the engineering feat of the Hoover Dam. It might not have mattered what he said, but any mention of the president at that moment was more than people wanted to hear. A heckler called out, "Why didn't you feed some of those ex-soldiers?" The vice president did not hesitate to respond, and the "Curtis ire was roused."

> "I've fed more than you, you dirty coward," retorted the Vice-President, pounding the rail of the observation platform with his fist.
> He shouted that he had fought for veterans' legislation through two administrations.
> "Come up here and talk like that," he said. "I've worked for the bonus during President Coolidge's Administration and I forced passage of the bill through the Senate this term."[40]

The next day, Charley arrived in Los Angeles, as reported in that city's *Evening Post-Record*. But the story of the vice president's arrival was directly underneath a photograph of mounted soldiers on the streets of Washington routing their fellow soldiers. The headlines were chilling:

NEW ARMY RAID ON VET CAMP
Rush More Gas Bombs
HOOVER TELLS WHY HE CALLED OUT ARMY
TORCH, GAS, SABERS WIPE OUT VET CAMPS
DON GAS MASKS IN WHITE HOUSE
As Bonus Army Fled
Hoover Happy Over Routing
And,
VICE PRESIDENT ARRIVES HERE TO OPEN GAMES

The caption under the only photograph on the page read:

Only after masked cavalrymen laid down a gas attack against world war veterans in the streets of Washington did the bonus forces retreat from their encampment. Here the mounted troops with masks are shown marching on the veterans. A short time before this picture was taken police had killed one of the bonus marchers and injured others. Many were overcome by the gas attack.[41]

News reports also described the gates of the White House being locked while motorcycle police continually circled the building. Ammunition and gas masks were stockpiled inside.[42]

Everywhere Charley went, people were reading the news and listening to the reports on the radio. A group of fifty to sixty heavily armed guards were on hand to protect him and the Assistant Secretary of the Navy, Ernest Lee Jahncke on the train platform as two hundred people welcomed them. Among the throng was Charley's friend and prominent Republican Louis B. Mayer. Charley hurried to his suite at the Biltmore Hotel, no doubt eager to be away from the public before the next reception and ball that evening. President Hoover went to sleep that night with the sight of the veterans' shanties in flames.

The next day, before a crowd of 105,000 people, the only vice president (and the first of only three Americans) to open the Olympic Games received wave after wave of cheers.

Maybe being in second place was sometimes preferable to being number one.

CHAPTER 13

A Good Loser 1932–1936

But still when the mists of doubt prevail,
And we lie becalmed by the shores of age,
We hear from the misty troubled shore
The voce of children gone before.
Drawing the soul to its anchorage.

—BRET HARTE

WILL ROGERS REPORTED ON THE 1932 REPUBLICAN CONVENTION IN Chicago:

Well, got some scandal for you today, for it wouldn't be a Republican convention without some sort of under-cover "finagling." They are out now to throw poor old Injun Charley Curtis off and get another Vice-President.

Now they are trying to do this at the last minute. They wouldn't tell him a few months before and let him run and get his seat back in the Senate. They wait till now to root him out. Their alibi is that he is too old in case something happened to the President. Well, didn't they know a few months ago how old he would be about now. Anyhow, how can you tell when a Vice-President makes good and when he don't? They have never given one anything to do yet to find out.

What they are after, only they haven't got the decency to come out and say it is, "we are in the hole and we got to try and dig up somebody that will help us swing some votes. It's not your age, Charley; it's not your party loyalty. You got to be the goat, not us."[1]

As usual, the Cherokee Kid had hit the nail on the head.

Charley was completely blindsided. A year earlier, he had considered running for his old Senate seat. When he had resigned to become vice president, Republican Henry Allen was appointed to fill his term but he lost the election to finish it. Democrat George McGill had been elected. The party faithful in Kansas wanted Charley back. But his advisors in Washington wanted him to stay on the presidential ticket. Otherwise,

When Vice President Charles Curtis's renomination was in doubt at the 1932 Republican Convention, Dolly Curtis Gann, center, campaigned tirelessly to insure he was the nominee. The vice president, with most of the Republican leadership, remained in Washington debating the "Bonus Army Bill" and did not attend. At left is Harry King Curtis, Charles Curtis's son, and at right is Edward Everett "Billy" Gann, Dolly's husband.
COURTESY LIBRARY OF CONGRESS

his actions would demonstrate he had no faith in the national ticket's chances of being reelected.

Charley agreed that it was best for the party for him to remain on the national ticket, and he let it be known that he would accept the nomination. He and many other members of Congress were not able to attend the convention because of the real work to be done in Washington—namely, voting on a bonus for the Great War veterans. Dolly and Billy headed to Chicago totally unprepared for what was to come.

It was all over beer, Dolly said. "[T]he evening before the convention opened, it became clear that the 'wet' element would dominate the proceedings, and as this certainty developed," she wrote, "the candidacies of Vice Presidential aspirants increased so fast that we could barely keep track of them. I seemed to hear a new name everywhere I turned."[2]

The *Emporia* Gazette reported:

> For a time, even toward the end, it appeared that Curtis was on the verge of defeat, despite the fact that every key man in the convention understood President Hoover wanted his running mate of 1928 kept on the ticket. There was wet opposition to him. There was a movement for a younger and more spectacular figure. And there was an important undercurrent of opposition growing out of the social war which had been waged in Washington, over precedence, between Mr. Curtis' sister, Mrs. Dolly Gann, and Alice Longworth.
>
> Against this combined opposition the Curtis people played an interesting game. At their head was Mrs. Gann herself, receiving constantly at her hotel, present in a box at every convention session. She had been at work in fact for months beforehand, making speeches to Republican gatherings far and wide, and in every one of them she had praised the achievements of the Hoover administration.[3]

If there had been a Most Valuable Player Award in the Republican Party, it would have gone to Dolly.

The situation was compounded by a lack of leadership. With so many of the veteran campaigners still back in Washington, disorganization reigned. Dolly was constantly running back and forth from the Palmer House, where she and Billy had rooms, to the Hotel Stevens, where the

Kansas Delegation was staying, to the Blackstone Hotel, which was a quasi-administration headquarters, to the Congress Hotel for the activities of the National Committee. Alice Roosevelt Longworth was staying at the Blackstone, but she walked the floor of the convention visiting with delegates and making note of the vice presidential hopefuls.[4]

Dolly denied that she and Alice were social rivals (though the evidence would indicate otherwise), but they were always friends in public and Alice was a valuable ally. While Alice might have hoped her brother, Theodore Jr., would get the vice presidential nod, or even Senator Borah of Idaho, once Charley was again on the ticket she went to work to reelect Hoover and Curtis. It is likely, though, that she was working harder to keep her cousin Franklin out of office. At the Democratic Convention, New York Governor Franklin D. Roosevelt was nominated for the presidency with Texas Congressman John Nance "Cactus Jack" Garner, Speaker of the House, as his running mate. Garner was fairly conservative and actually opposed many of Roosevelt's programs. It was a perfect pairing.

"The thought of FDR in the White House so appalled Alice," wrote biographer Stacy A. Cordery, that she took every opportunity to undermine his candidacy. At the request of Mrs. Hoover, Alice used her many connections to wealthy and influential friends who might turn the tide for the Republicans.[5]

Alice, Theodore's daughter, was from the Republican side of the Roosevelt clan—the Oyster Bay Roosevelts—while Franklin's had been nurtured in the Democratic Party—the Hyde Park Roosevelts. Eleanor was Alice's first cousin and a distant cousin to Franklin, who became her husband. Politics had not always stood between them until Teddy Jr. insulted Franklin when he ran for vice president in 1924, saying that he "didn't wear the brand of the family." Rather than giving as good as he got, Franklin was wounded. Then when Teddy was running for the governorship of New York, Eleanor followed on his speaking tour with a steaming teakettle rigged to the top of her car, leading people to believe that he had been involved in the Teapot Dome scandal associated with the Harding administration. The chasm between the two Roosevelt families widened.[6]

While Dolly worked every minute to keep Charley on the ticket, the business of Congress went on just as vigorously. The convention coincided with the debates on the "Bonus Army." Chicago was hardly far enough away to escape the fallout from the fiasco in Washington. The Republicans would have a tough time selling themselves to the American public this election.

In the end, nobody campaigned harder than Dolly, and much of the time she was on her own, with Charley committed to work as well as campaigning and Billy as ever working behind the scenes and keeping up his own career. She was feted and dined from one corner of the country to the other. In Buffalo, New York, she was met by forty children, mounted escorts (horses and motorcycles), and a fife and drum corps. In June alone she spoke in Detroit, Manchester (NH), Boston, Asbury Park, Lancaster (PA), Altoona (PA), St. Louis, Philadelphia, and Saginaw. She also ventured into "enemy country."[7]

The Deep South had become solidly Democratic. The Republicans had made gains, but in many ways, it was a given the South would vote with the Democrats and not a lot of effort was wasted currying favor there. But Dolly had been invited to speak to a luncheon in Greensboro, and she was hosted by Mr. and Mrs. Jefferson Penn at their home, Chinqua Penn, in Reidsville, North Carolina. Mr. Penn was a Virginian who had sold his tobacco company to American Tobacco (the Duke family) and made a fortune. Mrs. Penn, "Betsy," was a gracious hostess. Dolly said it was one of the most beautiful homes she had ever seen. Several Republican ladies had been invited to breakfast, and Mr. Penn was the only man. When he left the table he said, "Good-bye, ladies—I love you, but I am going to vote against you."[8]

While in Greensboro, Dolly was also invited to address the local Democrats—"a delightful ten minutes with 'our enemies.'"[9]

It may have been a sign, however, when Dolly was on a train in St. Louis and found two ladies staring intently at her. Finally, one of the women asked if they had met her or perhaps seen her picture? Dolly responded that she "had probably seen photographs, as I happened to be the sister of the Vice President. Her reply was, 'Why, Miss Garner, we are on our way South to work for your brother.'"[10]

Charley was pushing his legendary stamina to the limits with work and campaign travel. His last big appearance before the election came in Pittsburg, Kansas, the Friday evening before Tuesday's election. Thousands attended, making it the largest such gathering in at least thirty years. He was warm, told jokes, shared stories, and the audience loved the "old, native Kansan."

Two high school seniors arose at five o'clock the next morning to try to catch the vice president for an interview as he left town. He had stopped in every Kansas location possible and was squeezing in several more before arriving in Topeka, where he would vote. He was "weary, worn, and tired" but gracious to the young men.

By the time the newspaper account of his visit was released, Roosevelt had been elected. But in what must have been a rare occurrence, the headline, "Vice-President Honors Pittsburgers," ran across the top of the page and underneath, in a slightly smaller font, "Roosevelt Heads Nation." Charley's picture was the only one on the page.[11]

Meanwhile, Dolly was in Manhattan, Kansas, sharing the stage with Republican gubernatorial candidate Alf Landon. The young businessman from Pennsylvania was cut from the Republican cloth—practical solutions, real concerns, balanced budgets. There were at least two thousand people in the community center, with people crowded outside and behind the stage.[12]

It was a chilly morning when Charley arose and walked the four blocks to Polk School to cast his ballot. Sister Libby, relied upon to keep things in order in Topeka, was there too, casting her vote for Brother. He then boarded a train back to Washington, passing through Chicago.[13]

With so little good news to report, the election was lost no matter how badly Alice or Dolly or any other Republican wished otherwise. Will Rogers rightly commented, "Well its [sic] over and while everybody is not happy, everybody is at least glad, glad the thing is over."[14]

Franklin Delano Roosevelt and John Nance Garner won by a landslide. Roosevelt-Garner carried forty-two states compared to six for Hoover-Curtis and swept the Electoral College 472 to 59. Roosevelt had gotten over 57 percent of the popular vote. No matter how you counted it, it was a crushing defeat for the Republicans.

"I was totally unprepared for the avalanche of ballots which went against us on Election Day," wrote Dolly.[15]

Charley was between trains in Chicago when the news reached him. Caught by surprise, his reply was characteristically politely sarcastic:

> "I cheerfully accept the verdict," he said between trains, "and eagerly if not confidently await the return of abundant prosperity that the democrats have assured the American people they will bring about firmly and certainly when they take over the national government on March 4.
>
> "Let us hope they prove equal to the great responsibilities that await them and that they fulfill their solemn obligation to the people."[16]

What must have been the most difficult blow for Charley personally was the loss of Kansas. Roosevelt received about 75,000 more popular votes, giving him all nine of Kansas's electoral votes. While Hoover-Curtis carried Charley's home county of Shawnee, nearly all of the rural counties voted Democratic.

In the meantime, winners or losers, the work went on until spring. Official duties continued—hosting dignitaries, the lame duck session of Congress—and the Hoovers and the Curtises stayed in the spotlight.

In December, Charley delivered the official radio address to the nation on Christmas Eve. It was rainy and overcast as the crowds gathered to welcome Santa Claus and light the community Christmas tree in Sherman Park, just south of the Treasury Building. Senator Capper oversaw the event and invited the president-elect to listen on the radio. The honor of tree-lighting usually fell to the president, but the Hoovers were out of town. With Charley were Dolly and Billy; his daughter Perm; her husband, Toddy; and their children, Ann and Curt.

It was the first "singing Christmas tree," with loudspeakers concealed within the tree connected to a Victrola that was concealed in a nearby police booth. Two officers were kept busy changing records from six to ten o'clock each evening from Christmas Eve to New Year's.[17]

The dreaded New Year was further marred by the sudden death of Calvin Coolidge on January 5. In keeping with his personality, the former president had a modest funeral in Northampton, Massachusetts, where

Vice President Charles Curtis often performed ceremonial duties on behalf of the president, including the official Christmas tree lighting ceremony in the nation's capital. He is pictured on Christmas Eve 1932 with Dolly Curtis Gann and Kansas Senator Arthur Capper, who organized the event.

COURTESY LIBRARY OF CONGRESS

the family made their home. Several dignitaries, including President and Mrs. Hoover and Charley, attended and the president traveled on to Vermont for the private burial service.

Flags were ordered at half-mast and Washington began an official thirty-day period of mourning, so no invitations were sent or accepted by the Hoovers or by Charley and Dolly during that time, including a dinner hosted by the Kansas Society in Washington. Charley may have been very disappointed since they were honoring native Kansan Walter Johnson, the former pitcher and manager of the Washington Senators baseball team.

Almost as soon as the stalwart Republicans realized they had lost the election, they began planning a comeback. It seemed Hoover was ready to retire from public life (if not politics altogether), but Charley was not. The Republican League was established with Charley at the helm as chairman. The group's purpose was "to attempt restoration of the G. O. P. from the tremendous drubbing the voters gave it last November."[18]

"It has long occurred to me," Charley wrote in accepting the chairmanship of the organization, "that some such organization should be formed for the education of the youth of the country in the principles of the Republican party."[19]

The "Party Machine" was still controlled by former president Hoover, "but whether it could remain so if he wished to retain control and point for renomination in 1936 has yet to be shown." General dissatisfaction was expressed with the chairman of the National Committee, who had been put there by Hoover. In fact, the first order of business for the Republican League was to get rid of the current chairman. The new league was composed of members who were "strictly regular Republican."[20]

Charley had been loyal to Hoover and the party, and if he had been anyone else, he would have been second-guessing his decision not to get his old seat in the Senate back. But Charley was not one to look back. He didn't like losing, but he was always focused on the next opportunity to win.

Probably one of the most unpleasant duties left to him was certifying the votes in the 1932 election. It was a very formal and somewhat old-fashioned process. On February 8, the House was in session when the senators marched in with two pages carrying the sealed boxes that contained the votes of the Electoral College. No sooner than the senators had taken their seats than Charley began. He wanted to get this over.

After rapping the podium and calling the group to order, he reached into the box and pulled out the first envelope, Alabama. He cut it open and passed it to a representative who read the enclosed vote—eleven votes had been cast for Roosevelt and Garner and the "certificate seems to be regular in form and authentic."[21]

The Democrats applauded and the vice president pounded his gavel and called for order. He continued the process, finally reaching Connecticut, the first state that had gone to Hoover and Curtis. The Republicans applauded and Charley once again banged the gavel and demanded order. The entire Congress rose and applauded him.[22]

When the count for Kansas was read with the votes going to Roosevelt and Garner, Charley turned to his successor, Speaker Garner, and shook his hand.[23] When they were done, Franklin D. Roosevelt of New York and John Nance Garner of Texas were announced formally elected president and vice president.

Charley soon moved out of the Mayflower Hotel, where he had kept that apartment that people had been so concerned about his paying for. There were rooms for Dolly and Billy there as well, and they would stay through the winter. She packed their things, and they were established in the Gann Home on Macomb Street once again.

On March 3, Charley's colleagues in the Senate presented him with a three-foot oval silver tray with each of their names engraved upon it. Senator Robinson, the Democratic leader, told the vice president that when "you leave the Senate tomorrow . . . you will carry with you the confidence, the respect, and the admiration of all the members of this body."[24]

At last the time came for Charley to turn over the gavel. In his final address on March 4, he spoke of the "common good" and expressed confidence in the new administration and everyone's willingness to work together. He became emotional and spoke haltingly, recalling that only one man in Congress—Swanson of Virginia—was in the House when he entered in 1893. (Swanson was also leaving to become Secretary of the Navy for Roosevelt.) Only one member of the Senate—Smoot of Utah—was there when Charley was sworn in in 1907:

> "To me personally," he said, "this is one of the most important days of my life. It marks my leave-taking as your presiding office[r], my leave-taking as a member in the halls of congress where I have been present as vice president of the United States, as senator, and as congressman, for 40 years.
>
> "It is with deep emotion that I bid you good-bye and shortly go forth from here a private citizen."[25]

In the inaugural parade, Charley rode with Garner and Dolly in the car with Mrs. Garner. Mrs. Garner remarked that she had known Dolly years ago but looked forward to getting her advice on the duties that awaited her. She also mentioned that they had been through many experiences since that time and that Dolly would be meeting a new "Mrs. Garner" and likely she would be meeting a new "Mrs. Gann."[26]

The weather for this ceremony was much better than what had greeted Hoover and Curtis four years earlier, but still a pall hung over the event.

Montana Senator Thomas J. Walsh was to become the Attorney General in the new cabinet. He was traveling from Havana, Cuba, where he had been married the Saturday before, when he suffered a heart attack and died on the train while passing through North Carolina. His bride was hysterical and suffered a mild heart attack. The senator's body was taken to a funeral home in Rocky Mount, North Carolina, and prepared for burial. The attendants dressed him in his wedding suit, and Mrs. Walsh accompanied her husband's body to Washington on a later train. Two days after the inaugural, Charley and another former senator returned to the Senate Chamber for the funeral of their colleague.[27]

The year was proving to be even sadder than anticipated. Like his friend Senator Capper, however, Charley's answer for every problem was work. And now his job was to get the Republican Party back on track for 1936 and the interim elections.

One bright spot in Kansas had been the election of Republican Alf Landon as the governor. As talk grew about nominating the Kansas governor for the presidency in 1936, Charley was fully supportive.

He reestablished his law practice but did not solicit clients. He spent his time keeping abreast of political developments and, in season, watching the thoroughbreds run at Maryland's Bowie, Laurel, and Pimlico tracks.[28]

The Gann household fell into a happy routine, not as demanding as before. It was generally agreed they had accepted loss graciously:

> Together, Charles Curtis and Dolly Gann took political defeat gallantly. Hers was the last, most vigorous wave as officials went down the ramp at the close of the Roosevelt inauguration ceremonies. She and her brother and her husband went to the inaugural ball and have continued to mingle in Washington society ever since, less frequently than when in official life, but always on the best of spirits. "Good losers," Washington said.[29]

Often while Charley was in office, he and Billy had ridden to work together. They truly were the inseparable pals that Dolly had described when she married.

There were trips to Topeka, to check on property and business and to visit with his sister Libby. In the summer of 1935, Charley told some friends that he hoped to move back when he "retired from his law practice." That November, he returned once more and spoke to a meeting of Young Republicans. He also called on Governor Landon and expressed his confidence in the 1936 race for the presidency.

The following February, Charley had been suffering from a cold but was feeling better. On the night of the 7th he sat up late listening to the radio, and had breakfast in bed reading the paper the next morning. Billy went into his office and Dolly went out to do some shopping. A frantic maid called her—something was terribly wrong. The maid had gone to check on him and found him dead.[30]

Dolly bore up well in those first hours dealing with the press, until she said, "He was the perfect brother," and her voice broke, and she left the room weeping.[31]

In the last months of the Hoover administration, Charles Curtis was a weary public servant. The stinging defeat of the Republican ticket by Franklin D. Roosevelt and John Nance Garner was very personal, especially the fact that Kansas had gone for the Democrats. He returned to private practice in Washington, DC, after leaving office but did not solicit new clients. He often visited the horse racing tracks in nearby Maryland.
COURTESY LIBRARY OF CONGRESS

Arthur Capper was one of the first to arrive at the home of his old friend and he helped with the funeral arrangements. Charley's body was placed in a black coffin in the Gann living room with a full-length portrait of him on a nearby wall. Secretary of War and Mrs. George Henry Dern led hundreds of mourners "high in officialdom" through the home to pay their respects. A congressional delegation was present at the train station when his body was placed on board for the trip home to Topeka for burial. Dolly, Billy, and Leona traveled with the coffin.[32]

Tributes poured in—the president, the former president, senators, congressmen, governors, members of the Kaw Nation. The accolades were numerous and sincere.

From President Roosevelt: "I am deeply distressed to learn of the sudden passing of my old friend, Charles Curtis. Whether they knew him as a Senator, as the Vice-President of the United States, or as the man he was in his own right, his legion of friends will remember him, always affectionately, and will mourn his passing."[33]

"I was always fond of him," said Vice President Garner, who had served with him in the House and the Senate. "He was a fine man and a good friend."[34]

Senator Charles McNary of Oregon succeeded Charley as the Republican leader and described him as "quiet and yet successful" and "popular and efficient" as the presiding officer of the Senate. "He was an able and loveable character," Senator McNary added.[35]

Even the opposition paid homage. Senator Joe T. Robinson of Arkansas, Democratic leader, said Charley was "an outstanding factor in public affairs." Speaker of the House Jo Byrns of Tennessee was more effusive in his praise: "[H]e rendered long and distinguished service to his country and was a splendid public servant . . . whose death will be universally mourned."[36]

Fond and colorful memories were also shared, like his famous "nickel bets." Senator J. Thomas Heflin of Alabama would begin speaking and Charley would pull out a nickel and bet the others that within five minutes the speaker would be trashing Wall Street. As vice president, he demanded order, and broke several gavels trying to maintain it.

Governor Landon issued this statement:

> The people of Kansas will receive the unexpected news of Senator Curtis's death with deep sadness. His service for Kansas and the nation was after a distinguished and useful one which occupied his splendid faculties for the best part of two generations. Countless friends today find comfort in the realization that before he died he had completed a career distinguished in every way for its success.[37]

As the train bearing Charley's body left Washington, a blizzard gripped the Midwest. Senator Capper was to be the official representative of the administration and he had gone to Topeka a day or so early for the funeral of a longtime editor in his employ, so he was there ahead of the family.

Perm traveled to Topeka from Fort Sam Houston, where her husband was stationed, and was on hand for the train's arrival. Harry came from Taos, New Mexico, where he was living at the time, and Libby's sons came up from Oklahoma. Libby waited at the Curtis home for the brother she idolized to return for the last time.[38]

All government offices in the city were ordered closed that afternoon; other Kansas cities, like Wichita, did the same out of respect. The casket was taken from the train depot to the Kansas Statehouse, where his body lay in state prior to the funeral. Thousands of his fellow Kansans crowded into the capitol. Floral tributes from President Roosevelt, former president Hoover, the Osage Nation, and other dignitaries and organizations flanked the coffin, so many that one side of the rotunda was covered.

The bronze casket was simply inscribed "Charles Curtis 1860–1936." Atop the casket were placed a bow and arrows in honor of Charley's Native ancestry, a gift from Chief Deerfoot of the Apache tribe. Dolly had brought them with her from Washington, and they were to be buried with him. As mourners passed, two little blonde girls each placed a rose at the foot of the bier. They passed—great and ordinary alike—and most of them felt as if they had lost a friend.[39]

"In the long lines of spectators were women in rich furs, gray old men who shuffled past with red-rimmed eyes, thousands of girls and boys from Topeka's schools dismissed to honor the man who rose to the highest place ever accorded a Kansan," observed the Associated Press reporter assigned to cover the funeral. "A military guard of honor of officers of the Kansas national guard—a rank never before accorded even public officials in Kansas—stood at the bier."[40]

At the appointed time, the casket was moved into the House Chamber, where the representatives' chairs had been moved out and other chairs moved in to accommodate the crowds. Organ music was transmitted from the nearby Methodist Church, and WIBW radio broadcast the funeral. The family listened to the services from the Speaker's room, adjacent to the chamber, to offer them privacy. A loudspeaker had been placed in the room as well as others throughout the building for the hundreds of people who would not fit inside the room where the funeral was conducted. Motion-picture cameras were there as well, and newsreels of the funeral were later shown at movie theaters across the nation.[41]

The active pallbearers were Harry W. Colmery (who would later be credited as an architect of the G.I. Bill), W. L. Dean, D. R. Kircher, Hugh McFarland, Holmes Meade, and Edward Rooney, "all business and professional men of Topeka." The honorary pallbearers were Senator Capper; Judge George T. McDermott of the US Supreme Court of Appeals; Judge Richard J. Hopkins of the Federal District Court; W. A. Johnston, former Chief Justice of the Kansas Supreme Court; former senator Henry J. Allen; Homer Hoch, chairman of the State Corporation Commission; Charles F. Scott, Iola publisher; Charles H. Sessions, editor of the *Topeka Daily Capital*; Arthur Carruth Jr., managing editor of the *Topeka State Journal*; District Judge Otis E. Hungate; and other prominent men.[42]

Following the service, Charley was buried next to Annie in Topeka Cemetery.

Across the state and nation, acquaintances shared their memories of long relationships or brief encounters, favors done or campaign escapades. The stories were as varied as Charley's life experiences had been.

"He was a friend of all Indians," said his friend Mose Bellmard, assistant chief of the Kaw Council. "[W]e asked his advice on almost everything because he had our interests at heart." Bellmard added that he was "a great leader of our people."[43]

The Topeka Public Schools eulogized Charley as "an inspiration to all young manhood" and reminded the public that it was by his request that the Department of the Navy presented to Topeka High School the flagstaff, the "original lower fore yard of the United States frigate 'Constitution,' famous as 'Old Ironsides,' in the war of 1812 and many later naval encounter[s]. The spar will stand as a memorial to Charles Curtis, to those who knew him."[44]

William Allen White had known Charley for years, understood him well, and succinctly summarized his political career:

> Charles Curtis always played personal politics. Issues, causes and the warring feuds and factions that produce public questions interested him

little. He built his career on what was known, in the heyday of his maturity, as the personal touch. When he came into his day of power in the twenties, he rose to prominence and garnered his strength, which was exceptional, from the loyalties of men. He did a man a good turn and expected the man to be grateful. Generally speaking, his theory worked.[45]

White reflected on the 1928 Republican Convention and said, "Curtis was easily the most popular figure there. More fellows loved him and were loyal to him than even to Mr. Hoover." He said that when Charley's name was presented as a candidate, the demonstration for him overshadowed that for Hoover, and it was sincere and genuine. "But it was a hollow shell," White observed. Charley was shocked and saddened that those he believed would back him did not.

He recovered for his was a resilient blood and he bounced back in a few months to the full strength of his ardor and love for men. He was too old to acquire an interest in issues and causes and his next sorrow came in 1932 when Kansas voted against him and turned to Roosevelt. He could not believe it would happen. And when it came, his surprise was mingled with sadness.

Probably this shock of surprise and sadness at the end is the inevitable fate of men who linger too long in politics. A crash almost invariably ends their careers unless death is kind and hurries to their aid.[46]

It seems a harsh assessment, but it is true that the loss hurt Charley deeply. His politics had always been personal, just as White said, and the rejection of his home state after all those years was a hard blow. "He must have known that the odds were against the Hoover-Curtis national ticket in 1932 but he was not prepared for the defection of Kansas," eulogized the *Parsons Sun*. "He took that as a sort of personal matter and it hurt him much. He was never just the same afterward."[47]

The *Marshall County News* in Marysville, Kansas, compared Charley to Abraham Lincoln. As the funeral fell so close to Lincoln's birthday, reminders of the sixteenth president were everywhere. With so many references to Charley's having been born in a log cabin, the comparison was inevitable:

He went at life like Abraham Lincoln did—studied long hours, went through many hardships and won. There is a lesson in the life of Charles Curtis that every young boy should learn. And our country is almost the only country in the world where it is possible for any person of humble beginning to reach the top, not only in politics, but in business life. . . .

Charles Curtis reached his success by service to his friends, to his party, to his state and to his nation. He never forgot a friend.

He made an earnest effort to take care of every reasonable request that was made of him. He probably knew more people in Kansas by their first names than any other man in public office and he was a friend of all poor or rich.[48]

The *Manhattan Mercury* quipped, "Supposedly up where Charles Curtis is he is obliged to associate with nothing but loyal republicans."[49]

His idea of heaven may have included as many horses as Republicans. Had he lived, according to reports, he was set to become the racing "Czar," a position the media compared to the Commissioner of Baseball job held by Judge Kenesaw Mountain Landis. Charley would have been the ultimate arbiter in horse racing. His friend and legal associate, Robert Miller, said the offer had come from a group composed of half a dozen state racing groups. Miller said that Charley "practically had made up his mind to take the post which it had been planned to create April 1."[50]

Others also bemoaned Charley's loss in a very practical, and political, vein:

Had former Vice President Curtis lived until the coming presidential campaign entered the really crucial stage, his contribution undoubtedly would have been an important one. As far back as last August he announced his support of Governor Alfred M. Landon for the republican nomination.

Always a colorful campaigner, Curtis doubtless would have been a valued ally for the Kansas governor and his presidential aspirations. Few men knew the inside of politics, both from the standpoint of pre-nomination maneuvers and the rough and tumble of the hustings, as did the former vice president.[51]

The next items to make news were the beneficiaries of Charley's estate. He left $25,000 to Dolly, $10,000 to Libby, and $2,000 to his "faithful and efficient" secretary, Lola Williams. Miss Williams had come to Topeka to take over funeral arrangements for the family and was a trusted employee who had become more like family. Charley also left a parcel of land to his son, Harry, and described it as Harry's "surplus allotment as a member of the Kansas tribe of Indians, which he deeded to me March 10, 1932." The remainder of the estate was to be divided equally among his children. "I hope they may agree upon a fair and equal division of stocks and bonds, furniture, silver, plate, and other personal property," he instructed, "so that each may have one-third in value, and I suggest the sale of such if they cannot agree to divide, and that the proceeds be divided between them, share and share alike."[52]

Billy, Harry, and Miss Williams were his executors. When Billy filed the paperwork with the district supreme court in Washington, DC, the estate was listed at $187,000, with $12,000 in real estate (allotment lands in Oklahoma) and $175,000 in personal property including stocks and bonds.[53] Certainly an indication that Charley was a successful man, but it is only a fraction of the wealth of either of the Roosevelts or President Hoover or Secretary Mellon, or many of his contemporaries in Congress. It is more in line, however, with the financial status of Charley's friend, President Coolidge.

At the Republican National Convention that summer, Alf Landon did indeed get the nomination and it was another hard-fought campaign. Dolly immersed herself once again in Republican politics. In October, she was campaigning for Landon in Evansville, Indiana, where she was to be one of the speakers. She received a wire from Billy informing her that he was feeling better, recovering from the slight illness he had when she left. A few moments later, she received word that he had died of a heart attack at their home. "She was near a nervous collapse as she left by auto to take a train at Terre Haute," according to news reports.[54]

A friend accompanied her on the trip to Washington, but for the first time since her mother's death when her big brother had come to take her home, Dolly was alone.

LEGACY

Life is not a matter of holding good cards, but sometimes, playing a poor hand well.

—JACK LONDON

IT WOULD BE A KANSAN WHO BROUGHT THE REPUBLICANS INTO THE White House, but it would not be Alf Landon. Alf lost in a bigger landslide than Hoover. It was General Dwight D. Eisenhower from Abilene, Kansas, who led the Republican ticket in the election of 1952.

Dolly lived to see Eisenhower in office. After the devastating year of 1936—losing both Billy and Charley, nephew Harry's publicized divorce and remarriage later in the year, another Republican loss at the polls— Dolly somehow found her strength. She remained a pillar of the party. In 1944, in the waning days of the Second World War with Roosevelt still at the helm, the Republicans were floundering to find a candidate. One observer suggested the GOP should use Dolly as a role model. "The trouble with the Republican party is this," wrote columnist Helen Essary. "It hasn't wit enough to see that it should be more like Mrs. Dolly Gann."[1]

The columnist noted that administrations come and go, but "Dolly goes on forever":

> The same bright, eager look shines on Dolly's friendly face. The same sort of hat with the same sort of feather adorns Dolly's head. (She always was and always will be a pretty woman.) I venture to say she hasn't gained or lost a pound since the Charlie Curtis days. I also venture to say that she has not changed her mind or her loyalties an iota in

the years that have passed. . . . She marches straight ahead. Complete with orchids and the conviction of the infallibility of Brother Charlie's party. It is possible she has more spunk than the rest of the Republicans lumped together.[2]

She remained a thorn in the side of the Democrats, and that kept her going.

Dolly kept scrapbooks of her brother's life and accomplishments and she wrote a book, published in 1933, about campaigning and entertaining in Washington. True to her straightforward manner, it was aptly titled *Dolly Gann's Book*. She was kind in her commentary on friends and foes alike. Her scrapbooks, crammed with clippings pasted on top of each other, are in the archives of the Kansas State Historical Society. While many are undated, no doubt because she was so busy, nothing speaks as eloquently to her devotion to Charley and his career. His achievements and those of his children were hers as well. If there is any lesson to be drawn from the life of Charley Curtis, it is the importance of family and having that core of support upon which one can always rely.

Charley was a self-made man fortunately surrounded by encouraging women—his grandmothers, his wife, his sisters, his daughters—all committed to his realizing every ambition. It is no surprise that such a man would champion equal rights for women. The official program for the 1928 inaugural read, "Probably no man in Congress has been more active in behalf of women's rights. As whip of the Senate in 1919, he virtually led the fight for adoption of the resolution submitting the suffrage amendment to the States. He also sponsored a bill protecting the rights of American women who marry foreigners, and another creating federal women's prisons." While championing a prison for women might not appear pro-woman, it absolutely was viewed as a safer environment and more appropriate.

In May 1952, Dolly was walking through Oak Hill Cemetery in Georgetown, stepped in a hole, and fell, breaking her hip. The following winter, she caught a cold—or maybe the flu—and passed away on January 30. Ever the dutiful niece, Leona came to Washington to make the arrangements for her funeral, and Dolly was laid to rest beside Billy in

Maryland. She was eighty-one (again, best guess) years old. Every obituary rehashed the social feud with Alice Roosevelt Longworth.

Alf Landon became the Grand Old Man of the party, and on his one hundredth birthday, President Ronald Reagan came to celebrate with him. Landon's most valuable contribution to public service was his daughter, Nancy Landon Kassebaum Baker, elected to three terms as US Senator from Kansas, a seat once held by Charles Curtis. Her famous colleague, another presidential contender from Kansas, Senator Robert Dole, also served in a seat once held by Charley. When Charley ran for reelection in 1914, it was for the alternating Senate seat, making him the only senator to have served Kansas from both.

Charley's two namesakes—Charles Curtis George and Charles Curtis Knight—had distinguished careers. "Curt" George rose to the rank of major in the US Army, serving in World War II. Charles Curtis Knight became an industrialist, like his father, but his son, Steven Curtis Knight, joined the US Navy. He was tragically killed in a mine field at Guantanamo Bay in 1964. Both of his granddaughters, Ann and Connie, married and had children.

As the years went by, Charley's life and career faded into historical footnotes. The Curtis Act has been the most visible piece of his legacy, and the most controversial. Rightly so. The sovereignty of tribal governments continues to be debated and defined as the descendants of Charley's kinsmen struggle to maintain their identity in a world that has tried to destroy it. To hold Charley accountable for his role in that is appropriate, but it is also incumbent upon us to understand the world in which he lived, to discover the unique qualities that he may have possessed and the forces that shaped his choices. He was a wave, not the water.

Charley did not invent the allotment system; he was born on an "allotment," the lands inherited by his grandmother when her grandfather signed a treaty with the US government. All Charley ever knew, his entire background, was one of compromise. Combined with the fact that he was born into a world that would not accept someone of mixed blood, or dark-skinned peoples at all in most circumstances, he had the choice of being white, of fitting it. But the truth is he did not fit in. No matter what he achieved or what clothes he wore, he was still an "Indian," and that carried the connotation of being ill-suited for success. Charley broke free from that stereotype. He proved that a "person of color" could achieve anything a white person could achieve.

He said: "Obviously there was little in my early days that offered me particular advantages in reaching this goal. Since this journey has been possible for me who started so obscurely and who had so many early handicaps, is there any reason why any boy anywhere should not consider that to him all things are possible?"³

Then, he was the exception to the rule, but not anymore.

It is difficult to navigate the complex history of Native citizenship and voting rights. There is no doubt that Charley wanted his people, his Kaw relatives, to fully participate in government and society. How to achieve that was problematic. Professor Don Fixico, Regents and Distinguished Foundation Professor of History at Arizona State University, explained what a quagmire the process has been:

> From my perspective, as a Native scholar who focuses on American Indian history, trying to construct an accurate timeline for the U.S. citizenship of Native people is enormously complex. The various treaties, laws, and court cases involving Native Americans and citizenship are almost too challenging for most people to understand. For example, in the U.S. Constitution people who are born in the U.S. are American citizens. However, this portion of the Constitution did not include Native people, the original inhabitants of what became the United States. Some Native people became citizens of various states if they did not remove from their original homeland to the West, such as the Choctaws in Mississippi. The question remained were they U.S. citizens? In some cases, Native Americans became U.S. citizens according to their treaties. Federal law made some Native people U.S. citizens. For example, a federal law passed in 1901 designated members of the Five Civilized Tribes as American citizens. In 1919 all American Indian veterans from WW I became U.S. citizens as well. In 1924, the Indian Citizenship Act remedied the inconsistencies, and all Native Americans were made U.S. citizens.⁴

Charley and his fellow lawmakers were navigating a swamp.

As others study Charley Curtis more carefully and scrutinize his votes and stands while in Congress, and his relationship to his constituents and to his Kaw tribe, he may emerge as a self-serving politician with no loftier goals than his own power and comfort. But I think the evidence will lead elsewhere. No public servant is consistently noble, and there is no doubt that Charley benefited personally from the Kaw allotment program. But his wealth was not extreme. He achieved comfort, not wealth. In an era of self-made men, he stood out as one of the most accomplished and determined. "The last of the log-cabin candidates" it was said when he passed, again emphasizing the parallels to Lincoln, who had been deified by that time.

There is little danger of the deification of Charley Curtis, nor would he have wanted it. He was far too practical, if not humble. But he does deserve to be judged fairly. Perhaps the qualities that made Charley so popular during his lifetime are the reasons he has been largely forgotten—personal politics. He built his career on relationships, his grin, his handshake, his responding to letters and requests. As was often said, his name was rarely attached to legislation but in the cloakrooms he brokered the deals that passed bills.

It is natural to look back into the pages of history and categorize people, to put them on one side or the other of our dividing line—but people won't stay there. People were, and are, complicated. They may achieve great good while failing miserably. They may champion high ideals in one respect while wearing blinders in another. They do favors for one person and disappoint a dozen more.

Perhaps it is more accurate to describe Charley as a Kansan rather than as a Kaw, for the term *Kansan* comes from the Kaw but encompasses the totality of his story, a story that began in a log cabin on the north bank of the Kaw River and ended in the marble halls of Congress.

Richard Bergen's bronze sculpture of a Kanza warrior aiming his arrow toward the north star was placed on the capitol dome in Topeka in 2002. Named *Ad Astra*, from the state's motto *Ad Astra Per Aspera* ("to the stars through difficulty"), it stands over twenty-two feet and weighs more than two tons.

APPENDIX

Remedy by existing law not impaired.

SEC. 2. That nothing in this act contained shall prevent, lessen, impeach, or avoid any remedy at law or in equity which any owner of letters patent for a design, aggrieved by the infringement of the same, might have had if this act had not been passed; but such owner shall not twice recover the profit made from the infringement,

Approved, February 4, 1887.

Feb. 8, 1887.

CHAP. 119.—An act to provide for the allotment of lands in severalty to Indians on the various reservations, and to extend the protection of the laws of the United States and the Territories over the Indians, and for other purposes.

President authorized to allot land in severalty to Indians on reservations.

Be it enacted by the Senate and House of Representatives of the United States of America in Congress assembled, That in all cases where any tribe or band of Indians has been, or shall hereafter be, located upon any reservation created for their use, either by treaty stipulation or by virtue of an act of Congress or executive order setting apart the same for their use, the President of the United States be, and he hereby is, authorized, whenever in his opinion any reservation or any part thereof of such Indians is advantageous for agricultural and grazing purposes, to cause said reservation, or any part thereof, to be surveyed, or resurveyed if necessary, and to allot the lands in said reservation in severalty to any Indian located thereon in quantities as follows:

Distribution.

To each head of a family, one-quarter of a section;

To each single person over eighteen years of age, one-eighth of a section;

To each orphan child under eighteen years of age, one-eighth of a section; and

To each other single person under eighteen years now living, or who may be born prior to the date of the order of the President directing an allotment of the lands embraced in any reservation, one-sixteenth of a section:

Provisos.

Provided, That in case there is not sufficient land in any of said reservations to allot lands to each individual of the classes above named in quantities as above provided, the lands embraced in such reservation or reservations shall be allotted to each individual of each of said classes pro rata in accordance with the provisions of this act: *And provided further,* That where the treaty or act of Congress setting apart such reservation provides for the allotment of lands in severalty in quantities in excess of those herein provided, the President, in making allotments upon such reservation, shall allot the lands to each individual Indian belonging thereon in quantity as specified in such treaty or act: *And provided further,* That when the lands allotted are only valuable for grazing purposes, an additional allotment of such grazing lands, in quantities as above provided, shall be made to each individual.

Allotment pro rata if lands insufficient.

Allotment by treaty or act not reduced.

Additional allotment of lands fit for grazing only.

Selection of allotments.

SEC. 2. That all allotments set apart under the provisions of this act shall be selected by the Indians, heads of families selecting for their minor children, and the agents shall select for each orphan child, and in such manner as to embrace the improvements of the Indians making the selection. Where the improvements of two or more Indians have been made on the same legal subdivision of land, unless they shall otherwise agree, a provisional line may be run dividing said lands between them, and the amount to which each is entitled shall be equalized in the assignment of the remainder of the land to which they are entitled under this act: *Provided,* That if any one entitled to an allotment shall fail to make a selection within four years after the President shall direct that allotments may be made on a particular reservation, the Secretary of the Interior may direct the agent of such tribe or band, if such there be, and if there be no agent, then a special agent appointed for that purpose, to make a selection for such Indian, which election shall be allotted as in cases where selections are made by the Indians, and patents shall issue in like manner.

Improvements.

Proviso.

On failure to select in four years, Secretary of the Interior may direct selection.

Acts of the Forty-Ninth Congress of the United States

amended by adding thereto the following proviso, to wit: *Provided* further, That no suit against the Government of the United States, brought by any officer of the United States to recover fees for services alleged to have been performed for the United States, shall be allowed under this Act unless an account for said fees shall have been rendered and finally acted upon according to the provisions of the Act of July thirty-first, eighteen hundred and ninety-four (chapter one hundred and seventy-four, Twenty-eighth Statutes at Large, page one hundred and sixty-two), unless the proper accounting officer of the Treasury fails to finally act thereon within six months after the account is received in said office.

—filing of account necessary.
Chap. 359, vol. 24, p. 505, amended.
Post, p. 649.
Vol. 28, p. 206.

SEC. 2. That section two of the Act aforesaid, approved March third, eighteen hundred and eighty-seven, be, and the same is hereby, amended by adding thereto at the end thereof the following: "The jurisdiction hereby conferred upon the said circuit and district courts shall not extend to cases brought to recover fees, salary, or compensation for official services of the officers of the United States or brought for such purpose by persons claiming as such officers or as assignees or legal representatives thereof."

—concurrent jurisdiction of United States Courts not to extend to.
Post, pp. 649, 650.

Approved, June 27, 1898.

CHAP. 504.—An Act To amend an Act entitled "An Act to establish a Court of Private Land Claims and to provide for the settlement of private land claims in certain States and Territories," approved March third, eighteen hundred and ninety-one, and the Act amendatory thereto, approved February twenty-first, eighteen hundred and ninety-three.

June 27, 1898.

Be it enacted by the Senate and House of Representatives of the United States of America in Congress assembled, That section eighteen of an Act entitled "An Act to establish a Court of Private Land Claims and to provide for the settlement of private land claims in certain States and Territories," approved March third, eighteen hundred and ninety-one, as amended by the Act approved February twenty-first, eighteen hundred and ninety-three, be, and the same is hereby, further amended by striking out the words "within two years after the first day of December, eighteen hundred and ninety-two," as they stand in said Act as amended, and inserting in lieu thereof the words "before the fourth day of March, nineteen hundred and one," so that the first clause of said section shall read as follows, namely: "That all claims arising under either of the next two preceding sections of this Act shall be filed with the surveyor-general of the proper State or Territory before the fourth day of March, nineteen hundred and one, and no claim not so filed shall be valid."

Court of Private Land Claims.
Time extended to file claims under adverse possession.
Vol. 26, p. 862.
Vol. 27, p. 470, amended.

Approved, June 27, 1898.

CHAP. 517.—An Act For the protection of the people of the Indian Territory, and for other purposes.

June 28, 1898.
Post, pp. 770, 1099, 1233.

Be it enacted by the Senate and House of Representatives of the United States of America in Congress assembled, That in all criminal prosecutions in the Indian Territory against officials for embezzlement, bribery, and embracery the word "officer," when the same appears in the criminal laws heretofore extended over and put in force in said Territory, shall include all officers of the several tribes or nations of Indians in said Territory.

Indian Territory.
Protection of the people, etc.
"Officer," defined.

SEC. 2. That when in the progress of any civil suit, either in law or equity, pending in the United States court in any district in said Territory, it shall appear to the court that the property of any tribe is in any way affected by the issues being heard, said court is hereby authorized and required to make said tribe a party to said suit by service

Suits affecting tribal property, tribe to be made party.

Curtis Act

NOTES

PROLOGUE
1. Gilbert, *Eat, Pray, Love*, 165.
2. Dolly Curtis Gann, Undated Clipping, Dolly's Scrapbook, Charles and Anna B. Curtis Collection, Kansas Historical Society.

CHAPTER 1
1. Calloway, *Victory with No Name*, 116–17.
2. Ibid., 122.
3. Ibid., 96, 116.
4. Turner, *Red Men Calling*, 3–4.
5. Calloway, *Victory with No Name*, 5.
6. "From Thomas Jefferson to White Hair and Others, 16 July 1804," Founders Online, National Archives, https://founders.archives.gov/documents/Jefferson/01-44-02-0083.
7. Ibid.
8. Ibid.
9. Ibid.
10. Ibid.
11. "Fort Osage History," Fort Osage National Historic Landmark, accessed January 10, 2024, https://fortosagenhs.com/history.
12. Wallace, *Before Kansas Bled*, 81–88.

CHAPTER 2
1. Curtis, *In His Own Words*, 4. There are many variations in the spelling of Oran Curtis's name, but this is the spelling Charles Curtis used so that will be our preferred spelling.
2. Cody, *Life and Adventures of "Buffalo Bill*," 21.
3. Cyrus K. Holliday to Mary Holliday, December 31, 1854, Kansas State Historical Society.
4. Bisel, *Civil War in Kansas*, 35–36.
5. Ibid., 40.
6. Cody, *Life and Adventures of "Buffalo Bill*," 32.

7. Ibid.

8. Goodrich, *War to the Knife*, 125–26.

9. Ibid.

10. Bisel, *Civil War in Kansas*, 73.

11. *Evening Republic*, 1882.

12. Bisel, *Civil War in Kansas*, 98–99.

13. *Topeka Tribune*, December 1, 1860, 4.

14. *Evening Republic*, August 28, 1888.

15. Ibid.

16. Ibid.

17. Curtis, *In His Own Words*, 9.

18. *Tribune* (Scranton, PA), February 3, 1907, 12.

19. Ibid.

20. Ibid.

CHAPTER 3

1. *Topeka Tribune*, August 22, 1863, 2.

2. Ibid.

3. Ibid.

4. Goodrich, *Black Flag*, 90–95.

5. Thomas Goodrich, personal interview, July 15, 1999.

6. *Kansas State Record*, September 16, 1863, 5.

7. Ibid.

8. Ibid.

9. Jim Benbrook, "Joe Bellmard—Kaw Civil War Veteran," KSGenWeb Project, accessed January 5, 2024, https://www.ksgenweb.org/civilwar/Joebellmard.html.

10. *Kansas State Record*, September 23, 1863.

11. Goodrich, *Black Flag*, 99–100.

12. *Leavenworth Times*, March 1, 1864, 3.

13. Crawford, *Kansas in the Sixties*, viii.

14. *Border Sentinel*, September 2, 1864, 2.

15. Ibid.

16. Greene and Scott, *Finding Sand Creek*, 3–4.

17. Kraft, *Sand Creek*, 221.

18. *Nebraska City News*, January 21, 1867, 2.

19. Goodrich, *Black Flag*, 178.

20. *Border Sentinel*, February 24, 1865, 3.

21. Ibid.

22. *Topeka Weekly Leader*, May 3, 1866, 3.

23. Ibid.

24. Ibid.

25. *Topeka Tribune*, October 19, 1866, 2; *Topeka Weekly Leader*, November 1, 1866, 3.

CHAPTER 4

1. Curtis, *In His Own Words*, 8.
2. Ibid.
3. *Kansas Chief*, July 17, 1873.
4. Curtis, *In His Own Words*, 8.
5. Inman, *Ranche on the Oxhide*, 181–83.
6. Ibid.
7. Ibid.
8. Ibid.
9. Ibid., 184–87.
10. Curtis, *In His Own Words*, 8.
11. Ibid.
12. Cody, *Life of Hon. William F. Cody*, 161.
13. *New York Daily Herald*, February 24, 1867.
14. *New York Daily Herald*, July 18,1867.
15. *Philadelphia Evening Telegraph*, November 22, 1867, 2.
16. Ibid.
17. *Philadelphia Evening Telegraph*, May 20, 1867, 1.
18. Unrau, *Kansa Indians*, 43.
19. *Emporia News*, March 10, 1860.
20. Curtis, *In His Own Words*, 8–9.
21. Parks, *Darkest Period*, 200.
22. Ibid.
23. Alexander Gardner, photographer, "Lewis V. Bogy and Charles E. Mix in Council with the Sac and Foxes, and Kanza," 1867, Kansas State Historical Society Item # 25107, Call #E93 C.1867*1.
24. *National Republican*, January 26, 1867, 2.
25. Curtis, *In His Own Words*, 8–9.
26. E. S. Stover, U.S. Indian Agent, Washington Superintendency Report No. 70, September 10, 1868, in US Department of the Interior, Office of Indian Affairs, *Annual Report 1868*, 260–61.
27. Ibid.
28. Ibid.
29. Parks, *Darkest Period*, 181–82.
30. Ibid., 185.
31. "An Intersection of Cultures: Two Cultures—The Kaw," Kaw Mission, https://www .kawmission.org/places/kawmission/kansaeverydaylife.htm, February 22, 2024.
32. Curtis, *In His Own Words*, 10.
33. Stover, Washington Superintendency Report No. 70, 260–61.
34. Curtis, *In His Own Words*, 10.
35. Crawford, *Kansas in the Sixties*, 288–89.
36. Curtis, *In His Own Words*, 10–11.
37. Stover, Washington Superintendency Report No. 70, 260–61.

38. Charles Curtis to Mrs. Lalla Maloy Brigham, February 3, 1922, Charles and Anna B. Curtis Collection, Kansas State Historical Society.
39. Crawford, *Kansas in the Sixties*, 288–89.
40. Ibid.
41. Ibid.
42. Curtis, *In His Own Words*, 11.
43. resource.nlm.nih.gov/101716180, January 15, 2024.
44. Ibid.

CHAPTER 5

1. *Tribune* (Scranton, PA), February 3, 1907, 12.
2. Ibid.
3. Ibid.
4. *Lawrence Daily Journal*, June 10, 1868, 4.
5. Ibid.
6. Curtis, *In His Own Words*, 7.
7. Ibid.
8. Ibid., 29.
9. Ibid.
10. Crawford, *Kansas in the Sixties*, 318
11. Ibid.
12. Ibid., 320.
13. Ibid., 320–21.
14. Hoig, *Peace Chiefs of the Cheyennes*, 120.
15. Crawford, *Kansas in the Sixties*, 329–30.
16. Curtis, *In His Own Words*, 11.
17. Ibid., 12.
18. Ibid., 14–15.
19. Ibid., 15.
20. Ibid.
21. Ibid., 15–16.
22. Gray, *Desperate Seed*, 94–95.
23. Ibid.
24. Ibid.
25. *Sedalia Democrat*, September 27, 1872, 4.
26. Ibid.
27. Curtis, *In His Own Words*, 20–21.
28. Ibid., 29.
29. Ibid., 38.
30. Douglas, *Timeline History of the Kaw Nation*.
31. *Alma Daily News*, July 2, 1873, 4.
32. Dolly Curtis Gann, Undated Clipping, Dolly's Scrapbook, Charles and Anna B. Curtis Collection, Kansas Historical Society.
33. Curtis, *In His Own Words*, 37.

34. Dolly Curtis Gann, Undated Clipping, Dolly's Scrapbook, Charles and Anna B. Curtis Collection, Kansas Historical Society.

35. Curtis, *In His Own Words*, 37.

CHAPTER 6

1. *Daily Kansas Tribune*, October 28, 1873, 4.
2. Ibid.
3. *Junction City Weekly Union*, April 12, 1873, 3.
4. *Western Home Journal*, April 24, 1873, 5.
5. Curtis, *In His Own Words*, 42.
6. Ibid., 34.
7. Ibid., 35.
8. Jauken, *Moccasin Speaks*, 62.
9. Ibid., 63–67.
10. Ibid.
11. Leiker and Powers, *Northern Cheyenne Exodus*, 32.
12. *Austin Weekly Statesman*, December 3, 1874, 3.
13. Curtis, *In His Own Words*, 31–32.
14. Ibid., 33.
15. Dolly Curtis Gann, undated clipping. Dolly's Scrapbook, Charles and Anna B. Curtis Collection, Kansas Historical Society.
16. *Courier*, July 25, 1928, 16.
17. Curtis, *In His Own Words*, 43.
18. Ibid., 8; *Topeka Daily Capital*, March 17, 1910, 4.
19. Dolly Curtis Gann, Undated Clipping, Dolly's Scrapbook, Charles and Anna B. Curtis Collection, Kansas Historical Society.
20. Seitz, *From Kaw to Capital*, 8.
21. Dolly Curtis Gann, Undated Clipping, Dolly's Scrapbook, Charles and Anna B. Curtis Collection, Kansas Historical Society.

CHAPTER 7

1. Curtis, *In His Own Words*, 43
2. *Topeka Daily Capital*, January 14, 1907, 6.
3. *Topeka Weekly Times*, August 8, 1881, 4.
4. *Topeka Daily Capital*, June 2, 1882, 6.
5. Ibid.
6. *Topeka Daily Capital*, May 20, 1882, 6.
7. *Topeka Daily Capital*, June 2, 1882, 6.
8. *Topeka Weekly Times*, July 7, 1882, 6; *Topeka Weekly Times*, August 4, 1882, 6; *Topeka Daily Capital*, July 31, 1882, 6.
9. Curtis, *In His Own Words*, 105–6.
10. Ibid., 65.
11. *Topeka Weekly Times*, June 21, 1881, 1.

12. Curtis, *In His Own Words*, 54.
13. *Topeka Daily Commonwealth*, October 1, 1884.
14. Curtis, *In His Own Words*, 56.
15. Ibid., 60.
16. Ibid., 58.
17. Ibid., 58–59.
18. *Weekly Capital and Farmers Journal*, February 25, 1886, 3.
19. *Topeka Daily Capital*, January 13, 1887.
20. *Topeka Daily Capital*, February 16, 1887, 5.
21. *Weekly Commonwealth*, February 24, 1887, 3.
22. *Daily Commonwealth*, May 27, 1888, 3.
23. *Salina Daily Journal*, April 19, 1887, 2
24. *Indian Journal*, June 9, 1887, 8.
25. Ibid.
26. *Cherokee Advocate*, January 18, 1888, 1.

CHAPTER 8
1. Gann, *Dolly Gann's Book*, 4.
2. Ibid., 1.
3. Ibid., 4–5.
4. Collins, *Kansas County Seat Conflicts*, 146.
5. *Emporia Weekly Gazette*, June 27, 1891, 1.
6. Ibid.
7. Curtis, *In His Own Words*, 99.
8. Ibid., 100.
9. Ibid., 102.
10. Ibid., 98.
11. White, *Autobiography*, 304.
12. *Topeka State Journal*, May 19, 1892, 5.
13. Ibid.
14. Ibid.
15. *Osage County Graphic*, May 12, 1892, 2.
16. Curtis, *In His Own Words*, 114.
17. Ibid.
18. White, *Autobiography*, 304.
19. *Holton Signal*, February 8, 1893, 4.
20. Ibid.
21. Curtis, *In His Own Words*, 116.
22. *Topeka Daily Capital*, July 15, 1906, 4.

CHAPTER 9
1. Gann, *Dolly Gann's Book*, 8.
2. Ibid.

NOTES

3. Ibid., 25.
4. White, *Autobiography*, 196.
5. *Topeka State Journal*, August 24, 1893, 8.
6. White, *Autobiography*, 196.
7. *Topeka Mail*, November 3, 1893, 5.
8. *Emporia Gazette*, May 11, 1893, 7; *Topeka Weekly Times*, August 8, 1872, 3.
9. *Topeka Mail*, December 22, 1893, 1.
10. *Lawrence Daily Gazette*, March 29, 1894, 3.
11. *Topeka Mail*, April 27, 1894, 8.
12. *Topeka State Journal*, April 28, 1896, 2.
13. *Arkansas City Traveler*, Sept 9, 1897, 5.
14. *Topeka State Journal*, March 31, 1898, 7.
15. Ibid.
16. *Weekly Chieftain*, March 19, 1896, 2.
17. Ibid.
18. Ibid.
19. Ibid.
20. *Weekly Chieftain*, September 29, 1898, 1.
21. Curtis, *In His Own Words*, 29.
22. *Weekly Chieftain*, September 29, 1898, 1.
23. *Leavenworth Weekly Times*, June 29 1899, 6.
24. [1] *Arkansas City Traveler*, December 26, 1900, 5.[1]
25. Ibid.
26. *Baraboo Republic*, February 12, 1902, 5.
27. *St. Louis Republic*, February 9, 1902, 1.
28. *Topeka Plaindealer*, June 20, 1902, 1.
29. Curtis, *In His Own Words*, 135–36.
30. Ibid., 136.
31. Ibid.
32. Ibid., 137.
33. Ibid.
34. *Wichita Beacon*, June 9, 1903, 2.
35. *Topeka Daily Capital*, November 18, 1903, 4.
36. Cordery, *Alice*, 115.
37. *Topeka Daily Herald*, June 24, 1905, 5.
38. Ibid.

CHAPTER 10
1. *Topeka Daily Herald*, February 17, 1906, 8; *Topeka Daily Capital*, February 4, 1906, 1.
2. *Topeka Daily Capital*, February 13, 1906, 5.
3. *Topeka Daily Capital*, January 23, 1907, 1.
4. *Girard Press*, January 14, 1907, 2.
5. Gann, *Dolly Gann's Book*, 9.
6. *Topeka Daily Capital*, January 13, 1907, 5.

7. *Topeka State Journal,* January 17, 1907, 5.
8. Ibid., 1.
9. *Topeka Daily Herald*, March 28, 1907, 6.
10. Ibid.
11. *Pawhuska Capital*, January 7, 1915, 7.
12. *Sheboygan Press*, February 28, 1908, 1.
13. Ibid.
14. Ibid.
15. Ibid.
16. *Arkansas City Traveler*, February 18, 1908, 1.
17. *Twice a Week Plain Dealer*, August 9, 1910, 4.
18. Curtis, *In His Own Words*, 155.
19. Ibid., 158.
20. *Topeka State Journal*, January 3, 1914, 17.
21. *Topeka Daily Capital*, July 1, 1914, 6.
22. Gann, *Dolly Gann's Book*, 11.
23. Ibid.
24. *Topeka Daily Capital*, July 2, 1926, 23.
25. Gann, *Dolly Gann's Book*, 13.
26. Curtis, *In His Own Words*, 164–65.

CHAPTER 11

1. *Wichita Beacon*, November 10, 1906, 8.
2. https://www.ancestry.com/discoveryui-content/view/901488362:61381?tid=&pid=&queryId=7a672974-c6aa-4063-85fa-4887e650d61c&_phsrc=Mbc1225&_phstart=-successSource.
3. *Evening Star*, June 18, 1915, 8.
4. Gann, *Dolly Gann's Book*, 20.
5. Ibid., 19.
6. Ibid., 18.
7. *Topeka Daily Capital*, July 2, 1916, 23.
8. *Washington Post*, April 3, 1917, 1.
9. Ibid., 2.
10. *Washington Post*, April 7, 1917, 2.
11. *Ponca City News*, March 28, 1948, 8.
12. Gann, *Dolly Gann's Book*, 47.
13. Ibid., 44.
14. Charles Curtis to William E. Connolly, June 1, 1916, Kenneth Spencer Research Library, University of Kansas.
15. Gann, *Dolly Gann's Book*, 46.
16. "Embroidered Flour Sacks," Kansas State Historical Society, accessed January 10, 2024, https://www.kshs.org/kansapedia/embroidered-flour-sacks/16791.
17. "1918 Flu Epidemic More Deadly than Germans," *Kansas Journal of Military History* 1, no. 1 (Spring 2005): 37.

18. Gann, *Dolly Gann's Book*, 50.

19. Ibid., 51.

20. Ibid., 55.

21. *McCracken Enterprise*, October 22, 1920, 1.

22. Gann, *Dolly Gann's Book*, 60.

23. *Daily Capital*, July 10, 1919, 6.

24. Douglas, *Timeline History of the Kaw Nation*.

25. *Wichita Eagle*, February 4, 1923, 30.

26. Ibid.

27. Ibid.

28. *Wellington Daily News*, December 28 1922, 5.

29. Ibid.

30. Ibid.

31. Ibid.

32. *Evening Star*, August 3, 1923, 1.

33. Gann, *Dolly Gann's Book*, 62.

34. *Evening Star*, August 3, 1923, 1.

35. Ibid.

36. Gann, *Dolly Gann's Book*, 62–63.

37. Ibid., 63–64.

38. Ibid., 84.

39. "Indian Citizen Act of 1924," Immigration History, accessed January 29, 2024, https://immigrationhistory.org/item/1924-indian-citizenship-act.

40. Gann, *Dolly Gann's Book*, 66.

41. Ibid.

42. Ibid.

43. Ibid., 74.

44. Ibid., 88.

CHAPTER 12

1. *Philadelphia Inquirer*, March 5, 1925, 6.

2. *Baltimore Sun*, October 14, 1923, 97.

3. Gann, *Dolly Gann's Book*, 83.

4. Ibid., 18.

5. Ibid., 18–19.

6. "The Congress: Quiet Leader," *Time*, December 20, 1926, https://content.time.com/time/subscriber/article/0,33009,711494,00.html.

7. Gann, *Dolly Gann's Book*, 90.

8. Ibid., 92.

9. Ibid., 93.

10. *Daily News*, June 8, 1928, 236.

11. *Baltimore Sun*, June 15, 1928, 2.

12. Ibid., 1.

13. Ibid.

14. Gann, *Dolly Gann's Book*, 95.
15. *Chicago Tribune*, June 16, 1928, 2.
16. *Baltimore Sun*, June 16, 1928, 1.
17. *Daily Press*, June 16, 1928, 1.
18. Ibid.
19. Gann, *Dolly Gann's Book*, 99.
20. Ibid., 100.
21. *Warren Tribune*, June 16, 1928, 1.
22. Ketchum, *Will Rogers*, 247.
23. *Baltimore Sun*, June 15, 1928, 1.
24. Grant, *Report of the Inaugural Committee*, March 4, 1929.
25. *Henryetta Daily Free Lance*, March 5, 1929, 1.
26. Gann, *Dolly Gann's Book*, 108.
27. Ibid., 109.
28. *Durant Weekly News* and *Bryan County Democrat*, March 8, 1929, 7.
29. *Ponca City News*, March 3, 1929, 2.
30. Gann, *Dolly Gann's Book*, 110; *Evening Star*, March 6, 1929, 1.
31. Gann, *Dolly Gann's Book*, 111.
32. Ibid., 113–15.
33. Ibid., 118
34. Hatfield, *Vice Presidents of the United States*, 373–81.
35. Ibid., 373.
36. Charles Curtis to W. A. Row, August 8, 1931, Kaw City Museum.
37. "National Affairs: Nobody's Business," *Time*, April 29, 1929, https://content.time.com/time/subscriber/article/0,33009,769216,00.html.
38. Ibid.
39. *Burlington Free Press*, June 21, 1932, 1.
40. *News Herald*, July 29, 1932, 6.
41. *Los Angeles Record*, July 29, 1932, 1.
42. Ibid.

CHAPTER 13

1. *Los Angeles Times*, June 14, 1932, 9.
2. Gann, *Dolly Gann's Book*, 99.
3. *Emporia Gazette*, June 17, 1932, 1.
4. Cordery, *Alice*, 365; Gann, *Dolly Gann's Book*, 198.
5. Cordery, *Alice*, 304.
6. Ibid., 364
7. Gann, *Dolly Gann's Book*, 210–12.
8. Ibid., 212–13.
9. Ibid., 213.
10. Ibid., 216.
11. *Booster*, November 11, 1932, 1.
12. *Manhattan Mercury*, November 3, 1932, 1.

13. *Leader*, November 10, 1932, 6.

14. *Sunday Times Democrat*, November 13, 1932, 1.

15. Gann, *Dolly Gann's Book*, 218.

16. *Leader*, November 10, 1932, 1.

17. "1924–1933 National Christmas Trees," National Park Service, updated October 22, 2019, https://www.nps.gov/whho/learn/historyculture/1924-1933-national -christmas-trees.htm.

18. *Iola Register*, February 6, 1933, 1.

19. Ibid.

20. Ibid.

21. *Emporia Gazette*, February 8, 1933, 4.

22. *Iola Register*, February 8, 1933, 2.

23. Ibid.

24. *Iola Register*, March 8, 1933, 2.

25. *Parsons Sun*, March 4, 1933, 2.

26. *Wichita Eagle*, March 1, 1933, 1.

27. *Evening Star*, March 6, 1933, 1.

28. *Evening Star*, February 9, 1933, 6.

29. Ibid.

30. *Kansas City Star*, February 8, 1936, 1.

31. *Evening Star*, February 9, 1936, 6.

32. *Wichita Eagle*, February 10, 1936, 1.

33. *St. Louis Globe Democrat*, February 9, 1936, 2.

34. Ibid.

35. Ibid.

36. Ibid.

37. *Kansas City Star*, February 8, 1936, 2.

38. *Wichita Eagle*, February 10, 1936, 6.

39. Ibid., 9

40. Ibid.

41. Ibid.; *Frankfort Index*, February 12, 1936, 2.

42. *Parsons Sun*, February 10, 1936, 2.

43. Ibid.

44. *Night Hawk*, February 13, 1936, 2.

45. *Wichita Beacon*, February 12, 1936, 9.

46. Ibid.

47. *Parsons Sun*, February 10, 1936, 6.

48. *Marshall County News*, February 20, 1936, 8.

49. *Manhattan Mercury*, February 12, 1936, 4.

50. *Wichita Beacon*, February 11, 1936, 3.

51. *Manhattan Mercury,* February 14, 1936, 4.

52. *Iola Register*, February 19, 1936, 1.

53. *New Castle News*, March 16, 1936, 8.

54. *Indianapolis News*, October 3, 1936, 3.

LEGACY

1. *Naugatuck Daily News*, February 28, 1944, 4.
2. Ibid.
3. *Baltimore Sun*, October 14, 1923, 97.
4. Dr. Don Fixico, personal correspondence, February 3, 2024.

Bibliography

Bisel, Debra Goodrich. *The Civil War in Kansas: Ten Years of Turmoil.* Charleston, SC: History Press, 2012.

Calloway, Colin G. *The Victory with No Name: The Native American Defeat of the First American Army.* New York: Oxford University Press, 2015.

Cody, William F. *Life and Adventures of "Buffalo Bill."* Chicago: John R. Stanton Co., 1917.

———. *The Life of Hon. William F. Cody: Known as Buffalo Bill.* Lincoln: University of Nebraska Press, 1978.

Collins, Robert. *Kansas County Seat Conflicts: The Elections, the Feuds, and the Wars.* Self-published, CreateSpace, 2013.

Cordery, Stacy A. *Alice: Alice Roosevelt Longworth, from White House Princess to Washington Power Broker.* New York: Penguin Books, 2007.

Cordry, Dee. *Children of White Thunder: Legacy of a Cheyenne Family, 1830–2020.* Piedmont, OK: Independently published, 2022.

Crawford, Samuel J. *Kansas in the Sixties.* Chicago: A. C. McClurg & Company, 1911.

Curtis, Charles. *In His Own Words.* Edited by Kitty Frank. Self-published by Kitty Frank, CreateSpace, 2019.

Douglas, Crystal. *A Timeline History of the Kaw Nation.* Kaw City, OK: Kaw Nation, 2011. http://www.kawnation.com/wp-content/uploads/2012/03/Timeline.pdf.

Drumm, Stella M., ed. *Down the Santa Fe Trail and into Mexico: The Diary of Susan Shelby Magoffin, 1846–1847.* New Haven, CT: Yale University Press, 1876.

Du Val, Kathleen. *The Native Ground: Indians and Colonists in the Heart of the Continent.* Philadelphia: University of Pennsylvania Press, 2006.

Edmunds, R. David. *The Potawatomis: Keepers of the Fire.* Norman: University of Oklahoma Press, 1978.

Eldridge, S. W. *Early Days in Kansas.* Topeka: Kansas State Historical Society, 1920.

Fisher, H. D. *The Gun and the Gospel.* 2nd ed. Chicago: Medical Century Company, 1899.

Gann, Dolly. *Dolly Gann's Book.* Garden City, NY: Doubleday, Doran & Company, 1933.

Gilbert, Elizabeth. *Eat, Pray, Love.* London: Bloomsbury, 2007.

Giles, F. W. *Thirty Years in Topeka: A Historical Sketch.* Topeka: George W. Crane & Company, 1886.

Goodrich, Thomas. *Black Flag: Guerilla Warfare on the Western Border, 1861–1865.* Bloomington: Indiana University Press, 1995.

————. *War to the Knife: Bleeding Kansas, 1854–1861*. Lanham, MD: Stackpole Books, 1998.

Grann, David. *Killers of the Flower Moon: The Osage Murders and the Birth of the FBI*. New York: Vintage Books, 2017.

Grant, U. S., III. *Report of Inaugural Committee for the Inauguration of Herbert Hoover as President, Charles Curtis as Vice President, March 4, 1929*. Washington, DC: Crane Printing Co., [1929?].

Gray, Jim. *Desperate Seed: Ellsworth, Kansas, on the Violent Frontier*. Ellsworth, KS: Kansas Cowboy Publications, 2009.

Greene, Jerome A. *Washita: The U.S. Army and the Southern Cheyennes, 1867–1869*. Norman: University of Oklahoma Press, 2004.

Greene, Jerome A., and Douglas D. Scott. *Finding Sand Creek: History, Archeology, and the 1854 Massacre Site*. Norman: University of Oklahoma Press, 2004.

Hatfield, Mark, with the Senate Historical Office. *Vice Presidents of the United States, 1789–1993*. Washington, DC: Government Printing Office, 1997.

Hoig, Stan. *The Battle of the Washita*. Lincoln: University of Nebraska Press, 1976.

————. *The Peace Chiefs of the Cheyennes*. Norman: University of Oklahoma Press, 1980.

Inman, Henry. *The Ranche on the Oxhide: A Story of Boys' and Girls' Life on the Frontier*. New York: Grosset and Dunlap, 1913. Archived at https://archive.org/details/rancheonoxhidest00inma.

Jauken, Arlene Feldmann. *The Moccasin Speaks: Living as Captives of the Dog Soldier Warriors*. Lincoln, NE: Dageforde Publishing, 1998.

Ketchum, Richard M. *Will Rogers, His Life and Times*. New York: American Heritage Publishing Company, 1973.

Kraft, Louis. *Sand Creek and the Tragic End of a Lifeway*. Norman: University of Oklahoma, 2020.

Leiker, James N., and Ramon Powers. *The Northern Cheyenne Exodus in History and Memory*. Norman: University of Oklahoma Press, 2011.

Levine, Lawrence W., and Cornelia R. Levine. *The Fireside Conversations: America Responds to FDR During the Great Depression*. Los Angeles: University of California Press, 2002.

Miner, H. Craig, and William E. Unrau. *The End of Indian Kansas: A Study of Cultural Revolution, 1854–1871*. Lawrence: Regents Press of Kansas, 1978.

"1918 Flu Epidemic More Deadly than Germans," *Kansas Journal of Military History* 1, no. 1 (Spring 2005): 37.

Olson, Greg. *Ioway Life: Reservation and Reform, 1837–1860*. Norman: University Press of Oklahoma, 2014.

Parks, Ronald D. *The Darkest Period: The Kanza Indians and Their Last Homeland, 1846–1873*. Norman: University of Oklahoma Press, 2014.

Shlaes, Amity. *Coolidge*. New York: Harper Perennial, 2013.

Tibbles, Thomas Henry. *Buckskin and Blanket Days*. Garden City, NY: Doubleday & Company, 1957.

Treadway, William E. *Cyrus K. Holliday: A Documentary Biography*. Topeka: Kansas State Historical Society, 1979.

Turner, Katherine C. *Red Men Calling on the Great White Father*. Norman: University Press of Oklahoma, 1951.

Unrau, William E. *Indians of Kansas: The Euro-American Invasion and Conquest of Indian Kansas*. Topeka: Kansas State Historical Society, 1991.

———. *The Kansa Indians: A History of the Wind People, 1673–1873*. Norman: University of Oklahoma Press, 1971.

Unrau, William E., and H. Craig Miner. *Tribal Dispossession and the Ottawa Indian University Fraud*. Norman: University of Oklahoma Press, 1985.

US Department of the Interior, Office of Indian Affairs. *Annual Report of the Commissioner of Indian Affairs for the Year 1868*. Washington, DC: Government Printing Office, 1868.

Utley, Robert M. *The Indian Frontier of the American West, 1846–1890*. Albuquerque: University of New Mexico Press, 1984.

Wallace, Douglass, ed. "Shawnee County's First Towns." *Before Kansas Bled*, Bulletin 82. Topeka: Shawnee County Historical Society, 2007.

White, William Allen. *The Autobiography of William Allen White*. New York: MacMillan Company, 1946.

Newspapers

Alma Daily News, Alma, KS
American Nonconformist and Kansas Industrial Liberator, Indianapolis, IN
Arkansas City Traveler, Arkansas City, KS
Austin Weekly Statesman, Austin, TX
Baltimore Sun, Baltimore, MD
Baraboo Republic, Baraboo, WI
Booster, Pittsburg, KS
Border Sentinel, Mound City, KS
Bryan County Democrat, Bryan County, OK
Burlington Free Press, Burlington, VT
Cherokee Advocate, Tahlequah, OK
Chicago Tribune, Chicago, IL
Courier, Waterloo, IO
Daily Commonwealth, Topeka, KS
Daily Kansas Tribune, Lawrence, KS
Daily News, New York, NY
Daily News Tribune, Greenville, OH
Daily Press, Newport News, VA
Durant Weekly News, Durant, OK
Emporia Gazette, Emporia, KS
Emporia News, Emporia, KS
Emporia Weekly Gazette, Emporia, KS
Evening Post-Record, Los Angeles, CA
Evening Republic, Topeka, KS
Evening Star, Washington, DC

Frankfort Index, Frankfort, KS
Girard Press, Girard, KS
Henryetta Daily Free Lance, Henryetta, OK
Holton Signal, Holton, KS
Indian Journal, Eufalala, OK
Indianapolis News, Indianapolis, IN
Iola Register, Iola, KS
Junction City Weekly Union, Junction City, KS
Kansas Chief, Troy, KS
Kansas City Star, Kansas City, MO
Kansas State Record, Topeka, KS
Lawrence Daily Gazette, Lawrence, KS
Lawrence Daily Journal, Lawrence, KS
Leader, Hinton, WV
Leavenworth Times, Leavenworth, KS
Leavenworth Weekly Times, Leavenworth, KS
London Times, London, England
Los Angeles Record, Los Angeles, CA
Los Angeles Times, Los Angeles CA
Manhattan Mercury, Manhattan, KS
Marshall County News, Marysville, KS
McCracken Enterprise, McCracken, KS
National Republican, Washington, DC
Naugatuck Daily News, Naugatuck, CT
Nebraska City News, Nebraska City, NE
New Castle News, New Castle, PA
New York Daily Herald, New York, NY
News Herald, Franklin, PA
Night Hawk, Topeka, KS
Osage County Graphic, Lyndon, KS
Parsons Sun, Parsons, KS
Pawhuska Capital, Pawhuska, OK
Philadelphia Evening Telegraph, Philadelphia, PA
Philadelphia Inquirer, Philadelphia, PA
Ponca City News, Ponca City, OK
Salina Daily Journal, Salina, KS
Sedalia Democrat, Sedalia, MO
Sheboygan Press, Sheboygan, WI
St. Louis Globe Democrat, St. Louis, MO
St. Louis Republic, St. Louis, MO
Sunday Times Democrat, Okulgee, OK
Times Journal, Mound Valley, KS
Topeka Daily Capital, Topeka, KS
Topeka Daily Commonwealth, Topeka, KS

Topeka Daily Herald, Topeka, KS
Topeka Mail, Topeka, KS
Topeka Plaindealer, Topeka, KS
Topeka State Journal, Topeka KS
Topeka Tribune, Topeka, KS
Topeka Weekly Leader, Topeka, KS
Topeka Weekly Times, Topeka, KS
Tribune, Scranton, PA
Troy Chief, Troy KS
Twice a Week Plaindealer, Topeka, KS
Warren Tribune, Warren, PA
Washington Post, Washington, DC
Weekly Capital and Farmers Journal, Topeka, KS
Weekly Chieftain, Vinita, Indian Territory
Weekly Commonwealth, Topeka, KS
Wellington Daily News, Wellington, KS
Western Home Journal, Lawrence, KS
Wichita Beacon, Wichita, KS
Wichita Eagle, Wichita, KS

Index

Lane, Jim, 34
La Tourette, Charlie, 66
La Tourette, Emma Curtis, 32
law: Charley and, 96–101, 103–7,
   113–18, 151, 189; Curtis
   Act and, 128–29; Jack and,
   98–100, 104
Lawrence, KS, 7, 26–27, 33–36
leadership, Charley and, 176–77
League of Nations, 164, 166
Leiker, James N., 88–89
Lewis, Meriwether, 15
Lincoln, Abraham, 31–32, 209–
   10, 217
liquor cases, 98–100, 103–4
Little Robe, 82
London, Jack, 213
Long, Chester, 144
Longfellow, Henry Wadsworth, 47
Longworth, Alice Roosevelt, 138,
   141, 142f, 185–86, 196
Longworth, Nicholas, 138, 141,
   142f, 186
Loose, Mrs. Jacob, 178
Louisiana Purchase, 15

MacArthur, Douglas, 190
Maine, USS, 131–32
Man-ah-to-wah, 56f
Marquette, Jacques, pere, 47
Martin, H. W., 56f
Mayer, Louis B., 191
Mayflower Hotel, 188–89, 202
McCandless, Byron, 160
McCarty, Mike, 75

McClellan Creek, Battle of, 88
McDermott, George T., 208
McFarland, Hugh, 208
McGill, George, 194
McKinley, William, 127, 132–
   36, 144
McNary, Charles, 206
McNeive, Sarah, 1, 3
Meade, Holmes, 208
media: and Annie, 145; and Bonus
   Army, 191; and Captain Jack,
   43; and Charley, 6, 199, 208,
   210; and Corbett case, 107;
   and elections, 143–44, 195; and
   Hoover nomination, 181–83;
   and liquor cases, 104; and
   Mayflower Hotel, 189; and mil-
   itary brutality, 41; and Native
   Americans, 24f, 55, 89–90, 121,
   133; and Roosevelt wedding,
   141; and Wood case, 115–16
Medicine Water, 88
Mehojah, William, 7
Mellon, Andrew, 166, 188
memory, Charley and, 121
Metzger, Phillip, 155
Miami people, 12
Miles, John D., 81–82
Miles, Nelson, 88
militias, 33–36, 38, 42–43. *See also*
   Kansas Volunteers
Miller, Robert, 210
Missouri Compromise, 22
Mitcher, O. A., 135
Mix, Charles E., 56f